TREATING DEPRESSION

TREATING
DEPRESSION

A VOLUME IN THE JOSSEY-BASS
LIBRARY OF CURRENT CLINICAL TECHNIQUE

Ira D. Glick, EDITOR
Irvin D. Yalom, GENERAL EDITOR

Jossey-Bass Publishers • San Francisco

Substantial discounts on bulk quantities of Jossey-Bass books are available to corporations, professional associations, and other organizations. For details and discount information, contact the special sales department at Jossey-Bass Inc., Publishers.
(415) 433–1740; Fax (800) 605–2665.

For sales outside the United States, please contact your local Simon & Schuster International Office.

Jossey-Bass Web address: http://www.josseybass.com

 Manufactured in the United States of America on Lyons Falls Turin Book. This paper is acid-free and 100 percent totally chlorine-free.

Library of Congress Cataloging-in-Publication Data

Treating depression/Ira D. Glick, editor.
    p.   cm.—(The Jossey-Bass library of current clinical technique)
Includes bibliographical references and index.
ISBN 0-7879-0144-X (hardcover)
ISBN 0-7879-1585-8 (paperback)
    1. Depression, Mental—Treatment. I. Glick, Ira D., 1935-. II. Series.
RC537. T734 1995
616.85'270651—dc20   95-16853
                                                                          CIP

FIRST EDITION
HB Printing 10 9 8 7 6 5 4 3 2 1
PB Printing 10 9 8 7 6 5 4 3 2 1

CONTENTS

FOREWORD ix
Irvin D. Yalom

INTRODUCTION xiii
Ira D. Glick

CHAPTER 1
FAMILY THERAPY 1
Carol M. Anderson, Sona Dimidjian, and Apryl Miller

CHAPTER 2
COGNITIVE BEHAVIOR THERAPY 33
Michael E. Thase

CHAPTER 3
INTERPERSONAL PSYCHOTHERAPY 71
Holly A. Swartz and John C. Markowitz

CHAPTER 4
INDIVIDUAL PSYCHOTHERAPY 95
Jules R. Bemporad

CHAPTER 5
GROUP THERAPY 123
Joan L. Luby

CHAPTER 6
SOMATIC THERAPY 153
Charles DeBattista and Alan F. Schatzberg

CHAPTER 7
COMBINED TREATMENT 183
Michael E. Thase and Ira D. Glick

ABOUT THE AUTHORS 209

INDEX 213

*To those patients with mood disorders who have
had the courage to rise above the pain caused by the
disease and gone for help. And especially to Susan
Dime-Meenan, executive director of the National
Depressive and Manic-Depressive Association,
a group that has pioneered helping others find
the way to effective treatment.*

FOREWORD

At a recent meeting of clinical practitioners, a senior practitioner declared that more change had occurred in his practice of psychotherapy in the past year than in the twenty preceding years. Nodding assent, the others all agreed.

And was that a good thing for their practice? A resounding "No!" Again, unanimous concurrence—too much interference from managed care; too much bureaucracy; too much paper work; too many limits set on fees, length, and format of therapy; too much competition from new psychotherapy professions.

Were these changes a good or a bad thing for the general public? Less unanimity on this question. Some pointed to recent positive developments. Psychotherapy was becoming more mainstream, more available, and more acceptable to larger segments of the American public. It was being subjected to closer scrutiny and accountability—uncomfortable for the practitioner but, if done properly, of potential benefit to the quality and efficiency of behavioral health care delivery.

But without dissent this discussion group agreed—and every aggregate of therapists would concur—that astounding changes are looming for our profession: changes in the reasons that people request therapy; changes in the perception and practice of mental health care; changes in therapeutic theory and technique; and changes in the training, certification, and supervision of professional therapists.

From the perspective of the clientele, several important currents are apparent. A major development is the de-stigmatization of psychotherapy. No longer is psychotherapy invariably a hush-hush affair, laced with shame and conducted in offices with separate entrance and exit doors to prevent the uncomfortable possibility of patients meeting one another.

Today such shame and secrecy have been exploded. Television talk shows—Oprah, Geraldo, Donahue—have normalized psychopathology and psychotherapy by presenting a continuous public parade of dysfunctional human situations: hardly a day passes without television fare of confessions and audience interactions with deadbeat fathers, sex addicts, adult children of alcoholics, battering husbands and abused wives, drug dealers and substance abusers, food bingers and purgers, thieving children, abusing parents, victimized children suing parents.

The implications of such de-stigmatization have not been lost on professionals who no longer concentrate their efforts on the increasingly elusive analytically suitable neurotic patient. Clinics everywhere are dealing with a far broader spectrum of problem areas and must be prepared to offer help to substance abusers and their families, to patients with a wide variety of eating disorders, adult survivors of incest, victims and perpetrators of domestic abuse. No longer do trauma victims or substance abusers furtively seek counseling. Public awareness of the noxious long-term effects of trauma has been so sensitized that there is an increasing call for public counseling facilities and a growing demand, as well, for adequate treatment provisions in health care plans.

The mental health profession is changing as well. No longer is there such automatic adoration of lengthy "depth" psychotherapy where "deep" or "profound" is equated with a focus on the earliest years of the patient's life. The contemporary field is more pluralistic: many diverse approaches have proven therapeutically effective, and the therapist of today is more apt to tailor the therapy to fit the particular clinical needs of each patient.

In past years there was an unproductive emphasis on territoriality and on the maintaining of hierarchy and status—with the more prestigious professions like psychiatry and doctoral-level psychology expending considerable energy toward excluding master's level therapists. But those battles belong more to the psychotherapists of yesterday; today there is a significant shift toward a more collaborative interdisciplinary climate.

Managed care and cost containment is driving some of these changes. The role of the psychiatrist has been particularly affected as cost efficiency has decreed that psychiatrists will less frequently deliver psychotherapy personally but, instead, limit their activities to supervision and to psychopharmacological treatment.

In its efforts to contain costs, managed care has asked therapists to deliver a briefer, focused therapy. But gradually managed care is realizing that the bulk of mental health treatment cost is consumed by inpatient care and that outpatient treatment, even long-term therapy, is not only salubrious for the patient but far less costly. Another looming change is that the field is turning more frequently toward the group and family therapies. How much longer can we ignore the many comparative research studies demonstrating that the group therapy format is equally or more effective than higher cost individual therapies?

Some of these cost-driven edicts may prove to be good for the patients; but many of the changes that issue from medical model mimicry—for example, efforts at extreme brevity and overly precise treatment plans and goals that are inappropriate to the therapy endeavor and provide only the illusion of efficiency—can hamper the therapeutic work. Consequently, it is of paramount importance that therapists gain control of their field and that managed care administrators not be permitted to dictate how psychotherapy or, for that matter, any other form of health care be conducted. That is one of the goals of this series of texts: to provide mental health professionals with such a deep grounding in theory and such a clear vision of effective therapeutic technique that they will be empowered to fight confidently for the highest standards of patient care.

The Jossey-Bass Library of Current Clinical Technique is directed and dedicated to the frontline therapist—to master's and doctoral-level clinicians who personally provide the great bulk of mental health care. The purpose of this entire series is to offer state-of-the-art instruction in treatment techniques for the most commonly encountered clinical conditions. Each volume offers a focused theoretical background as a foundation for practice and then dedicates itself to the practical task of what to do for the patient—how to assess, diagnose, and treat.

I have selected volume editors who are either nationally recognized experts or are rising young stars. In either case, they possess a comprehensive view of their specialty field and have selected leading therapists of a variety of persuasions to describe their therapeutic approaches.

Although all the contributors have incorporated the most recent and relevant clinical research in their chapters, the emphasis in these volumes is the practical technique of therapy. We shall offer specific therapeutic guidelines, and augment concrete suggestions with the liberal use of clinical vignettes and detailed case histories. Our intention is not to impress or to awe the reader, and not to add footnotes to arcane academic debates. Instead, each chapter is designed to communicate guidelines of immediate pragmatic value to the practicing clinician. In fact, the general editor, the volume editors, and the chapter contributors have all accepted our assignments for that very reason: a rare opportunity to make a significant, immediate, and concrete contribution to the lives of our patients.

Irvin D. Yalom, M.D.
Professor Emeritus of Psychiatry
Stanford University School of Medicine

INTRODUCTION

Ira D. Glick

*They had practically raised me, and now they would wonder what
had gone wrong. There was no way I could possibly explain to them
that I was suffering from an acute depression, that it was so intense
that even when I wanted to get out of my own head and attend
other people's needs—as I had so much wanted to do that day—I
couldn't. I was consumed by depression and by the drugs I took to
combat it, so there was nothing left of me, no remainder of the self
that could please them even for a few hours. I was useless.*

E. WURTZEL

Although "depression" is still not generally recognized by the
public as being an illness (as opposed to being a moral failing),
changing patterns of medical care are bringing increasing num-
bers of patients who are depressed to the attention of mental
health professionals. As a result, most of us have busy practices
with lots of depressed people in our caseloads. We recognize
that therapists have their hands full with this population and
that this is pervasive, hard work. This book aims to help by providing the specific guidelines and techniques for when to do
what and for whom.

Fortunately, treating depression in the 1990s is a far more
rewarding enterprise than it was up to several decades ago, when
no therapies could be proven more useful than a placebo. Today,
we are fortunate to have treatments that can change the life
course of those afflicted with this illness.

What else has changed? First, research has begun to integrate
the two developmental (and presumed etiological) pathways representing biological/genetic factors and psychosocial/environ-
mental factors. Second, treatment outcome (how an episode is

resolved) has become a window into pathogenesis for understanding the interaction of biological and psychosocial parameters in onset and recovery. For example, the response of an adolescent who is "depressed" after a breakup with a girlfriend or boyfriend and who remits after three sessions of psychotherapy suggests this is situation related. Conversely, a patient who remits within six months of medication and no psychotherapy suggests a biologically based etiology. Accordingly, new medication and psychotherapeutic strategies have been developed to manage these illnesses in ways very different from those two decades ago. Finally, new diagnostic criteria (*DSM-IV*) identify different subtypes of depression and, by implication, effective therapies for a particular type. This book details some of the most important models for understanding and treating all of these types and subtypes.

So what are the key issues for clinicians treating depression? The aim is to find the best combination of therapies for a particular individual, given his or her life circumstances, developmental phase, and particular type of depression. Our text aims to be helpful (1) when one uses medication alone, (2) when one uses psychotherapy alone, and (3) when one combines them.

This volume covers six approaches. For each, we spell out what it is (a definition of the therapy), how to do it (the model and process), and whom to do it with (indications) and present the data to support its efficacy.

We begin with the modality most recently developed—family therapy. The family is not only where depression plays out but, as it happens, also the crucial system for the long-term management of this disorder. Carol Anderson and her co-workers discuss the *psychoeducation model* as it applies to patients with depression and their families. This model has two formats—group and individual—and you will want to use them differentially in your practice.

Next, we present three models of individual therapy. The significant change in this field is the development of specific "brands" of individual therapy, which for the most part are now manualized and have been tested in controlled trials. Michael Thase discusses *cognitive-behavioral therapy*. Holly Swartz and John Markowitz discuss *interpersonal psychotherapy*, and Jules Bemporad discusses *psychodynamic psychotherapy*. Each of these modalities works somewhat differently, and obviously they have overlapping spheres. We outline for whom each model is indicated and how each technique can be applied.

Finally, Joan Luby discusses *group psychotherapy* for the depressed patient. This modality has reached full flowering with the recognition that, for some patients, a group setting is ideal for working out interpersonal problems consequent to their illness—such as maintaining a relationship—and in part caused by the often lifelong residue of the illness (lowered mood, irritability, oversensitivity).

We conclude by presenting the treatment modality that has been shown in controlled studies to be most beneficial for this disorder—psychopharmacotherapy. As presented by Charles DeBattista and Alan Schatzberg, this chapter also examines how to combine medication with psychotherapy for *which* patients under *what* circumstances. Because the most common treatment mix is combining medication with psychotherapy, hand in hand, Michael Thase and I devote another entire chapter to this modality.

We are also concerned throughout this book with how the conscientious and caring therapist can deal with issues raised by managed care. Here, we recommend a proactive stance based on principles elucidated in each chapter. The therapist first formulates a careful diagnosis of relevant issues of not only the patient but also the family. Second, a treatment plan based on one or more models of intervention presented here is laid out. Third, the case is presented to the new "member of the treatment team"—a managed care supervisor.

From our perspective, the major goal is quality, rather than limitations to treatment. The practitioner should not be sidelined by the attempts to cut costs as a by-product of managed care. We emphasize educating the payer and taking charge of the treatment plan.

What we are hearing more and more is that HMOs and MCIs are realizing that "quick and dirty" costs them more in the long run—in expensive hospitalization, residential treatment, and other costly emergency interventions. So, managed care supervisors are becoming more open and flexible about necessary outpatient treatment as preventive early intervention. This flexibility requires the therapist to be adept at persuasion and negotiation. It also requires a willingness to provide the required paperwork—treatment plans, progress notes, utilization reviews, even outcome data—that can help make the case. And it means thoroughly understanding the internal structure of the insurer so that the proper appeals can be initiated if necessary. New trends in managed care, moreover, seem to favor a capitation rather than fee-for-service approach, which means that many therapists will be working in groups, practices, networks, and clinics that contract to provide all necessary services for a predetermined total fee. This group work means we decide how much of what to do, without external approvals or review. Overall, however, we want to take a more work-together, pragmatic approach.

Finally, let's summarize the current treatment of depression. At this point, the symptoms and severity can be reliably rated, and as mentioned, particular subtypes can be defined. The severity of symptoms can also suggest the intervention: severe depression requires medications. The psychotherapeutic models may be more appropriate for the mild to moderate depression—that is, dysthymia, grief, or subsyndromal levels of the symptoms. At the same time, the following warning from a clinical social worker is relevant:

> Therapists need to be careful not to misdiagnose the dysthymic patient as suffering from a personality disorder or a depression that is simply a reaction to personal problems. Misdiagnosis may lead the therapist to mistakenly treat this illness with psychotherapy alone. Since dysthymia is often due to abnormalities in brain biochemistry, it is best to treat it with

antidepressants. Medication should not be reserved solely for depressed patients suffering gross impairments in functioning.

However, not every "depressed" patient needs medication.

Let's close by reviewing some of the basic epidemiology of depression—putting aside "grief" and the normal "ups and downs" with which all people suffer.

> Depressive illness is a very common condition affecting at least 5 percent of the general population over 18 at some point in their lives. It is more common in women than men. Depressive illness is severely disabling, adversely affecting working capacity and disrupting family and social life. The disability found in major depression exceeds that of most severe medical illnesses, such as diabetes and hypertension. Depressive illness can be lethal. At least 15 percent of patients with depressive illness have a lifetime expectation of committing suicide, a figure which has scarcely changed since the introduction of antidepressants unless systematic long-term treatment has been used.

Psychotherapeutic and rehabilitative strategies, with and without medication, can profoundly benefit the patients and families that therapists see daily. So we hope this book provides the specific guidelines and concrete methods for successful treatment of this very large and difficult population.

ACKNOWLEDGMENTS

I am especially grateful to our editor, Alan Rinzler, who has been crucial to the coherence and readability of this work. In addition, I wish to acknowledge the efforts of those researchers in the field of mood disorders who have done the hard work of finding the "facts" underlying the understanding and treatment of these diseases.

NOTES

P. xiii, *E. Wurtzel:* Wurtzel, E. (1993). *Prozac nation: Young and depressed in America, a memoir.* New York: Houghton Mifflin.

P. xvi, *impairments in functioning:* Quinn, B. (1994). Chronic depression: The danger of misdiagnosis and inadequate treatment. *NAFDI News, 7,* 1.

P. xvii, *long-term treatment has been used:* Task Force of the Collegium Internationale Neuro-Psychopharmacologicium (CINP). (1993). Impact of neuropharmacology in the 1990s: Strategies for the therapy of depressive illness. *European Neuropsychopharmacology, 3,* 153–156.

TREATING DEPRESSION

I

FAMILY THERAPY

Carol M. Anderson, Sona Dimidjian, and Apryl Miller

Those who have major depressive disorders or chronic dys-
thymias, almost regardless of their attitude and temperament
prior to becoming ill, tend to view themselves and their relationships in a negative and sometimes hopeless way. Withdrawn,
amotivated, lacking in energy or interest—it's as if they are
wearing dark glasses that color their view of the world around
them. As they selectively attend to negative events and feelings,
their sensitivity to criticism, feelings of worthlessness, and compromised self-esteem make it difficult for them to accept positive feedback and support. In fact, their depression often makes
them more frustrated and irritable when support is offered.

It is not surprising, then, that families of depressed patients
are almost always distressed. Depression acts like a magnifying
glass, highlighting all of the normal problems of families and
family members, making these issues seem more serious, and
adding stressful and worrisome troubles of its own. Anyone who
has observed the struggles of depressed patients and their families knows there is a powerful and complicated relationship
between depression and family life. Although biology and genet-
ics may play a significant role in the etiology and course of
depression, a variety of psychosocial issues, especially family
variables, is also crucial. Families have an influence over the
onset and course of the disorder, and the ways in which they
respond to depression influence both the lives of the individuals and each family as a whole.

LIVING WITH DEPRESSION

Most family members report that it's extremely difficult to live with someone who is depressed—so difficult, in fact, that over time their own mood and well-being are compromised. These complaints by family members are supported by observations of researchers that depression has a dramatic negative impact on those who come into contact with it even briefly. For instance, a limited telephone conversation with a depressed person can influence the mood of a nondepressed listener. Given such findings, it is not surprising that depression places great stress on family members and intimate relationships.

Trying to Cope

The way in which family members cope changes over time. Initially, many attempt to deal with the symptoms of depression by accommodating, adapting, and gradually centering their lives around their relative in an effort to help. They become highly attuned to needs and moods, attempting to protect the depressed person from criticism and life stress. They try to be reassuring or, by using logic, to make a case that life is not as bad as the depressed person perceives it to be. The husband of a thirty-five-year-old depressed woman responded to her repeated complaints about feeling depressed, isolated, and overwhelmed with household and child-care chores by listing all the people who cared about her and all the labor-saving devices she had that had not been available in their parents' generation. As other patients frequently report, this strategy did not help. When a depression is severe—as hers certainly was—such logic and reassurances only cause the depressed persons to feel alienated, to believe that their family members simply don't understand, don't want to hear about their troubles, or don't take their pain seriously.

Coping can be especially difficult for partners of adults who are depressed, because the disorder almost always compromises the spouses' ability to meet the responsibilities of their family roles. If the patient is a parent of small children, all family members may be required to shift responsibilities and to absorb additional household tasks, often without receiving much appreciation for doing so. Over time, reassurance become less genuine and support more sporadic as family members neglect their own needs. They begin to feel drained, overburdened, exhausted, and angry and to perceive that their efforts to help have little effect. In fact, family members often find that "helpful" strategies that might brighten their loved one's mood under "normal" circumstances produce, at best, no effect on someone who is depressed and may even exacerbate the problem.

The Impact of Relationships

Unlike many physical illnesses or even other major psychiatric problems that lead to unusual or aberrant behaviors (schizophrenia, bipolar disorders), many of the symptoms of depression can be deceptively similar to the ordinary mood swings and "blues" almost everyone experiences from time to time. It isn't surprising, therefore, that family members often do not perceive depression as an illness. As a result, they find its symptoms more difficult to tolerate and are likely to personalize the depressed person's negative communications and behaviors. The depressed person's relentless focus on the negative aspects of life is perceived, not as a consequence of depression, but as a reflection of how he or she actually feels about marital and family relationships. Family members tend to interpret symptoms of withdrawal, fatigue, diminished libido, and anhedonia as reflective of a lack of feeling and affection or commitment to the relationship.

In another example, the wife of a depressed forty-year-old man reported that he not only ruminated about the purpose and relevance of his life and work but also expressed many doubts about their marriage and even about his ability to love anyone. She had been trying to be supportive but found it very difficult not to take these comments personally. Like many other spouses of those who are depressed, she worried that he did not really love her, was not trying to get better, and was actively avoiding working on their marriage.

The Effect on Children

Children react to depression in one of their parents in their own way. They often feel responsible for the parent's apparent unhappiness and assume that they are defective or unworthy when they cannot arouse much interest or attention. Not surprisingly, they, too, can become symptomatic as their needs are neglected over time. Frequently, children presenting to child guidance clinics with acting out or school problems turn out to have mothers who are seriously depressed. Although it is not always clear which problem came first, often these children appear to be responding to the psychological unavailability of the depressed parent.

For instance, ten-year-old Katie experienced a precipitous drop in school performance and a sudden increase in defiance at home. These symptoms dramatically improved after an assessment by a family therapist who noted the mother's depression and began to deal with it in treatment, while simultaneously facilitating an evaluation for medication. In this case, Katie's symptoms acted as a cry for help, not just for herself, but for her mother.

Long-Term Impact

Eventually, if family members do not come to perceive depression as a legitimate disorder, they become increasingly critical and intolerant of the depressed person's mood and behavior. To some extent, intolerance is supported by the prevailing values of the wider culture, which extols the ability to "pull yourself up by your bootstraps" and to "stand on your own two feet." These attitudes give rise to impatience with the symptoms of prolonged depression and tend to promote views of depressed individuals as lazy, self-pitying, self-centered, selfish, and even manipulative.

This cultural context can lead both patients and their families to experience a sense of stigma and shame about symptoms and reactions that are beyond their control. These feelings, combined with the inherently demobilizing nature of depression, can make it very difficult for patients and families to maintain supportive links with the wider community. The resultant isolation can increase the intensity of family relationships, thereby increasing frustration and criticism and draining a family system whose resources are already taxed.

Unfortunately, most of the challenges of coping with depression do not influence family relationships in isolated or circumscribed ways. Because depression is often recurrent, and in some cases chronic, individuals and families can become locked in seemingly endless cycles of stress and conflict. Even after a particular depressive episode has resolved, the difficulty of coping with depression can have a lingering effect on family relationships. The scars of disappointment, resentment, and anger can persist long after depressive symptoms have abated.

Moreover, the stressors precipitated by the demands of coping with depression can also be complicated by already existing marital or parent-child difficulties, as well as by unrelated problems in other family members that may make it more difficult to manage the current crisis of a depressive episode.

The following story demonstrates the way depression can invade a family and progressively affect relationships in a spiraling, negative way:

JENNY

Jenny, a thirty-eight-year-old married woman, had been seriously depressed for over a year. She had multiple somatic complaints, sleep problems, lack of motivation and energy, and a diminished appetite. Over time, she had become increasingly unable to get her housework done, displayed little interest in either her husband or her three children, and experienced deepening feelings of worthlessness. She had never been treated for depression but could recall other times in her life when she had "had the blues." She noted that her husband had tried to be helpful, taking on many of the household chores, as well as the task of helping the children with their homework, an activity she once enjoyed. Nevertheless, their marital relationship had deteriorated to the point where they hardly spoke to one another, and she couldn't recall the last time she had been interested in having sex. She reported that, now, in fact, it was a struggle to remember whether she ever really loved her husband. She also reported that she longed for the time when she did not feel dominated by guilt for not wanting to be with her family and to meet their needs.

Sam, Jenny's husband, reported that Jenny was once vivacious and attractive. When she first became depressed, he had tried to be helpful and understanding, attempting to cheer her up and keep the children off her back. As the months had passed and as he continued to be burdened with managing the household, he began to resent her. He believed that taking care of these tasks takes time away from his job (which he was worried about losing). The fact that he was shouldering so much responsibility without any sign of gratitude from Jenny made it even worse. To Sam, it seemed that Jenny did not care about anyone else, that she was just wallowing in her misery. She "overreacts," he complained, to even the slightest criticism or negative event. Their three children, once the light of Jenny's life, seemed to have become a burden to her, and he was very concerned that they were being neglected. Their thirteen-year-old was spending most of her time with her friends; their ten-year-old was doing poorly in school; and their five-year-old was relentlessly demanding of attention. They all had become more withdrawn and insecure. Sam reported that their five-year-old complained she thought her mommy didn't love her. He knew it didn't help to nag Jenny to get moving, but his patience had worn thin. What bothered him most was that he wasn't sure she really wanted to get better. He also admitted that he was afraid that Jenny would end up like her mother, who "took to her bed" for much of her adult life.

Jenny, for her part, knew that her children weren't doing well and that her husband had about had it. Even when Sam tried to be supportive, she sensed an irritable tone in his voice that signaled his frustration. This only made things worse. Moreover, when he didn't help, she resented him; and when he did help, she felt more worthless than ever. She increasingly felt she was a burden to her family and wondered whether they wouldn't be better off without her. Their entire family was caught in a cycle of guilt, blame, and frustration.

Effective coping strategies have the potential to minimize the negative impact that depression can have on the vulnerable individual and on family relationships. Unfortunately, it is so challenging to cope effectively with depression, many families find that without information or knowledge their efforts can place increased stress on their depressed relatives, thereby aggravating the very behaviors and problems they want to eliminate.

WHY USE A FAMILY APPROACH?

Family intervention is likely to be relevant whether family problems precede and even precipitate episodes of depression, develop in response to them, or simply co-exist and interact to exacerbate one another. Interventions aimed at improving family coping and functioning can help protect both depressed individuals and their family members from stressful aspects of the current episode and prevent new ones. These family interventions can be used alone or in concert with a variety of other treatments, including medication and individual therapy.

An additional rationale for including a family approach to treatment is provided by today's changing patterns of health care reimbursement. In this era of managed care, an increasing number of families are being forced to become primary caregivers for patients with serious depressions, patients who may even be actively suicidal. Current health insurance policies provide relatively little financial coverage for treatment, and as a result, severely depressed patients are often denied admission to hospitals or are discharged after a week or two under tenuous control before the effects of medication begin. Even support for outpatient therapy is limited despite the fact that depression is not likely to be "cured" in eight, twelve, or sixteen weeks. Unfortunately, because many third-party payers fail to appreciate the power and relevance of families, support for family or marital interventions is often denied unless one member is designated the patient and sessions are listed as "collateral session with patient." Still, if family or marital therapists are willing to work under these constraints, it is possible to be helpful to patients and their families over time.

The majority (about 85 percent) of depressive episodes respond to treatment (or may even subside spontaneously), but recurrences are common. Thus, working with patients' support systems helps both patients and families develop ways to cope on their own and to use professionals sparingly. In short, depression is a "family affair" and often is a lifetime issue.

The approach described below is designed to deal with the families of both adults and children who are clinically depressed. It is based on the philosophy and structure of our psychoeducational model developed for schizophrenia. Although variations of this model have been described, no controlled clinical trials verify the effectiveness of this approach with depression. Nevertheless, because our previous experience has proven it effective in forestalling relapse in schizophrenia, we also rely heavily on psychoeducational interventions in our clinical work with depressed patients and their families.

Several reasons are relevant. First, the psychoeducational model is consistent with our understanding of depression as a disorder whose etiology and course are influenced by biological, genetic, and interpersonal factors. Second, it can easily be used in conjunction with medication or other treatment modalities, allowing therapists to simultaneously address both biological and psychosocial issues. Third, psychoeducation recognizes families as an invaluable resource for effectively managing psychiatric problems. For this reason, it strongly emphasizes the importance of working collaboratively with families as partners in the treatment process. Finally, the practical information provided in this treatment format can serve to decrease anxiety and increase the ability of both patients and families to cope effectively and reduce stress.

GOALS OF THE MODEL

The principal goals of this approach are to improve patient and family functioning and to decrease depressive symptomatology. These goals are achieved by working on the following goals for patients, family members, and the family as a whole:

For the patient:

Improved sense of self-worth and self-esteem

Increased responsibility for managing own depression

Increased ability to negotiate to have needs met in relationships

Increased activity and initiative

Increased skills for coping with crises

For family members:

Increased knowledge about depression (symptoms, treatments, impact on family life) and increased understanding of depression as a legitimate illness

Decreased stress/worry/guilt/anger about the illness

Increased coping skills for managing depressive behaviors

Increased ability to balance the need to respond to the patient's needs with the need to protect self from letting depression dominate life

For the family as a whole:

Increased hope and belief in change

Increased sense of mastery and self-determination

Decreased tension through increased use of skills for effective communication and conflict resolution

Increased connectedness with a wider community of support

These general goals vary as they are applied to the unique circumstances of each family. The specific goals of treatment depend on a number of factors, including the patient's degree of impairment, the patient's role, the family's strengths and resources, and the amount of time available for treatment.

The proposed treatment model is based on four phases of treatment: (1) connecting/assessment, (2) providing support and information, (3) application/maintenance interventions of this philosophy and information to everyday life, and (4) gradual termination. The primary tasks of each phase, along with common problems that clinicians encounter, are discussed below.

PHASE I: CONNECTING/ASSESSMENT

It is unlikely that any family treatment can be effective unless a strong and positive working relationship has been built between the family and the therapist. This relationship should be distinguished by a number of critical qualities, the most important of which are a spirit of collaboration and a genuine sense of respect for the family's strengths, autonomy, and right to make choices and decisions about treatment.

If the patient is acutely depressed, the patient's depressed mood may make it impossible to discern what is "real" and what is a part of a temporarily depressed worldview. For this reason, it may be necessary to restrict some of these early sessions to other family members only. This restriction allows an outlet for family frustrations and prevents the exacerbation of obsessions and self-destructive ruminations that might occur at this stage if the patient were encouraged to discuss family issues prematurely. As the patient improves, greater involvement in structured family sessions can be facilitated.

The main challenge of engaging successfully with families who are likely to have been demoralized by depression involves instilling a belief that change is possible, while respecting their inevitable skepticism about both treatment and the prospect that things can actually get better. Because most families, regardless of their problems, believe that they should be able to manage the needs and problems of all their members, by the time they reach a clinician's office, they are likely to feel frustrated and guilty about not having been able to help. Listening to the family's story, communicating that they have been heard, and affirming how difficult it is to cope with depression or come for help is an effective method of establishing an initial connection.

It is crucial that we as clinicians maintain an upbeat, active, but realistic stance. Given the powerful impact of depression, we, too, can become vulnerable to feelings of depression and hopelessness about the prospect of change. As a result, our perspective can become limited by a "depressed" worldview, and we can lose our ability to offer a "new lens." Alternatively, an unrealistically positive stance, one that is too divergent from the family's experience of reality, will diminish our credibility and compromise the connecting process. It is naive to attempt redefining a family's struggles or problems as blessings, but it is vital to offer them more usable ways of seeing their situation.

Reframing

Emphasizing the positives inherent in any situation, or "reframing," is one technique that can be used to provide a more positive but still realistic alternative worldview, a process that can begin during the assessment phase.

hough reframes must be tailored to each family's unique
rience, three types of reframes are most often useful in
working with depression:

1. Reframing symptoms by providing information
2. Reframing negative behaviors by emphasizing positive intentions
3. Reframing difficult situations in ways that emphasize the "good news about the bad news"

The following case study provides an example of how a therapist can use such reframes to engage with a family and begin to shift perceptions:

BRENDA

When Brenda, a seventeen-year-old African American female diagnosed with major depression, and her father, Jim, began family therapy, they were barely speaking to one another. In their early sessions, she explained that she thought her father was uncaring, critical, and insensitive. She explained that he lectured, nagged, and pressured her constantly and that she consequently had decided she wanted little to do with him.

Jim insisted that his lectures were necessary because Brenda was becoming a typical selfish, ungrateful teenager with little respect for adults. Brenda, he said, complained about everything in her life and refused to interact with others, isolating herself in her room for much of the day. In particular, he felt frustrated by the fact that Brenda spoke frequently about not wanting to live with him and her paternal grandparents, with whom she had resided since her mother left when she was four years old. Jim could not understand why Brenda wanted to be by herself so much or why she refused to acknowledge all the ways in which he and his parents had loved and cared for her.

As a way of connecting, the therapist began to emphasize the less negative aspects about their current struggles. She acknowledged that their conflict with one another was very difficult and stressful, but she also highlighted the ways in which these problems had precipitated a turning point in their relationship that was providing an opportunity to take stock and make some positive changes.

The therapist also talked with Jim about the difficulty of dealing with all the ways in which Brenda seemed unhappy. She then worked to provide information about common depressive symptoms to help him see Brenda's withdrawal, complaints, and negativity as part of her depression, not signs of selfishness or disrespect.

She also acknowledged that Jim wanted the best for his daughter and wished to help her feel happier. His concern and frustration with feeling unable to help her enjoy life were, she explained, natural. Acknowledging Jim's good intentions in these ways allowed her to introduce the idea that his efforts were counterproductive and exacerbated the very behaviors from Brenda that he hoped to minimize. Feeling supported and understood by the clinician and understanding his daughter's illness better allowed Jim to be more open to listening to new ideas about alternative strategies he could use to interact with Brenda. Moreover, Brenda began to feel less alienated as she began to see "nagging" as her father's misguided way of trying to protect and care for her.

This family's story demonstrates one way in which redefining the symptoms of depression as symptoms of a legitimate illness can help buy tolerance and time. Affirming how difficult it is to live with depression and recognizing how well everyone has coped helped decrease Brenda's father's feelings of guilt and helplessness. By emphasizing the good intentions behind his attempts to help, as opposed to behaviors that seemed to Brenda intrusive or controlling, the clinician decreased the tension between family members and laid the groundwork for conversations about what might be more helpful in the future. Shifting perspectives in these small ways can decrease blame and conflict, as well as change attitudes and behaviors.

Assessing Weaknesses and Strengths

During this initial phase of treatment, it is also important for you to begin the process of assessing the patient and the family environment for strengths that can be enhanced, as well as for vulnerabilities that must be minimized. An emphasis on strengths requires attention to such factors as how much family members care for and are committed to one another, their past coping abilities, their ability to ask for help, their ability to express their needs, their support network, and any other assets the clinician might observe. As these qualities are identified, they can be emphasized and reinforced, thus reminding both patient and family of positives that may have been neglected in their struggle to manage their current problems.

In assessing family vulnerabilities, it's important that clinicians assess current difficulties without assuming they are the only "real" or causative ones. This assessment includes an examination of the stresses and events family members might have recently experienced (for example, losses, job changes, life cycle changes) that could have left them with less than usual energy for coping with the current crisis. In assessing family interactional patterns, particular attention must be paid to (1) high levels of criticism, (2) interaction in which the verbal and nonverbal messages are not congruent, (3) caretaking that undermines the remaining skills of the patient, and (4) attempts to be so helpful and tolerant that family members exhaust their own resources.

These issues require attention and possible modification, not because they are pathological—they may be completely reasonable ways of coping with many everyday problems—but because those who are depressed find them particularly difficult to manage. In fact, the family's perfectly reasonable responses or natural efforts to help may actually undermine a patient's shaky sense of competence. One wife reported that her husband's tendency to take over what she viewed as her household chores made her feel worse because she was no longer "needed" by her family.

On the one hand, criticisms that are a normal part of family life may devastate someone who is depressed. On the other hand, attempts of family members to protect patients from criticism may backfire when the patient reads the nonverbal signals of irritation and begins to distrust all reassurance. Although those who are depressed respond with increased sensitivity to criticism, they are also very sensitive to the underlying messages sent by tone and posture.

For example, Mary, a fifty-year-old depressed woman, noted her husband's attempts to make her feel better, but she also noted the edge in his voice that signaled impatience and frustration. Her depressed view caused her to interpret his ambivalent attempts at support as simply a desire to get her better so that he could leave without excessive guilt. Her husband, in turn, found this interpretation of his efforts to "do the right thing" to be so infuriating that it almost became a self-fulfilling prophecy. It is not surprising that family members also can become exhausted and overwhelmed from trying so hard to protect the patient from all of these normal stresses of family life.

Although common problems can be identified, the specific impact of depression on a given family will depend on a multitude of factors. Many are related to the developmental stage of the patient and the life cycle stage of the family. The impact of depression differs, depending on whether the patient is a child, an adolescent, or an adult and whether his or her role in the family is that of child, homemaker, caretaker, wage earner, or elderly parent. Assessment must also address the nature of the illness (chronic, acute, recurrent) and any other unique circumstances (for example, family financial stresses, other family member's medical and/or psychiatric illnesses, single parenthood).

The Treatment Contract

During the final stage of connecting/assessment, the patient, the family, and the therapist together negotiate the treatment contract, the terms of therapy that tell everyone involved what he or she can expect of the process. The treatment contract should be time limited but renewable and based on clear, specific, mutually agreed-on, and realistic goals. Contracting should also address who will be involved in treatment, the frequency of sessions, and the primary intervention strategies to be used. An explicit contract ensures a collaborative approach in working on the problem and provides a guide against which progress can be measured.

PHASE II: PROVIDING SUPPORT AND INFORMATION

After the clinician has begun to develop a relationship with the family and has negotiated a contract with clear goals, educating the family about the illness in a supportive context becomes the next focus and task of treatment. Providing information is a nonthreatening intervention strategy designed to reduce family stress, interrupt negative patterns of family interaction, and create a more supportive environment. Providing information also communicates respect for patients and families and reinforces the effort begun in the connecting/assessment process to build a collaborative relationship.

Information can reduce the anxiety most people feel when they do not understand significant events or experiences in their lives. It can also provide them with the necessary data to make informed choices about treatment and about which coping strategies and responses they might prefer to employ in responding to behavior and events. Knowledge and the sense of mastery it can bring helps people manage all kinds of stress, including the stress of needing to cope with upsetting moods and behaviors in a family member. Consequently, a number of specific con-

tent areas should be addressed to help family members understand and better cope with depression (see Table 1.1).

Key Content Areas

To make it clear to families that the clinician knows what the
patient and family are experiencing and understands the difficulties inherent in coping with the illness, it is often helpful to
begin by describing depression, how it differs from the "blues"
all people experience, and the common responses that patients
and family members are likely to have. This description also lays
the groundwork for discussing the possible etiologies of depression.

Most family members worry that they have somehow caused
or contributed to the patient's illness, and too often they assume
they are to blame if the professionals with whom they interact
do not specifically refute this assumption. The guilt generated
in this way can add to the family's level of stress and interfere
with their coping and the development of the treatment relationship.

In explaining theories about the etiology of depression, we
have found it useful to highlight the stress-vulnerability model
while emphasizing that this model is a theory and that a definitive cause of depression has not been established. Feedback from
family members confirms that viewing depression as a disorder
produced in the context of some sort of genetic or biological vulnerability by ordinary or extraordinary stresses makes sense to
them. It is not uncommon for family members to remark, as one
spouse did, "Her depressions never made sense to me until now.
I think this will help me to help her."

Patients and family members should also be provided with the
most up-to-date information regarding currently available treatments and their demonstrated efficacy. Specific data about the
course and outcome of the disorder and its response to medication, psychotherapy, or (as usual) both can be used to help families understand the complex nature of the disorder and its

Table 1.1
Agenda for Patient-Family Psychoeducational
Sessions on Depression

I. Defining depression
  A. How depression differs from normal variations in mood ("blues")
     Description: Length of time it lasts, impact on functioning, self-esteem, responsiveness to the environment
  B. Possible causes: The stress-vulnerability model
     1. Genetic factors
     2. Biochemical factors
     3. Life events, stressors, and family problems

II. Depression and the interpersonal environment
  A. What depression looks like: interpersonal difficulties
     1. Oversensitivity and self-preoccupation
     2. Unresponsiveness to reassurance, support, feedback, sympathy
     3. Behaviors that appear willful
     4. Apparent lack of caring for others, unrealistic expectations
     5. Apparent increased need to control relationships
     6. Inability to function in normal roles, tasks
  B. Negative interactional sequences
     1. Family attempts to help by coaxing, reassuring, protecting (potential for overinvolvement)
     2. Patient is unresponsive, family escalates attempts to help or withdraws
     3. Patient feels alienated; family becomes withdrawn, angry, or both
     4. Family feels guilty and returns to overprotective stance
     5. Patient feels unworthy, hopeless, infantilized
     6. Families burn out over time but remain caught in guilt/anger dilemma
     7. Alienation and/or overprotection

Table 1.1 *Continued*
Agenda for Patient-Family Psychoeducational
Sessions on Depression

III. Treatments
  A. Psychotropic medication
  B. Psychotherapies
  C. Other treatments

IV. Families with depression
  A. What to avoid
    1. Reassuring too rapidly
    2. Taking communications literally
    3. Attempting to be constantly available and positive
    4. Allowing the disorder to dominate family life
  B. Creating a balance of protectiveness (neither over nor under)
    1. Recognizing multiple realities
    2. Distinguishing between the patient and the disorder
    3. Temporarily decreasing expectations
    4. Providing realistic support and reinforcement
    5. Avoiding unnecessary criticism (but providing feedback when necessary)
    6. Communicating clearly and simply (preverbially)
    7. Providing activity and structure
  C. Skills for family's self-preservation
    1. Taking time out (away from patient)
    2. Avoiding martyrdom
    3. Accepting own negative feelings
    4. Minimizing the impact of the disorder
  D. Coping with special problems
    1. Suicide threats and attempts
    2. Medication
    3. Hospitalization
    4. Atypical responses

ramifications on family life. This information also helps family members understand why it isn't possible for most patients simply to "get on with life" and overcome depression by sheer force of will. This information helps increase family members' tolerance of behaviors that might otherwise be irritating or unacceptable, thus buying time for the depression to remit or treatments to take effect.

Finally, information should be shared about psychosocial stressors that can affect the onset or course of depression, including the possible impact of certain inevitable aspects of family life. Strategies and coping skills can be emphasized that may help mitigate the severity and impact of a patient's depressive symptoms. The useful nature of activity and structure for the patient can be highlighted. Families can also be helped to avoid too rapid reassurance, too much support, and too much criticism. The needs and vulnerabilities of the patient clearly must be a focus, but family members must also be encouraged to take care of themselves to avoid the burnout that would otherwise occur from attempting to provide a constantly supportive environment. These efforts may include helping family members identify ways to avoid allowing the depression to dominate family life, including learning to realize their own limits, to accept their own inevitable negative feelings, to take respite "time-outs," and to connect with their networks for support.

Children and Adolescents

When the patient is a child or an adolescent, the educational sessions will differ somewhat. Much of the same information about symptomatology is relevant, but information about the prevalence of specific symptoms for specific age groups differs.

For instance, prepubertal children are more likely to show depressive appearance, physical complaints, separation anxiety, and agitation, whereas adolescents are more likely to complain of changes in vegetative signs, such as appetite impairment, weight loss, sleep problems, more general complaints about hopelessness, and phobias.

In child or adolescent depression, the request for help may have come as a result of crisis, such as a suicide attempt, or it may be the result of more chronic difficulties, such as withdrawal or underachievement. Because parents are more likely to be aware of overt behavioral manifestations of depression than of the child's thoughts and feelings, the presenting complaint often involves the secondary complications of the disorder.

In these cases, considerable family dissension may be present, dissension that may be complicated by the likely history of affective disorder, substance abuse, or anxiety in the parents. As a result, these families are more likely to be multiproblem and to require sensitive attention to a variety of possible problems among other family members. In addition, because parents usually feel responsible for the well-being of their children, special attention should be paid to alleviating their guilt and anxiety, thus freeing up their ability to cope effectively.

Parents will need the information that all family members need about how much to monitor someone who is depressed; how to differentiate normal fluctuations in mood from the symptoms of depression; whether or not to protect the child from their negative feelings, concerns, and other potentially distressing information; and how to deal with a recovery process that seems to be unpredictable and intermittent. For instance, parents, like any other family member of someone who is depressed, may well need help sorting out when to be available and supportive to their offspring. For depressed adolescents, however, this decision is made more sensitive by the high value they often place on their parents allowing them privacy and independence. For depressed children and adolescents, specific additional topics that must be addressed include how to handle resistance to treatment, how to set appropriate limits, and how to differentiate normal developmental changes from behaviors that signal a need for help. For instance, because parents may have had recent alarming experiences with more severe symptoms, they may need support as they try to cope with general adolescent moodiness without overresponding. They may also need suggestions for finding ways to keep their child involved in treatment without letting this issue become a battleground for a major power struggle.

The Elderly

If the patient is an elderly family member, other issues require special attention. For instance, the central nature of both loss and the potential complications of medical problems must be addressed. Loss is always relevant as a factor associated with the onset of a depressive episode, but it is a particularly important factor for the elderly, given that they are likely to experience it with greater frequency. The multiple medical disorders associated with aging, and the medical interventions used to treat them, can also be associated with an increased risk for depression. Furthermore, the family members likely to be involved are most likely spouses, adult children, and siblings. Special attention should be given to the possibility that the nondepressed spouse is overburdened or that adult children, as the "sandwich generation," are being pulled in many conflicting directions. Because some family members are more likely to volunteer to help or are more easily called on, it is often helpful to take a look at who is performing what tasks. With these data in hand, some of the chores can be more equitably divided among family members, or additional network members can be drawn in to help.

Format of Treatment

The most effective format for providing information to families is that of multiple family group sessions. Such large group sessions are particularly valuable as an efficient and cost-effective way to impart a great deal of information to several families at a time. Moreover, they simultaneously provide contact with other families, which is a powerful way to help decrease the sense of isolation and stigma that people coping with depression often experience. Not only can families and patients see others struggling with similar issues, but those who might not feel able to ask questions or challenge professionals can also benefit from hearing clinicians respond to other families.

It is our experience that families ask many questions about causes and treatments once it is clear that asking questions is acceptable. Responding to these questions honestly, particularly acknowledging what is *not* known, helps clinicians continue to build the treatment alliance.

Typically, such group sessions include six to eight families. They can be given in a one-day "survival skills group" format lasting four to six hours or in a series of four to six briefer sessions over several weeks. We have tried both methods and have concluded that each has advantages. The one-day format allows an accelerated engagement process with the clinicians involved and establishes a sense of comfort and support from one another for families. The extended format allows family members the chance to think about issues between sessions, to prepare their questions and comments, and gradually to develop relationships with both the team and other families over time.

When offering multiple family groups is not feasible, the provision of information can be easily integrated into individual family sessions, a method that still makes the treatment relationship a more collaborative one. The information may be provided by any one of a number of professionals. Frequently, a psychiatrist or a master's level nurse provides a review of theories of etiology and medication management, whereas a nonmedical professional, such as a social worker or psychologist, discusses the psychosocial ramifications and possible psychotherapeutic interventions.

Whatever the format, clinicians can increase their effectiveness by using a variety of tools and techniques for presenting information to families and patients, including the provision of handouts on each of the specific content areas. Booklets available from

NIMH, NAMI, and other self-help organizations are often helpful. The distribution of such printed materials increases the legitimacy of depression as a disorder and additionally allows patients and families to take the information home and absorb it at their own pace.

PHASE III: APPLYING PRINCIPLES AND MAINTAINING GAINS

Because depression is often recurrent and sometimes chronic, patients and families must learn to cope with it over time, and they need support for their attempts to do so. Even when psychotropic medication works miracles in modifying acute episodes, dealing with the aftermath of depression often involves addressing entrenched marital and parent-child problems. Whether these problems preceded and contributed to depression or are a result of it, finding ways to mitigate these difficulties will improve family satisfaction and may also help forestall relapse.

Providing information, as described, is a critical part of learning to cope with depression, but information alone is rarely sufficient to produce significant and lasting change. A series of family sessions can be offered to help families apply the principles and themes of the educational sessions to their actual experience of daily life.

Setting Limits

Initially, the goal of these sessions is to begin to live with the symptoms of depression without allowing them to take center stage in family life. For adult patients, this goal is likely to require that the clinician help family members sort out temporary reallocation of household and child-care responsibilities. With child or adolescent patients, this goal means helping the family avoid any unnecessary influence on normal life cycle tasks by helping them facilitate small steps toward emancipation.

While the depression is still acute, family interaction usually will need to be modified in ways that may not be normal, to allow for temporary support of the depressed member and for special needs and sensitivities that accompany depression. For instance, when a family member is struggling with low energy and inertia, providing temporary relief from some of his or her ongoing family responsibilities may be necessary and feasible. Clinicians can use family meetings to develop a plan for coverage involving other family members or outsiders. Because it may not be possible to count on the patient for initiative during this early phase, it often falls to family members to get the patient moving. The art of this part of therapy is to help family members support the patient without getting overinvolved and overprotective and without depleting their own energy and coping resources.

An open discussion of this issue sometimes helps make patients less reactive as family members learn to set some limits on the amount of care they can provide. It is important to emphasize the temporary nature of these arrangements by encouraging the resumption of normal roles as soon as possible. This emphasis serves to reassure family members that there is light at the end of the tunnel and makes it clear to the depressed person that he or she continues to be competent, with a temporary problem, not a permanent disability. To prevent further erosion of self-esteem, it is also crucial to continue to support the sense that, even while ill, the depressed person has something to offer.

Related Problems

As the depression becomes less severe and as initiative returns, the contract for family sessions can be shifted to focus more on family issues of general concern, particularly those that may be stressful in ways that could precipitate further difficulties or trigger depressive episodes. The presence of depression is no guarantee that the family and its members do not have other problems as well.

"Assortive mating," the phenomenon of people tending to choose partners with similar psychiatric disorders, makes it more likely that more than one family member is vulnerable to mental health or substance abuse problems. When this is the case, clinician and family must negotiate to establish the priorities of treatment based on risk and pain experienced. Certainly, a wife's alcoholism may influence a husband's depression, as well as her ability to cope effectively to help both spouse and children. A child's chronic medical illness may have depleted family coping resources and may make it difficult to manage a depressive crisis. Each problem can contribute to another and needs to be evaluated in terms of its effect on the family as a whole.

The existence of independent or related problems, however, does not necessarily mean that the family will be willing to work on them. Members can be encouraged to put their concerns on the table, with the clinician adding and clarifying and helping to prioritize. The final decision belongs to the family. This process becomes the basis for establishing the goals of the treatment contract, which will be the focus of ongoing sessions. The most important guideline is to limit the number of items on the agenda at any given time so as not to overwhelm an already stressed system. Modifying these interactional patterns in families is often a difficult task because they are likely to be core components of the way a family operates.

Marital Issues

Two very common areas of focus at this stage of family work are (1) the balance of power and intimacy between marital partners and (2) the growing autonomy of adolescents or young adults whose emancipation has been hampered by depression.

Depression is more common in women and often affects the marital relationship. It influences a woman's ability to negotiate with her spouse about having her needs met in their relationship or even to believe that her needs are legitimate. A depressed woman is prone to low self-esteem and to giving away parts of her identity in the marital relationship. If she overaccommodates to the needs of others, she denies her negative feelings to the point of forgetting who she is. Thus, by the time she comes to treatment, she is likely to have developed a habit of deferral to her husband's choices that she may find less than satisfying, and she is also likely to have acquired a sense of helplessness that may contribute to her vulnerability to depression.

Working on this issue may initially make the marriage more troubled because although he may be eager to see her depression lift, he may not be prepared for her anger, her desire for more power or autonomy that may accompany recovery, and the increased focus on the negatives of their relationship. Additionally, he may have learned to cope with her unrealistically negative view of herself and family relationships by dismissing and minimizing her communications. So, you may have the task not only of helping her communicate her needs but also of helping him learn to listen all over again.

Family or marital therapy at this phase can help reestablish genuine communication, can help the depressed woman articulate her needs, and can help her husband adjust to a change in the balance of power/intimacy. It can also help him begin to expect more from her and to be freed from any excessive temporary responsibilities he may have assumed, which, in turn, should increase her sense of mastery.

In marital sessions, it is important not to pressure either partner to develop more intimacy than either can tolerate. Often, couples think they should use this opportunity to make their marriage a perfect one and feel pressured to raise all previous complaints for the agenda. Many spouses, not just depressed ones, think they *should* want more intimacy, without really thinking about the cost of what increased intimacy would mean. Clinicians should help partners move carefully into these issues and avoid blaming themselves or each other.

The issues in basically sound or moderately impaired relationships can easily be addressed in a brief treatment model such as this one. It may also be possible to improve more dysfunctional relationships if you are careful to negotiate very limited goals. An important factor will be the length of time and satisfaction in the marriage prior to the current crisis. Commitment to a marital relationship is more likely if there has been time to form a bond of good memories before the impact of any major negative event, including that of serious depression.

Adolescence

The family issues of depressed adolescents in this phase of treatment are somewhat different. Adolescence is clearly a time in any family's life when conflict is likely to occur as teenagers move toward greater independence and experimentation. Depression in these adolescents makes their parents understandably concerned. They become protective in ways that adolescents are likely to find constraining during a depressive episode, and intolerable once they are better.

Family sessions can be geared to help them negotiate a reasonable and increasing amount of independence and autonomy within the modified comfort levels of parent concern. Renegotiating a set of increasingly flexible family rules that allow for increased privacy and the expanding rights of young adulthood can begin to make room for more effective functioning. Still, parents of very impaired adolescents need to have ways of being reassured that suicide is not a risk or that the adolescent is not behaving in other self-destructive ways.

Parents may need help in learning to differentiate between normal adolescent moodiness and symptoms of serious depression. Sometimes, getting a contract from the adolescent to agree to signal a need for more help and support provides parents with enough reassurance to enable them to free some of the restrictions they have imposed. For example:

MELINDA

After sixteen-year-old Melinda had been released from the hospital after a suicide attempt, her parents remained understandably vigilant about her moods and behavior. Their concern became increasingly difficult for Melinda to tolerate, and she became surly and withdrawn. This behavior, of course, only made them more worried and more intrusive. She thought they did not respect her need for privacy and independence; they thought she could not be trusted. Family sessions centered on helping each faction understand the other's needs and on developing a contract they could both live with. Melinda agreed to tell her parents of any major upsets in exchange for being allowed to be in her room alone and to go out on weekend nights until 11 p.m. Her parents agreed to review this arrangement once a month and to consider allowing more freedoms if no evidence of increased depression or school problems occurred.

In all of these sessions, be they with adolescents or adults who are depressed, the theme of encouraging a sense of mastery in both the depressed person and the family is crucial.

Finally, as depression lifts, patient and family members must be helped to modulate their increasing expectations of each other. Too often, long-term problems are attributed to the depression and, as a result, everyone expects that once the illness is better, his or her life will all be conflict free and cozy. Problems are a part of family life, and those that existed before the depression will no doubt continue after it has ended. Reminding everyone about the normal vicissitudes of family life can help prevent unrealistic expectations and their resultant disappointments.

PHASE IV: GRADUAL TERMINATION

This model is meant to be time limited. The initial contract usually specifies a number of sessions despite the tendency of depression to be slow in remitting and the possibility that it will recur. Therefore, sessions of gradually decreasing frequency are advisable by moving from frequent contacts to monthly sessions and eventually quarterly or yearly checkups.

To make families more comfortable with the brief nature of treatment, clinicians can emphasize what both the patient and the family have come to know about depressive symptoms, how to identify them, and how to get help early in the course of an episode. Specific information about the early warning signs of depression can be shared and will allow family members to request help before symptoms have become full blown and entrenched. It is also helpful to teach families techniques for stress reduction and to provide the evidence of the advantage of maintenance medication.

Finally, stressing the fact that you will keep an open door, allowing them to return as necessary, is also advisable. Giving all family members permission or encouragement to recontact you if they should become worried or symptomatic helps make the cessation of sessions less upsetting. The model proposed is similar to that used in primary care, in which patients can use services as needed.

We designed our approach on the basis of the structure of psychoeducation, clinical experience with depressed patients and their families, and what we know from other studies about depression and families. It has been our observation that patients and families respond positively. In particular, this intervention seems to decrease the stress on family members and to increase their ability to cope effectively and get on with their lives.

No research evidence, however, confirms its effectiveness. We have made some attempts to assess the impact of the workshop for patients with affective disorders, but controlled clinical trials for this population have yet to be conducted. Until such studies are available, we believe that this model at least does no harm. It combines an awareness of family systems principles, avoids guilt-inducing interventions, attempts to empower family members, and restores patient functioning as quickly as possible. We believe that this intervention could become an important part of your treatment armamentarium because it also is relatively simple to employ and should work well in a managed care environment because it is time limited, not labor intensive.

NOTES

P. 2, *For instance, a limited telephone conversation:* Coyne, J. (1976). Depression and the response of others. *Journal of Abnormal Psychology, 85,* 186–193; Coyne, J., Kessler, R. C., Tal, M., Turnbull, J., Wortman, C. B., & Greden, J. F. (1987). Living with a depressed person. *Journal of Consulting and Clinical Psychology, 55*(3), 347–352; Hinchcliffe, M., Hooper, D., Roberts, F. J., & Pamela, W. V. (1975). A study of the interaction between depressed patients and their spouses. *British Journal of Psychiatry, 126,* 164–172.

P. 2, *Coping can be especially difficult:* Birtchnell, J., & Kennard, J. (1983). Does marital maladjustment lead to mental illness? *Social Psychiatry, 18,* 79–88.

P. 4, *They often feel responsible:* Beardslee, W. R., Bemporad, J., Keller, M. B., & Klerman, G. L. (1983). Children of parents with major affective disorder: A review. *American Journal of Psychiatry, 140,* 825–832; Orvaschel, H. (1983). Maternal depression and child dysfunction: Children at risk. In B. Lahey & A. Kazdin (Eds.), *Advances in clinical child psychology* (Vol. 6, pp. 45–51). New York: Academic Press; Widmer, R. B., Cadoret, R. J., & North, C. S. (1980). Depression in family practice: Some effects on spouses and children. *Journal of Family Practice, 10,* 45–51.

P. 5, *Even after a particular depressive episode:* Bothwell, S., & Weissman, M. (1977). Social impairments four years after an acute depressive episode. *American Journal of Orthopsychiatry, 47*(2), 231–237; Weissman, M. (1972, September). The depressed woman: Recent research. *Social Work,* pp. 19–25; Weissman, M., & Paykel, E. J. (1974). *The depressed woman: A study of social relationships.* Chicago: University of Chicago Press.

P. 8, *It is based on the philosophy and structure:* Anderson, C. M., Reiss, D. J., & Hogarty, G. E. (1980). Family treatment of adult schizophrenic patients: A psycho-educational approach. *Schizophrenia Bulletin, 6*(3), 490–505; Anderson, C. M., Reiss, D. J., & Hogarty, G. E. (1986). *Schizophrenia and the family.* New York: Guilford Press; Haas, G. L., & Clarkin, J. F. (1988). Affective disorders and the family context. In J. F. Clarkin, G. L. Haas, & I. D. Glick, *Affective disorders and the family: Assessment and treatment* (pp. 3–28). New York: Guilford Press.

P. 8, *Although variations of this model:* Anderson, C. M., Griffin, S., Rossi, A., Pagonis, I., Holder, D. P., & Treiber, R. (1986). A comparative study of the impact of education vs. process groups for families of patients with affective disorders. *Family Process, 25,* 185–206; Daley, D. C., Bowler, K., & Cahalane, H. (1992). Approaches to patient and family education with affective disorders. *Patient Education and Counseling, 19,* 163–174; Holder, D. P., & Anderson, C. M.(1990). Psychoeducational family interventions for depressed patients and their families. In G. Keitner (Ed.), *Depression and families: Impact and treatment* (pp. 159–184). Washington DC: APA Press.

P. 8, *First, the psychoeducational model is consistent:* Bromet, E. J., Ed, V., & May, S. (1984). Family environments of depressed outpatients. *Acta Psychiatrica Scandinavica, 69,* 197–200; Brown, G. W., Harris, T., & Copeland, J. R. (1972). Depression and loss. *British Journal of Psychiatry, 130,* 1–18; Vaughn, C. E., & Leff, J. P. (1976). The influence of family and social factors on the course of psychiatric illness: A comparison of schizophrenic and depressed neurotic patients. *British Journal of Psychiatry, 129,* 125–137.

P. 8, *Third, psychoeducation recognizes:* Hooley, J. M., Orley, J., & Teasdale, J. D. (1986). Levels of expressed emotion and relapse in depressed patients. *British Journal of Psychiatry, 148,* 642–647; Paykel, E. S., Myers, J. K., Dienelt, M. N., Klerman, G. L., Lindenthal, J. J., & Pepper, M. P. (1969). Life events and depression: A controlled study. *Archives of General Psychiatry, 21,* 753–760.

P. 10, *If the patient is acutely depressed:* McNabb, R. (1983). Family function and depression. *Journal of Family Practice, 16 (1),* 169–170.

P. 20, *For instance, prepubertal children:* Ryan, N., & Puig-Antich, J. (1986). Affective illness in adolescence. In A. J. Francis & R. E. Hales, *Psychiatry Update: American Psychiatric Association Review,* (p. 5). Washington DC: American Psychiatric Press.

P. 26, *"Assortive mating":* Merikangas, K. R., Bromet, E. J., & Spiker, D. G. (1983). Assortive mating, social adjustment, and course of illness in primary affective disorder. *Archives of General Psychiatry, 40,* 795–800.

P. 26, *A depressed woman is prone to low self-esteem:* Crowley-Jack, D. (1991). *Silencing the self: Women and depression.* Cambridge, MA: Harvard University Press.

P. 30, *confirms its effectiveness:* Frank, E., & Kupfer, D. J. (1992). Does a placebo tablet effect psychotherapeutic treatment outcome? Results from the Pittsburgh Study of Maintenance Therapies in Recurrent Depression. *Psychotherapy Research, 2,* 102–111.

P. 30, *We have made some attempts:* Anderson, C. M., Griffin, S., Rossi, A., Pagonis, I., Holder, D. P., & Treiber, R. (1986). A comparative study of the impact of education vs. process groups for families of patients with affective disorders. *Family Process, 25,* 185–206; Jacob, M., Frank, E., Kupfer, D., Cornes, C., & Carpenter, L. (1987). A psychoeducational workshop for depressed patients, family, and friends: Description and evaluation. *Hospital and Community Psychiatry, 38,* 968–972.

2

COGNITIVE BEHAVIOR THERAPY

Michael E. Thase

Cognitive behavior therapy (CBT) is the most widely studied form of psychotherapy for depression. Also called cognitive therapy, CBT has evolved during the past thirty years principally as a result of the work of Aaron T. Beck and his associates. CBT also draws on the seminal writings of Albert Ellis, Charles Ferster, and Joseph Wolpe. In this chapter, I first describe the basic principles of CBT and the corresponding model of depressive psychopathology. Next, I outline the methods commonly used in therapy and highlight typical problem areas. Third, I briefly review the results of studies examining the outcome of CBT. Finally, I consider the impact of managed care on the practice of CBT.

BASIC PRINCIPLES OF CBT

CBT is a structured, time-limited model of psychotherapy, typically conducted over a three- to six-month period. CBT centers around understanding the functional relationships between thought processes, thought content, overt behaviors, and mood

Note: This research was supported, in part, by grants MH–41884 and MH–30915 (MHCRC) from the National Institute of Mental Health, as well as the support of a grant from the John D. and Catherine T. MacArthur Foundation. We wish to thank Lisa Stupar and Andrea Emling for their assistance in the preparation of this manuscript.

disturbances (see Figure 2.1) and helping patients learn to use more efficient means to cope with depression. As therapy progresses, areas of potential vulnerability are examined, identified, and addressed, and prior to termination, relapse prevention techniques are practiced. CBT is delivered as either a group or individual therapy, and couples models of CBT have recently been developed. The therapy is best suited for people with mild to moderately severe nonbipolar, nonpsychotic forms of depression. The typical course of therapy ranges from eight to twenty sessions.

A number of characteristics differentiate CBT from both traditional models of insight-oriented psychotherapy and other, newer time-limited therapies, such as interpersonal psychotherapy (IPT). Perhaps most important, the CBT therapist's case formulations and interventions stem directly from cognitive and behavioral conceptualizations of depression. Second, CBT sessions follow a specific pattern or outline (see Table 2.1). Third, as revealed in the regular use of homework, CBT emphasizes a stepwise introduction to methods that patients begin to use in vivo to cope with depressive symptoms and other areas of difficulty. Fourth, the therapist uses a style of interaction known as *collaborative empiricism*. Beyond providing the so-called core therapeutic qualities (genuineness, accurate empathy, and respect), the therapist fosters an alliance in which problems are examined, alternative explanations are explored, and new approaches are tested in order to examine their utility. An empirical approach to therapy also is reflected in the regular use of problem lists and various types of assessment scales to monitor progress. As in IPT, cognitive therapists also make ample use of psychoeducational strategies to help patients gain more knowledge about depression and a more realistic understanding about what to expect from treatment.

The Cognitive Model of Depression

The cognitive model of psychopathology centers on the role of disturbances of thought content and thought process in the onset and maintenance of emotional disorders. I discuss abnormalities

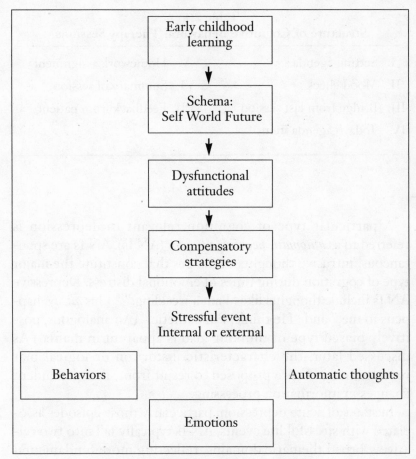

Figure 2.1
Cognitive Model of Psychopathology

of thought content first. The thought content of depressed people is characterized by a significant increase in self-depreciating, pessimistic, or apprehensive thoughts about the self, the world, and the future (Beck's cognitive triad). Studies document that an increasing frequency of negative thoughts covaries with depressive severity such that markedly hopeless, suicidal, or delusionally depressed patients may experience 80 percent, 90 percent, or an even greater proportion of negative thoughts and feelings. This type of depressive thought disturbance also includes negatively tinged daydreams, recall of memories, and dreams.

Table 2.1
Structure of Cognitive Behavioral Therapy Sessions

I. Setting agenda	V. Homework assignment
II. Mood check	VI. Summary of session
III. Bridge from last session	VII. Feedback from patient
IV. Today's agenda items	

A particular type of cognition relevant to depression is referred to as *automatic negative thoughts* (ANTs). ANTs are spontaneous, intrusive thoughts or images that constitute the major type of cognition during times of emotional distress. Depressive ANTs include thoughts like "I am a weakling," "This *always* happens to me," and "He thinks I'm pathetic." (An analogous, positively biased type of thinking also is apparent in mania.) As discussed later, the characteristic distortion or logical bias revealed in ANTs are proposed to result from state-dependent changes in information processing.

In states of acute depression, particularly those episodes associated with stressful life events, ANTs typically fall into two relatively broad thematic domains, reflecting more fundamental concerns related to issues of competence or lovability. The theme areas, in turn, are understood to reflect a deeper (unconscious) level of cognition referred to as a *schema*. Drawing on the Piagetian construct, schemata are developmentally influenced "silent" guiding principles shaped by the interaction of aptitude, temperament, and experience. In acute depression, depressogenic schemata are easier to infer because they typically have been activated by a relevant stressor. In chronic depression, persistently elevated levels of ANTs suggest the continued salience of these basic concerns.

A third and more intermediate level of cognition is referred to as *attitudes* or *beliefs* (see Table 2.2). These cognitions provide

Table 2.2
Common Dysfunctional Attitudes in Depression
and Anxiety Disorders

To be happy, I must be accepted by all people at all times.

If I make a mistake, it means that I am inept.

I can't live without you.

If somebody disagrees with me, it means that person doesn't like me.

My value as a person is dependent on what others think of me.

I must avoid embarrassment at all cost.

If I lose control of my emotions, I may go crazy.

I must hide my inner weaknesses from others in all circumstances.

Source: Adapted from Beck, 1976.

more specific rules of conduct and expectancy that are subordinate to the relevant schemata. Although clinicians' actual behavior in particular situations may be much less consistent with their attitudes than they realize, they nonetheless give personal credence to their attitudes about themselves, the future, and the world in general. Depression-prone people often have more rigid, demanding, or unrealistic beliefs and expectations. For example, perfectionistic attitudes may be developed, in part, to compensate for fundamental doubts about competency. These maladaptive cognitions are referred to as *dysfunctional attitudes*, and not surprisingly, they may be measured with a self-report inventory called the Dysfunctional Attitude Scale (DAS).

Dysfunctional attitudes may be most relevant for chronically depressed patients. The experience of being depressed, however, also will cause a state-dependent increase in dysfunctional attitudes that typically normalizes with effective treatment. As was the case with ANTs, dysfunctional attitudes may be recorded and collated according to themes, which in turn point to depressogenic schemata. To provide another example, dependent attitudes about the importance of maintaining romantic relationships (for example, "I must be in a relationship to be happy") would suggest a problematic schema in the area of lovability.

Attributional style represents another, more intermediate cognitive construct that may be inferred from a paper-and-pencil test (the Attributional Style Questionnaire). Attributional style stems from the reformulated learned helplessness model of depression and refers to the tendency for people to assign causality to events on the basis of three dimensions: internality versus externality, specificity versus globality, and transient versus enduring. A majority of studies indicate that depression-prone people are much more likely to attribute events to internal, global, and enduring factors. For example, a setback at work may be understood by a vulnerable person as being caused by personal inadequacy, and the event would be perceived to have much broader implications (for example, past and future failures) that might be unremediable.

Cognitive Distortions and Information-Processing Abnormalities

Depression, like other states of affective arousal, elicits characteristic changes in information processing. Some researchers have suggested that these changes actually are adaptive during life-threatening circumstances that require rapid, decisive action. Although the survival value of such changes is speculative, they do seem to shape the flow of information in such a way so as to clarify and intensify the prevailing affect. Thus, anxiety heightens vigilance and awareness of threatening cues, whereas anger increases the probability of defensive or aggressive responses. Sadness in general and depression in particular produce a number of changes in information processing, including overestimation of losses or limitations, undervaluation of one's strengths and resources, and increased recall of negative experiences. A list of such errors in personal logic and information processing is presented in Table 2.3.

Table 2.3
Common Patterns of Irrational Thinking in
Anxiety and Depression

1. *Emotional Reasoning:* A conclusion or inference is based on an emotional state; that is, "I *feel* this way, therefore I *am* this way."

2. *Overgeneralization:* Evidence is drawn from one experience or a small set of experiences to reach an unwarranted conclusion with far-reaching implications.

3. *Catastrophic Thinking:* An extreme example of overgeneralization, in which the impact of a clearly negative event or experience is amplified to extreme proportions; for example, "If I have a panic attack, I will lose *all* control and go crazy (or die)."

4. *All-or-None (Black or White; Absolutistic) Thinking:* An unnecessary division of complex or continuous outcomes into polarized extremes; for example, "Either I'm a success at this, or I'm a total failure."

5. *Shoulds and Musts:* Imperative statements about self that dictate rigid standards or reflect an unrealistic degree of presumed control over external events.

6. *Negative Predictions:* Use of pessimism or earlier experiences of failure to prematurely or inappropriately predict failure in a new situation. Also known as "fortune telling."

7. *Mind Reading:* Negatively toned inferences about the thoughts, intentions, or motives of another person.

Continued

Table 2.3 *Continued*
Common Patterns of Irrational Thinking in
Anxiety and Depression

8. *Labeling:* An undesirable characteristic of a person or event is made definitive of that person or event; for example, "Because I *failed* to be selected for ballet, I am a *failure*."

9. *Personalization:* Interpretation of an event, situation, or behavior as salient or personally indicative of a negative aspect of self.

10. *Selective Negative Focus:* Undesirable or negative events, memories, or implications are focused on at the expense of recalling or identifying other, more neutral or positive information. In fact, positive information may be ignored or disqualified as irrelevant, atypical, or trivial.

11. *Cognitive Avoidance:* Unpleasant thoughts, feelings, or events are misperceived as overwhelming and/or insurmountable and are actively suppressed or avoided.

12. *Somatic (Mis)Focus:* The predisposition to interpret internal stimuli (for example, heart rate, palpitations, shortness of breath, dizziness, tingling) as *definite* indications of impending catastrophic events (for example, heart attack, suffocation, collapse).

Source: Adapted from Beck, Rush, Shaw & Emery, 1979.

More severe depressive states also are associated with changes in concentration, attention span, and the capacity to use abstract thought. These neurocognitive abnormalities are, on occasion, severe enough to warrant the use of the term *depressive pseudodementia* in older patients. Neurocognitive abnormalities may impair an individual's capacity to benefit from the learning-based psychotherapies by affecting the recall, understanding, or generalization of therapy materials. Some evidence indicates that increased central nervous system arousal and persistently increased hypothalamic-pituitary-adrenocortical activity (for example, high plasma cortisol levels) may trigger the neurocognitive abnormalities of depression.

Behavioral Models of Depression

Observational studies of depressed people document a broad range of behavioral difficulties. Almost universally, a reduction of goal-directed behavior is observed, resulting in decreased pleasurable physical activity and a deficit of social reinforcement. Figure 2.2 describes this "downward spiral" resulting from the reciprocal interaction of mood, behavior, and cognition. At the same time, many depressed people also show decreased self-reinforcement for the activities and accomplishments they are able to complete. Such deficits lead to increased solitary time during which the increased frequency of negative thoughts may provoke a further reduction of mood. Procrastination resulting from decreased energy and/or reduced self-confidence may increase both subjective and objective stress as deadlines are missed; work may accumulate to an overwhelming level. Family members sometimes inadvertently reinforce dependent or depressive behavior by helping too much. Conversely, significant others may add to the patient's isolation as they begin to adjust their lives to take into account the depressed person's absence. Similarly, other sources of social support may be slowly extinguished by the depressed person's frequent decline of invitations to go out or be suppressed by the general aversiveness of repeated crying or complaining behavior.

At the same time, more long-standing or traitlike patterns may predispose to depressive difficulties. In particular, a more general tendency toward increased emotional and autonomic reactivity, referred to as *neuroticism*, has been associated with increased rates of depression. In a related manner, depression-prone individuals are more likely to manifest difficulties with interpersonal assertiveness and/or to have poor conflict resolution skills. Thus, a potentially vicious positive feedback loop is

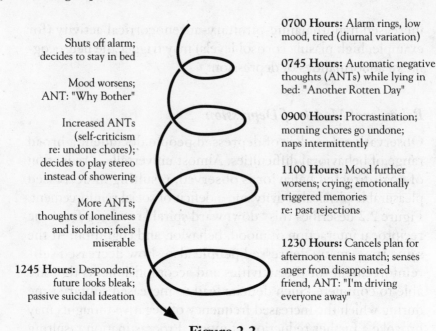

Shuts off alarm;
decides to stay in bed

0700 Hours: Alarm rings, low
mood, tired (diurnal variation)

Mood worsens;
ANT: "Why Bother"

0745 Hours: Automatic negative
thoughts (ANTs) while lying in
bed: "Another Rotten Day"

Increased ANTs
(self-criticism
re: undone chores);
decides to play stereo
instead of showering

0900 Hours: Procrastination;
morning chores go undone;
naps intermittently

1100 Hours: Mood further
worsens; crying; emotionally
triggered memories
re: past rejections

More ANTs;
thoughts of loneliness
and isolation; feels
miserable

1230 Hours: Cancels plan for
afternoon tennis match; senses
anger from disappointed
friend, ANT: "I'm driving
everyone away"

1245 Hours: Despondent;
future looks bleak;
passive suicidal ideation

Figure 2.2
The Downward Spiral: Interaction of Affect,
Behavior, and Cognition in Severe Depression

inherently primed, in which individuals with fewer coping abilities have a greater probability of encountering a threatening
stressor and a lower probability of resolving that difficulty satis-
factorily.

THE PROCESS OF COGNITIVE BEHAVIOR THERAPY

The structured, psychoeducational nature of CBT facilitates the
process of therapy to unfold in a slowly progressive manner.
Early sessions are devoted primarily to identification of a problem list, establishment of a solid therapeutic alliance, encultur-
ation into the model of therapy, and demonstration of the
methods and utility of therapy on pressing difficulties. The lat-

ter goal is specifically emphasized to counteract demoralization and hopelessness.

As described earlier, each session begins with setting an agenda outlining the tasks and/or goals for the session. It is the therapist's responsibility to set the agenda, monitor the session's flow, manage the pace and time, and maintain the focus on specified tasks. Structurally, each session of CBT shows some similarity to a teacher's lesson plan. Like a truly gifted tutor or a skilled coach, however, the therapist is sensitive to the patient's reservations and limitations. Moreover, the effective CBT therapist incorporates the patient's feedback liberally.

The First Session

Setting the agenda is a collaborative endeavor blending both the therapist's and patient's issues and concerns. I like to introduce the concept of an agenda within the first few minutes of the initial session, with a statement such as, "In this form of therapy, we've found that our work goes more efficiently if we follow an agenda or work plan. Today, clearly the first order of business is for us to discuss your history and the nature of your difficulties. I'd also like to develop a problem list and to have the opportunity to tell you a bit about this therapy. Do you have any questions up front? Can you think of anything else that should be added to today's agenda?" In this fashion, the directive yet collaborative style of CBT is illustrated almost immediately.

I have found that people with past experience in more expressive, unstructured therapies have, on occasion, some difficulty accepting such structure. Often, the person seeking therapy has learned to use the sessions as a sounding board or as a place for ventilation. Thus, people with prior therapy experience often have been enculturated to expect to spend a large proportion of time talking more generally about their concerns. The CBT therapist needs to gently interrupt long monologues and to help the depressed person get back on "track" (the agenda items) without feeling rebuffed or criticized.

It is important for the CBT therapist to recognize the potential for discrepancies in expectations and behavior and how these might affect the working alliance. Such early rifts may be apparent in the patient's body language, facial expression, inflection of speech, or noncompliance with the initial homework assignments. It is helpful if the therapist has the maturity of perspective so that the previous therapy is not presented as "bad" or "old-fashioned." Such experience also usually increases the therapist's intuitive recognition of opportunities to elicit thoughts and feelings about an affect-laden interchange. An example follows:

> *Therapist:* I noticed that when I interrupted you a moment ago, you seemed taken aback. Were you aware of any reaction?
>
> *Patient:* No. . . . Not really.
>
> *Therapist:* Well, people in general don't like to be interrupted, and after I interrupted you, I noticed that you crossed your arms over your chest (demonstrating) and your posture changed. If you don't mind taking a few minutes to discuss what might be going on, I'd like to, because it could be important. What was running through your mind just at that moment (when I interrupted you)?
>
> *Patient:* Well, like I said, it really didn't bother me much . . . maybe it did surprise me. . . . Dr. Johnson (previous therapist) didn't do things like that.
>
> *Therapist:* Okay, I may be making too much of this, but it does provide an opportunity for me to get to know you better and to teach a bit more about CBT. (On an eight-by-eleven-inch pad, the therapist draws three columns: Situation, Feelings, and Thoughts.) We call this a three-column sheet, and it's used in one of the first strategies we'll be working with. It helps to establish cause-and-effect relationships between events, feelings, and thoughts. I've written down the situation (being inter-

rupted by therapist), your initial description of the accompanying feeling (surprise), and the thought you reported (Dr. Johnson didn't do things like that). Now, let me ask you, if Dr. Johnson and I act differently, what might that say about me or our chances for working productively together?

Patient: Well, maybe nothing. But, it could mean you're not as good a listener.

Therapist: And if that's true, what might that mean?

Patient: Therapy might not be as helpful . . . or I might not get better.

Therapist: And if that's true?

Patient: Then I've wasted my time . . . another failure . . . I'll have to find another new therapist. Why did you interrupt me? Am I that boring? Was I just rambling?

Therapist: Your questions reflect just the type of thoughts we work with in CBT. We call them automatic negative thoughts. This is a really good example of how an event can elicit a whole chain of automatic thoughts about yourself, about me, and about your chances of getting better. You wondered aloud that I might find you to be boring or that you could be rambling. Can you think of any other explanations for my behavior?

Patient: Well, you could be rude. But, I don't think that's true. Maybe you just wanted to get back on track with the agenda.

Therapist: You're absolutely on target with the second possibility. But the most important point is what this illustrates about the way people think when they're depressed. Depressed people are much more likely to believe negative explanations, and this can lead to feeling even worse. By the way, I'm sorry if you felt criticized by the interruption, and my intention was not to hurt you. Perhaps I did it clumsily. I know Dr. Johnson, and I use different methods of treatment, and my methods tend to be more structured.

Patient: No, you weren't rude. I think I'm too sensitive.

Therapist: That could be. . . . We'll need to look at the evidence to see if that's accurate or if it's another example of an automatic negative thought. If it is a concern, we can certainly work on that specifically as part of our treatment plan. How do you feel about the work we've done so far?

Patient: Good. . . . I think I have a better understanding about how the therapy works.

Therapist: Great. . . . I'm glad we spent the time looking at that interchange. If it's okay with you, may I ask a few more questions about your condition?

Other illustrations of the cognitive model are pertinent to the first session of therapy. For example, when discussing symptoms, the therapist may ask about the patient's attributions or subjective appraisal. This often elicits verbalization of harsh, self-critical comments, such as laziness, stupidity, or weakness. Similarly, explicit questions about morale and expectations for the future naturally segue into a frank discussion of hopelessness and suicidal ideation. Another common strategy to introduce the cognitive model is to ask for the patient's thoughts and feelings about therapy before starting the session and to obtain feedback about his or her reaction so far. Such regular interest in patients' reactions and incorporation of their feedback further illustrate the collaborative nature of therapy.

When suicidal thoughts are present, it is important to elicit and understand the patient's perspective justifying such a desperate position. From the cognitive perspective, suicidal ideation is understood as a quasi-logical type of problem solving—contemplating an end to an apparently unbearable situation. Alternatively, a Reasons for Living Inventory may be collected to begin to marshall a list of the patient's assets and resources. This list provides an objective counterpoint to suicidal ideations. Given the loss of future perspective and undervaluation or even negation of positive attributes seen in depression, it is useful to ask the patient to also consider an external perspective, such as, "What would your spouse/parents/best friend/sibling say about your reasons for living?" Again, by modeling the use of an alternative perspective in order to examine the evidence in favor of and against suicide, basic cognitive interventions are introduced even during the first session.

The remaining goals of the first therapy session include a collaborative discussion of the case formulation, formulation of an initial problem list, and introduction of the use of homework assignments. Care is taken to fully integrate cognitive and behavioral concepts, as illustrated in the following summary:

> Let me sum up my understanding of your condition at this point, with the understanding that we can always fill in additional details in future sessions. Please feel free to interrupt if I've gotten something wrong or if I've overlooked an important detail. I understand that you've been increasingly more depressed over the past six months since the breakup of a stormy love relationship. As you felt more depressed, it's begun to affect your energy and you've been eating less. Your sleep also has been lighter and frequently disrupted by awakenings. You've been less interested in going out and less able to relax and have fun. You're getting behind in your work, and your boss has noticed that your performance has fallen off. When you're alone, it's hard to take your mind off your worries and loneliness, and you've begun to have thoughts like "why bother" and "things won't ever work out." You've also been more preoccupied with past memories about other romantic breakups, and you said that you've questioned whether there was something seriously wrong with you that causes women you love to ultimately reject you. Does this seem like a fair summary?

The initial homework assignment usually consists of a brief reading assignment, such as Aaron T. Beck and Ruth Greenberg's pamphlet "Coping with Depression" or the introductory workbook "Beating the Blues: Recovery from Depression" by Joe Howell and myself. Typically, an initial self-monitoring task also is assigned (see Figure 2.3). Homework is introduced as an essential component of therapy that builds logically on the material covered in sessions. Part of the skill of therapy is to communicate the significance of homework assignments, devise assignments that match the patient's readiness and capability, interweave completed homework within the next session, and supportively but decisively deal with noncompliance. Although many patients will not comply with homework assignments on occasion, the vast majority are able to actively collaborate on homework assignments if provided appropriate therapeutic support and encouragement.

In subsequent sessions, behavioral and cognitive interventions are selected as indicated by the case formulation and problem list. As described earlier, each session follows a structured plan that includes addressing one or two problem areas in detail. Early in the course of therapy, use of behavioral strategies may predominate. This use is particularly important for treatment of severe depressions. By the middle phase of therapy (for example, sessions six to twelve), most patients are able to master basic cognitive strategies. For patients responding to therapy, a final course of four to eight sessions is devoted to identifying, testing, and modifying basic assumptions and relapse prevention (for example, sessions twelve to twenty). In each case, however, the introduction of a particular strategy is prefaced by a concise description of the method and a demonstration of its relevance to the patient's problems. The major strategies employed in CBT are described below.

BEHAVIORAL TECHNIQUES

Behavioral techniques are particularly useful in the early stages of therapy. Their principal use is to help patients cope with symptoms and address interpersonal skills deficits. This use is especially true in the treatment of more severely impaired patients who are less active, socially withdrawn, and/or have marked difficulty with concentration. Although behavioral techniques thus tend to be more focused and concrete, they also are used as the vehicle to help patients identify, test, and modify dysfunctional cognitions. For example, a patient who complains of marked anhedonia often can use the results of a behavioral assignment specifically developed to increase pleasurable activity to also test the accuracy of the catastrophic thought "I don't enjoy anything!" The most commonly used behavioral methods are described in the following subsections.

Activity Scheduling

The activity schedule specifically helps the patient learn to monitor and modify behavior and to increase productivity. Patients are given a rating form and are instructed how to keep a record of their activities on an hour-by-hour basis. Ratings of mood may then be added to help establish functional relationships between the scheduled activity and changes in behavior and mood. Scheduling new activities is usually one of the first techniques used with a depressed patient and may be targeted to counteract hopelessness, inactivity, anhedonia, or loss of motivation. The therapist helps the patient identify unscheduled blocks of time that are empty and to consider alternative, potentially rewarding activities that may be scheduled into these time slots. Such activities include blocking out one hour to complete laundry or exercise or two hours to watch a videotape of a favorite movie or sporting event on TV.

Patients are often skeptical about the merits of activity scheduling. They point out that they've tried to do things and that they just don't feel any benefit. The collaborative-empirical approach taken by the CBT therapist is to acknowledge the skepticism and to point out that depressive anhedonia may make usual standards of fun or enjoyment temporarily unreachable. The patient is then engaged in trying out an experimental test of the hypothesis that the scheduled activity won't make a difference. An example of an experiment devised around an activity schedule is for the patient to monitor his or her mood and thoughts during an unstructured time period in comparison with a similar time period spent engaged in a preferred or potentially rewarding activity.

It is important to help the patient understand that his or her inactivity and loss of enjoyment are *symptoms* of depression and therefore likely to be transient (rather than enduring) and potentially amenable to change. Conversely, an informed therapist appreciates that the patient's anhedonia may actually be the result of dysfunction in the pleasure-reward centers of the brain, and as a result, the reinforcing aspects of many formerly desirable activities have a reduced salience. In cases of an apparently diminished capacity to enjoy, therapeutic expectations are temporarily set lower (to complete a task, rather than to enjoy it), and an illustration such as "priming a pump" or "establishing a foundation" to lessen dysphoria and build on is often helpful.

Mastery and Pleasure Ratings

Activity scheduling is often necessary because patients may feel too anergic and/or dysphoric to spontaneously seek out pleasurable activities. Moreover, many patients minimize or devalue their remaining intellectual and interpersonal assets and areas of competence. The process of gaining greater objectivity is facilitated by having patients begin to rate scheduled activities according to their experiences of mastery (M) or pleasure (P). Although most patients can readily identify with the concept of pleasure, the term *mastery* often requires a brief psychoeducational lesson. Mastery is used to refer to any required skill or competence. For example, completion of an overdue tax form is not likely to elicit pleasure, but it does require a certain measure of competence.

Once patients understand the concepts underlying M and P ratings, they are asked to use a scale from zero to ten to rate M and P experiences. These ratings are then used to identify areas of deficit in the experience of pleasure or mastery. Such deficits can then be addressed with new homework assignments emphasizing increased access to reinforcement or esteem-enhancing activities. Persistently low M and/or P ratings also often provide a helpful clue that the patient's perceptions about the assignments (negative predictions, ruminations, and automatic negative thoughts) may be interfering with their intended effect. Identification of such a process would readily lead to the therapist's use of cognitive interventions, as I describe later.

Diversion Techniques

These techniques are used to help patients cope with the most painful or overwhelming affects, including dysphoria, anxiety, and anger. The rationale for the use of diversion techniques (rather than methods intended to have more fundamental or enduring effects on cognitions or behaviors) is that strong affects may be too overwhelming to overcome early in the course of therapy. The use of diversion thus enables the patient to cope more effectively at times of intense distress and/or to "dampen" an otherwise escalating emotional reaction. Patients thus obtain the added benefit of being able to regain a sense of control. Diversion may be accomplished through the use of physical activity (for example, riding an exercise bike), a distracting social contact, or visual imagery. Thought stopping, a specific elaboration of a diversion technique, may be particularly useful in coping with more intrusive ruminations or images. The therapist teaches the patient to use a distressing rumination as the cue to visualize an alternate image, such as a stop sign or a mountain brook. By focusing intently on the visual image, the patient typically achieves some respite from the emotionally charged rumination.

Patients sometimes disparage diversion techniques as a superficial or "trivial" approach. It is important for the therapist to elicit negative cognitions at such times (for example, "My problems are overwhelming, and the only help you can offer is to ride an exercises bike!"). The therapist also must ensure that the rationale and time-limited nature of the use of diversion techniques are understood explicitly. Moreover, when the patient uses a negative image to describe the technique (for example, "This is just a Band-Aid"), it is helpful to use reattributions of that image to address the problem. For example, the therapist might ask, "What is it about the idea of our using a Band-Aid technique that is so upsetting for you?" and "Can you think of any real-life circumstances in which you would find a Band-Aid helpful?"

Graded-Task Assignments

To help severely depressed patients initiate more complex activities, the therapist often needs to break down an activity into a series of steps, beginning with the simplest part of the task and progressing to the most demanding. This step-by-step approach permits the patient to eventually complete assignments that at first seem impossible or overwhelming. Graded-task assignments thus serve as a key behavioral method of addressing problems associated with procrastination and inertia. In the early phases of treatment, graded-task assignments also may help a markedly depressed patient realize that some accommodations need to be made to cope with impairments caused by the disorder. Such graded tasks also teach the utility of a stepwise approach to problem solving and thus may be generalized and applied to more complicated life problems after discharge.

Behavioral Rehearsal and Role-Playing

Rehearsal strategies help patients prepare and ultimately accomplish difficult tasks or responses. Role-playing usually includes the therapist's use of modeling and coaching of the patient's approximations of the target behaviors. For example, the patient may be asked to play the role of a significant other while the therapist "models" an appropriately assertive or confrontational response in the patient's role.

The monitoring of automatic thoughts during the use of rehearsal methods also may help the patient identify cognitive distortions that may exacerbate an emotionally charged situation. Imagery also may be used to help a patient covertly rehearse for specific tasks that cannot be explicitly practiced. These methods may be modified or expanded to enable the patient to develop new patterns of behavior, such as enhanced social skills, assertiveness, or improved management of anger.

Relaxation Training

Progressive deep muscle relaxation is a useful adjunctive method for managing generalized anxiety, psychomotor agitation, and initial insomnia. Relaxation training has been shown to have a modest additive effect when used along with antidepressant therapy, and we have found it to be a particularly helpful adjunct to CBT when medications are not used.

Cognitive Techniques

Four general steps are involved in a cognitive intervention:

1. Eliciting automatic thoughts and understanding their personal significance in terms of the cognitive triad (the meaning of the perception with respect to thoughts about self, world, or future)
2. Testing the accuracy of the automatic thoughts
3. Identifying logical errors, distortions, or maladaptive underlying assumptions or schemata
4. Testing the validity of alternative, more adaptive cognitions

These methods are discussed in the following subsections.

Identification of Dysfunctional Automatic Thoughts

The patient is taught to identify automatic negative thoughts as the first step of cognitive intervention. Automatic thoughts are described to patients in a didactic manner, and relevant reading material is provided early in the course of therapy. The therapist and the patient next work collaboratively to identify examples of such thoughts in vivo. Through repetition of this process, the patient learns to become more aware of his or her internal dialogue and patterns of thinking. The central hypothesis of CBT—namely, that feelings of depression or anxiety are related to the patient's tendency to think in a distorted or unrealistically negative manner—is thus introduced. The therapist, however, does not explicitly try to "correct" the accuracy of a patient's thoughts until the process for identifying and evaluating negative automatic thoughts is established.

Several techniques are used to help the patient identify automatic negative thoughts. The therapist may ask about what "passed through" the patient's mind during an emotional state. Mood shifts that occur during the session provide a particularly timely opportunity for the therapist to ask about the patient's thoughts. Similarly, upsetting events from the patient's recent past can be examined by asking him or her to recall specific thoughts and feelings while imagining that the troubling event is taking place. Role-playing also may be used to facilitate recall of thoughts and feelings associated with an unpleasant circumstance. Once an automatic thought is identified, the "downward arrow" technique (illustrated in Figure 2.3) is useful to help the patient access deeper, maladaptive assumptions, or schemata.

Homework assignments are similarly used to improve the patient's recognition of automatic negative thoughts and their relation to emotional reactions. The Daily Record of Dysfunctional Thoughts (DRDT; see Table 2.4) is an especially helpful form for patients to use as they begin to record variations in mood in relation to the situations or events associated with dysphoric mood or, conversely, the automatic thoughts that accompany a change in emotions. Thought counting may be used as a

PATIENT	THERAPIST
"I think the date went poorly (chuckles with gallows humor) . . . I'm so depressed!	"Is it true that the date went that poorly? Could this be an example of how negative thinking is involved with feeling depressed?"

"No, it's true. He didn't mention another date and hasn't called me since."

"Okay . . . that sounds convincing enough. So, if the date went badly, what's that really say about you?"

"Stuff like this happens to me a lot!"

"And, if that's true?"

"There is something seriously wrong with me." (There is a visible shift in affect.)

"Such as . . ."

"I must be a reject . . . a social basket case . . . I'm so pathetic!" (tearful)

"And if that's true, which we still have to test out, what does that say about your world and future?"

"It says that no one will ever love me. . . . I'll be lonely forever . . . an old maid. . ." (more tears)

"I can see from your tears that these thoughts really hit you where it hurts. I've written down some of the more dramatic and hurtful statements. Do you feel up to taking a look at them and testing their accuracy?"

Figure 2.3
The Downward Arrow Technique

Table 2.4
Sample Daily Record of Dysfunctional Thoughts

Situation	Emotion(s)	Automatic Thought(s)	Rational Response	Outcome
Describe:	1. Specify sad/anxious/ angry, etc.	1. Write automatic thought(s) that preceded emotion(s)	1. Write rational response to automatic thoughts	1. Rerate belief in automatic thought(s), 0–100 percent
1. Actual event leading to unpleasant emotion, or	2. Rate degree of emotion, 1–100			2. Specify and rate subsequent emotions, 0–100
2. Stream of thoughts, daydreams, or recollection, leading to unpleasant emotion				
Date:				
12/23 Folding laundry	Sad, 50; Anxious, 60	1. There's so much to be done.	1. There *is* a lot to be done. I'll need to ask for help and use an activity schedule to manage my time. Bob (husband) and my mom both say that they don't mind helping.	Sad, 20 percent; Anxious, 30 percent
		2. I won't be able to pull my share of the load	2. I don't really know what I will or won't be able to do. If I can't work at 100 percent capacity at first, this will not be a tragedy. I am still recuperating, and it's okay to have help.	

Table 2.4 *Continued*
Sample Daily Record of Dysfunctional Thoughts

Situation	Emotion(s)	Automatic Thought(s)	Rational Response	Outcome
		3. I might get depressed again.	3. Yes, there is a chance of relapse. I know what the warning signs are, and I now can cope and manage symptoms a lot better. My therapist is available to help me if things get rough. Also, I can take an antidepressant if I have a severe relapse.	
		4. I'll let everyone down.	4. It's normal for people who care about me to be concerned about how I'm doing. However, my recovery is *not* something I owe them. My therapist says that the odds for doing well are very good.	

homework assignment when a patient is skeptical about the occurrence of a certain type of automatic thought. Patients may use a wrist counter or golf scorer to count the "targeted" thoughts.

Testing the Accuracy of Automatic Negative Thoughts

After the patient's pattern of automatic negative thoughts has been demonstrated to covary with disturbances of mood (a process that typically takes one to three sessions to establish), therapy shifts to testing the accuracy of the patient's thoughts. The goal of this step is to help the patient learn to think more objectively (like a scientist or judge). As a result, the patient learns through guided discovery that his or her thoughts and conclusions are hypotheses rather than facts and that because these hypotheses often have ominous implications, they require verification against all available evidence. A majority of therapist-patient interactions during the midphase of therapy (sessions five to fifteen) use this method. The novice CBT therapist must learn that this method differs from simple persuasion, in which an expert (the therapist) attempts to persuade or convince the patient that the automatic thoughts are wrong or irrational. This step represents a fundamental element of Beck's approach to CBT.

As described earlier, the patient records emotionally charged situations and the corresponding automatic negative thoughts during targeted periods of time. Material elicited during periods of increased depression may be particularly useful, as are the patient's thoughts and afterthoughts about stormy interactions with family members. These recordings are examined in the subsequent session to evaluate their accuracy. At the most pragmatic level, patients need to learn to ask themselves several basic questions regarding their automatic negative thoughts:

1. What is the evidence to support these thoughts?
2. Could my conclusions be distorted by depressive thinking?

3. Are there any alternative interpretations?

4. [If a negative event has happened] What is my honest, real role/responsibility for this problem, and what can I do to help correct it?

5. If my interpretation is true (or partly true), what does it really say about me (or the world, or my future)?

At another level, the therapist is teaching the patient to look at each ANT as an accusation or charge. As in a trial, the evidence in support of the charges is presented first, followed by the defense's presentation of their alternate view of the case. After the trial model, therapist and patient work together to build an ironclad defense, presenting contradictory evidence, raising alternate possibilities, and (when appropriate) acknowledging guilt but pointing out mitigating circumstances.

Learning to develop more rational responses to dysfunctional automatic thoughts accompanies the process described above. At first, patients are encouraged to write down their alternative explanations or more rational counterresponses to automatic negative thoughts within the session, followed shortly thereafter by written homework. Specifically, the fourth and fifth columns of the DRDT sheet are tailored for this purpose. The therapist often needs to help the patient flesh out or expand these rational alternatives. The therapist may suggest one or more less damning explanations. Similarly, the therapist may encourage the patient to look for other, more objective sources of information—for example, "What would your sister/brother/best friend say about that?" For patients who "freeze" during times of emotional upset, rational responses to frequent dysfunctional cognitions may be practiced and rehearsed and, if necessary, jotted down on three-by-five-inch coping cards, which are carried to help prompt rational responses. Subsequently, patients are encouraged to begin to tackle their dysfunctional automatic thoughts in vivo (first by writing them down and then, once successful, through covert verbalizations).

Many patients find that their initial efforts to construct rational responses trigger a new "wave" of automatic negative thoughts. Often, these thoughts undercut the mood-altering goal of the rational response intervention. The skilled CBT therapist learns to perceive when a patient is experiencing unstated thoughts that question the accuracy of his or her rational responses. Such reservations usually can be recognized, tested, and countered within therapy sessions if the patient is to reach maximum benefit from the rational response technique.

Identification of Schemata and Dysfunctional Silent Assumptions

In later stages of treatment, it is important for the patient to gain some understanding about his or her basic schemata. Because schemata must be inferred from more superficial levels of cognition, an assignment to review past homework assignments to collate themes or patterns of rigid, harsh, or maladaptive attitudes is often a useful gateway. An autobiography also may be assigned as a way to collect historical data to document the development of pertinent schemata. In my experience, it is of some comfort for most patients to understand the origin of a pathologic schema (analogous to the "intellectual insight" of psychodynamic therapy), but the real action takes place during periods in which dysphoria triggers "hot thoughts."

Testing the Validity of Modified Response

Several strategies are available to modify schemata and silent assumptions. A common initial task is to have the patient list the advantages and disadvantages of retaining the attitudes and beliefs that are derived from a schema. Drawing on a technique used in the behavioral treatment of obsessive-compulsive disorder, a modified form of response prevention also may be used. This technique involves encouraging the patient to conduct experiments in which he or she behaves oppositely to his or her normal tendency (the stereotypical response typically dictated by the attitude or silent assumption in question).

For example, a patient with perfectionistic attitudes may be encouraged to perform an experiment in which he or she must complete a task in an "only satisfactory" manner. While performing this experiment, a patient typically encounters automatic negative thoughts that trigger anxiety or dysphoria, which in turn may interfere with performance or trigger ruminations. The patient may then apply methods learned in therapy to cope with the symptoms in vivo. Parallels then can be drawn to circumstances from the past or anticipated situations in which the standard of perfection would be impossible to achieve.

ASSESSMENT OF OUTCOME

Depressed patients receiving any form of professional therapy warrant periodic review of the effects of treatment on their symptoms and functioning. The Beck Depression Inventory (BDI) is well suited for this purpose, and I strongly recommend its weekly administration. In fact, we use the BDI in our clinic as a standard metric of treatment outcome.

Generally, a score reduction of at least 50 percent is anticipated by the midphase of therapy (weeks six to ten). In my experience, most patients who have not achieved this level of improvement often require alternative interventions, such as the addition of an antidepressant or the inclusion of the spouse.

Other useful assessment measures include the Global Assessment Scale, the Hopelessness Scale, the Dysfunctional Attitude Scale, and the Attributional Style Questionnaire. The latter measures are also sometimes used to gather additional data on attitudinal or attributional correlates of depressive vulnerability. This information then may be used to help guide work in sessions.

TERMINATION OF THERAPY

Although research protocols typically provide a fixed, predetermined number of sessions (twelve to twenty), in practice I recommend that decisions to terminate therapy should be based entirely on the quality of the response. The aim of therapy is complete resolution of the depressive syndrome, and even minor residual symptoms appear to convey a higher risk for relapse. Persistently elevated levels of dysfunctional attitudes also appear to reflect greater vulnerability and thus would justify continued, targeted therapy.

One practical approach suggested by my group's research is to gauge the anticipated termination date for about eight weeks after the patient has achieved a stable degree of remission (consecutive BDI scores of six or less). This final phase of therapy then can be used to clarify areas of schematic vulnerability, to identify situations that may cause a reactivation of depressive thinking, and to practice the variety of relapse prevention techniques.

The value of long-term "maintenance" CBT has not yet been documented. It may or may not convey additional protection against relapse. I have not found regular "booster" sessions after termination of therapy to be of much use for patients who have remitted. Rather, I prefer to space the last few sessions, with at least two every-other-week sessions followed by a final session about one month later. An important part of relapse prevention is to inform the patient that depression may become a chronic and recurrent illness and that exacerbations of symptoms are to be expected, particularly during times of stress. Increased symptoms are framed to represent opportunities to practice the skills learned in therapy. Thus, denial of vulnerability and its opposite dysfunctional response, catastrophization, are dealt with proactively. Patients are encouraged to return to therapy should symptoms persist for longer than two weeks.

EFFECTIVENESS OF CBT

A majority of randomized clinical trials have examined the effectiveness of CBT in outpatients who would meet *DSM-IV* criteria for major depression and/or dysthymia. Across a number of trials, response rates to CBT have generally ranged from 50 percent to 80 percent. Keith Dobson reported the results of a meta-analysis of controlled studies available through 1989. This analysis indicates that CBT is greatly superior to low-contact control conditions and somewhat more effective than antidepressants, behavior therapy, and other forms of psychotherapy. In a commissioned review of a more narrowly defined sample of controlled studies, however, the Agency for Health Care Planning and Research drew a more modest conclusion, finding that CBT was generally comparable to other active treatments. Scant research has examined the utility of CBT as a primary treatment for hospitalized patients. Contrary to much prevailing psychiatric opinion, our group found that more than 60 percent of nonpsychotic inpatients responded to an intensive three- to four-week course of CBT. Increased severity, diagnostic comorbidity, and/or hypercortisolism were associated with poorer outcomes in our inpatient study.

Perhaps the most influential outpatient study, conducted under the auspices of the National Institute of Mental Health, compared CBT against IPT and a lower contact clinical management condition combined with either inert placebo (PBO) or the tricyclic antidepressant imipramine (IMI). The study took place at three university medical centers, and scrupulous attention was devoted to such issues as the training of the therapists and the reliability of clinical ratings. There were about sixty patients in each condition and eighty patients per site. The findings were notable in that the four treatment conditions were not significantly different across the sixteen-week treatment protocol, although IMI was more rapidly effective. In a subset of patients with more severe depressive symptoms, both IMI and

IPT were significantly more effective than PBO, whereas CBT had an intermediate effect. However, there is now evidence that CBT was differentially effective across the three sites, suggesting that the technical fidelity of CBT (how well it was delivered compared to the ideal) may have varied more than either IPT or IMI.

Another recent large study also failed to differentiate between the efficacy of CBT and other active interventions. In the Edinburgh Primary Care Study, 120 depressed outpatients were enrolled across sixteen inner-city sites. Patients were randomly assigned to CBT, amitriptyline (AMI, a tricyclic antidepressant) prescribed by a psychiatrist, social work counseling (SW), or treatment-as-usual as provided by a general practitioner (GP). All four conditions were associated with a clinically meaningful level of symptomatic improvement. Further, at the end of the sixteen-week trial, CBT did not differ significantly from either the SW condition or the AMI condition. Moreover, the social work condition received significantly higher ratings than CBT on several measures of patient satisfaction.

These studies indicate that CBT is not universally a superior treatment of depression, and in some settings, it may be no more effective than competently administered but less expensive therapies. Also, the fact that the largest negative reports concerning CBT stem from multicenter trials suggests that issues related to standardization and fidelity may be more critical to CBT's efficacy than the comparator treatments.

Correlates of CBT Response

An excellent review of the literature examining the correlates of CBT response was recently published by Mark Whisman. Across a number of studies, chronicity, unmarried status, higher levels of dysfunctional attitudes, and higher symptomatic severity have been associated with poorer outcomes. Homework compliance, optimism about the relevance of therapy, and the therapist's consistent use of CBT's structural elements also have been reported to predict favorable outcomes. A more self-reliant coping style, referred to as *learned resourcefulness*, has been associated with positive responses by several groups. Moreover, in a recent study by our group, high levels of learned resourcefulness were found to offset the negative effects of increased severity. CBT has not, however, been found to be more effective in patients with higher IQ scores, suggesting that not all cognitive skills are generalizable to this form of therapy. CBT appears to be equally effective for men and women.

Prophylaxis

At least 50 percent of patients treated with antidepressants will relapse within one year of successful treatment if not maintained on continued pharmacotherapy. By contrast, one-year relapses after CBT typically range from 10 percent to 30 percent. In one recent study by Mark Evans and colleagues, the magnitude of this preventive effect was comparable to that of continued drug therapy. Beyond suggesting that the coping skills learned in CBT may convey some degree of ongoing prophylaxis, these findings point out that simple cost comparisons based on the relative expense of twelve or sixteen weeks of CBT versus pharmacotherapy do not provide a fair cost-effectiveness assessment of CBT.

The major correlates of relapse following CBT are a history of prior episodes of recurrent depression, residual symptoms at the time of termination, and persistently high levels of dysfunctional attitudes. These clinical risk factors may be practically used to determine who might benefit from longer courses of therapy. For example, in my group's experience, incompletely remitted patients had five times the risk of relapse during the first year after termination when compared with fully remitted patients.

MANAGED CARE CONSIDERATIONS

Most therapists and patients have been touched by the changes in reimbursement of health care. So far, CBT has fared relatively well in the managed care arena. Although cost-containment measures are not always rational, it appears that CBT has done well because the treatment is well described, it has been empirically tested, outcomes are measured, and alternative strategies are generally pursued if treatment is not effective within a specified period (a two- or three-month trial of therapy). Although no data are available, it is my experience that an initial short-term treatment plan emphasizing CBT for treatment of a non-bipolar major depressive episode or dysthymia is acceptable to most reviewers.

The major tension about reimbursement for CBT concerns negotiations on the length of the course of therapy. Some managed care reviewers insist on an early termination if the patient is improving rapidly—that is, after only ten or eight or even six sessions. In our group's study, patients who had maintained a full remission for eight weeks prior to termination had a relapse rate of only 10 percent during the first year. By contrast, patients who had not achieved the eight-week remission prior to termination had a relapse rate of more than 50 percent during the same time frame. Therefore, it is important to assert that additional sessions are justified for partial responders in order to consolidate treatment gains and prepare for termination.

Beck's model of CBT is a practical, active treatment for nonpsychotic major depressive disorder. A majority of depressed outpatients will respond to twelve to sixteen weeks of therapy conducted by an appropriately trained and experienced therapist. For many patients, enduring prophylaxis may result. Although CBT has not been convincingly shown to be superior to other competently administered treatment options, its credibility (both clinically and empirically) has helped ensure its place in contemporary mental health care. So, if you have a patient appropriate for CBT, particularly one who might enjoy a structured, psychoeducational approach to therapy reinforced by homework and in vivo application, this may be the most suitable treatment for his or her depression.

FOR FURTHER READING

Beck, A. T. (1976). *Cognitive therapy and the emotional disorders.* New York: International Universities Press.

Beck, A. T., & Greenburg, R. L. (1974). *Coping with depression.* New York: Institute for Rational Living.

Beck, A. T., Rush, A. J., Shaw, B. F., & Emery, G. (1979). *Cognitive therapy of depression.* New York: Guilford Press.

Burns, D. (1980). *Feeling good: The new mood therapy.* New York: Morrow.

Burns, D., Rude, S. T., Simons, A., & Thase, M. E. (1994). Does learned resourcefulness predict the response to cognitive behavioral therapy for depression? *Cognitive Therapy and Research, 18,* 277–291.

Depression Guideline Panel. (1993). *Depression in primary care: Vol. 2. Treatment of major depression, clinical practice guideline number 5* (Publication No. 93–0551). Rockville, MD: Agency for Health Care Policy and Research.

Dobson, K. (1989). A meta-analysis of the efficacy of cognitive therapy of depression. *Journal of Consulting and Clinical Psychology, 57,* 414–419.

Elkin, I., Shea, M. T., Watkins, J. T., Imber, S. D., Sotsky, S. M., Collins, J. F., Glass, D. R., Pilkonis, P. A., Leber, W. R., Docherty, J. P., Fiester, S. J., & Parloff, M. B. (1989). National Institute of Mental Health Treatment of Depression Collaborative Research Program: General effectiveness treatments. *Archives of General Psychiatry, 46,* 971–982.

Ellis, A. (1962). *Reason and emotion in psychotherapy.* New York: Lyle Stuart.

Evans, M. D., Hollon, S. D., DeRubeis, R. J., Piasecki, J. M., Grove, W. M., Garvey, M. J., & Tuason, V. B. (1992). Differential relapse following cognitive therapy and pharmacotherapy for depression. *Archives of General Psychiatry, 49,* 802–808.

Ferster, C. B. (1967). Animal behavior and mental illness. *Psychological Record, 16,* 345–356.

Hollon, S. D., DeRubeis, R. J., Evans, M. D., Wiemer, J. J., Garvey, J. G., Grove, W. M., & Tuason, V. B. (1992). Cognitive-therapy and pharmacotherapy for depression: Singly and in combination. *Archives of General Psychiatry, 49,* 774–781.

Howell, J. R., & Thase, M. E. (1991). Beating the blues: Recovery from depression. In D. C. Daley (Ed.), *Insight to recovery: A practical workbook series for mental health disorders* (pp. 1–27). Skokie, IL: G. T. Rogers.

Persons, J. B. (1989). *Cognitive therapy in practice: A case formulation approach.* New York: W. W. Norton.

Scott, A. I. F., & Freeman, C. P. L. (1992). Edinburgh Primary Care Depression Study: Treatment outcome, patient satisfaction, and cost after 16 weeks. *British Medical Journal, 304,* 883–887.

Simons, A. D., Lustman, P. J., Wetzel, R. D., & Murphy, G. E. (1985). Predicting response to cognitive therapy of depression: The role of learned resourcefulness. *Cognitive Therapy and Research, 9,* 79–89.

Stuart, S., & Thase, M. E. (1994). Inpatient applications of cognitive behavior therapy: A review of recent developments. *Journal of Psychotherapy Practice and Research, 3,* 284–299.

Thase, M. E. (1992). Transition and aftercare. In J. H. Wright, M. E. Thase, A. T. Beck, & J. W. Ludgate (Eds.), *Cognitive therapy with inpatients: Developing a cognitive milieu* (pp. 414–435). New York: Guilford Press.

Thase, M. E. (1993). Inpatient cognitive behavior therapy of depression. In E. Leibenluft, A. Tasman, & S. A. Green (Eds.), *Less time to do more: Psychotherapy on the short-term inpatient unit* (pp. 111–140). Washington, DC: American Psychiatric Press.

Thase, M. E., & Beck, A. T. (1992). An overview of cognitive therapy. In J. H. Wright, M. E. Thase, A. T. Beck, & J. W. Ludgate (Eds.), *Cognitive therapy with inpatients: Developing a cognitive milieu* (pp. 3–34). New York: Guilford Press.

Thase, M. E., Reynolds, C. F. III, Frank, E., Simons, A. D., Garamoni, G. D., McGeary, J., Harden, T., Fasiczka, A. L., & Cahalane, J. F. (1994). Response to cognitive behavior therapy in chronic depression. *Journal of Psychotherapy Practice and Research, 3,* 204–214.

Thase, M. E., Simons, A. D., Cahalane, J., McGeary, J., & Harden, T. (1991). Severity of depression and response to cognitive behavior therapy. *American Journal of Psychiatry, 148,* 784–789.

Thase, M. E., Simons, A. D., McGeary, J., Cahalane, J. F., Hughes, C., Harden, T., & Friedman, E. (1992). Relapse after cognitive behavior therapy of depression: Potential implications for longer courses of treatment? *American Journal of Psychiatry, 149,* 1046–1052.

Thase, M. E., & Wright, J. H. (1991). Cognitive behavior therapy manual for depressed inpatients: A treatment protocol outline. *Behavior Therapy, 22,* 579–595.

Watkins, J. T., Leber, W. R., Imber, S. D., Collins, J. F., Elkin, I., Pilkonis, P. A., Sotsky, S. M., Shea, M. T., & Glass, D. R. (1993). Temporal course of change of depression. *Journal of Consulting and Clinical Psychology, 61,* 858–864.

Whisman, M. A. (1993). Mediators and moderators of change in cognitive therapy of depression. *Psychological Bulletin, 114*, 248–265.

Wolpe, J. (1958). *Psychotherapy by reciprocal inhibition.* Stanford, CA: Stanford University Press.

Wright, J. H., Thase, M. E., Beck, A. T., & Ludgate, J. W. (Eds.). (1992). *Cognitive therapy with inpatients: Developing a cognitive milieu.* New York: Guilford Press.

3

INTERPERSONAL PSYCHOTHERAPY

Holly A. Swartz and John C. Markowitz

When a patient complaining of feeling depressed comes to the office, it is almost second nature to inquire about the life events that led up to the current depressive episode, in addition to asking about the patient's symptoms. With that information in hand, we make sense of the depression for ourselves and for our patients, offering an explanation such as, "You became depressed soon after you lost your job. These two events are probably related." Connecting mood with environmental stress, in addition to holding true in empirical studies, is an acceptable path to understanding depression—both for ourselves as clinicians and for our patients.

Interpersonal psychotherapy (IPT) is a psychotherapeutic technique that focuses on the relationship between a patient's interpersonal issues and his or her depressive symptoms. Built around the clinically relevant and empirically demonstrated link between interpersonal events (for example, marital conflict, a new job, the loss of a spouse) and depression, we have found that IPT is both intuitively appealing and remarkably effective. With clearly defined treatment goals, a specified duration of treatment, and an excellent track record in clinical trials, IPT is a useful treatment option for a wide range of depressed patients in a clinic, private practice, or managed care setting.

WHAT IS IPT?

IPT is a codified, time-limited psychotherapy that was created in the 1970s by Gerald L. Klerman, M.D., and Myrna M. Weissman, Ph.D. IPT was originally developed for the outpatient treatment of moderately severe depression and has demonstrated efficacy in several large controlled clinical trials. During the past decade, researchers have expanded and adapted the technique for the treatment of many other clinical syndromes, including bulimia, late-life depression, dysthymia, and depression in HIV-positive individuals.

Unlike cognitive therapy (which focuses on the automatic negative thoughts associated with depression) or psychodynamic psychotherapy (which focuses on underlying unconscious wishes and conflicts), IPT focuses on *current* interpersonal issues. IPT employs a "medical model" in which the patient is informed that he or she suffers from an illness (depression) that can be treated. The premise of IPT (which is explicitly presented to the patient) is that, by working through present interpersonal problems, the patient will both resolve the interpersonal dilemma and treat the depression.

The techniques and interventions of IPT are published in a manual. From the manual and regular supervision of video-taped treatment sessions, therapists are trained to follow a consistent, specific approach for treating depressed patients, thereby ensuring intertherapist reliability in clinical trials. Although used primarily as a research tool, IPT can also be adapted for general clinical practice. Because it has been used in clinical trials, excellent data already have proven that it works!

Consequently, from both our research and clinical experience, we believe that IPT is an effective, systematized approach to the treatment of depressed outpatients that capitalizes on the well-established link between depression and interpersonal stressors.

THEORETICAL BACKGROUND

IPT has its theoretical roots in the work of Adolf Meyer and Harry Stack Sullivan. Meyer postulated that an individual's psychiatric symptoms emerged from a patient's attempt to adapt to his or her environment; Sullivan enlarged this concept to include a more general theory of interpersonal relationships. Empirical studies in the 1960s and 1970s added evidence to the theoretical work of Meyer and Sullivan. Bowlby, drawing on the work of ethologists demonstrating the importance of bonding among primates, emphasized the importance of human social attachment bonds. Studies of women in the 1970s demonstrated that intimate relationships provide protection against the onset of depression in the face of life stressors. Later epidemiological work demonstrated a positive association between marital disputes and major depression.

A "HERE AND NOW" TREATMENT

IPT is a "here and now" treatment. In contrast, psychotherapies such as psychoanalysis and psychodynamic psychotherapy focus on the "there and then," conceptualizing symptoms as manifestations of underlying conflicts originating in early development.

With IPT, the patient and the therapist identify the interpersonal issue most clearly tied to the *current* depressive episode and together work to find reparative strategies that can be applied to the problem *today*. The treatment does not attempt to change character or to understand the genetic evolution of the interpersonal problem; it targets recent problems and seeks practical solutions.

For example, Ms. A., a twenty-three-year-old single graduate student, developed a major depression after a semester of near-failing grades (Note: all case material has been altered to protect the identity of our patients). Ms. A. revealed that, during the preceding summer, she had become sexually involved with an older professor who ended the relationship with his student, Ms. A., at the beginning of the school year. Since that time, Ms. A. had been distracted and unable to complete her schoolwork. Over the period of a month, Ms. A. developed problems sleeping and lost ten pounds. She felt like "a failure in love and work" and was convinced that she "deserved to be alone forever."

Ms. A. grew up in a poor, urban family. Her father was imprisoned during most of her childhood and early adolescence. Her mother supported Ms. A. and her four siblings with checks from public assistance. An intellectually gifted child, she used school and her academic talents as a means of coping with the chaos and emotional turmoil of her home life.

At this point, one could consider approaching this case in several ways. A psychodynamically oriented treatment might seize on Ms. A.'s preoccupation with an inattentive, older professor as evidence of unresolved, ambivalent feelings about her incarcerated, unavailable father. Ms. A. could then embark on a several-year exploratory treatment that would allow her a deeper understanding of the unconscious meaning of her choice of the professor. Or, working in a cognitive model, Ms. A. could examine the negative automatic thoughts (such as, "I deserve to be alone forever") to understand the connection between her thoughts and mood state. Alternatively, a psychopharmacologist might elect to use an antidepressant (with or without supportive psychotherapy).

None of these approaches are inherently "wrong." Rather, each treatment offers different potential benefits and costs to the patient. A psychodynamically oriented treatment may take several years but would offer the patient an opportunity to better understand the origins of her problematic relationships with men and her compensatory drive to excel in school. Cognitive therapy, which will specifically treat Ms. A.'s depression, may appeal to this intellectually curious patient and could also be proposed as a treatment approach. Antidepressant medications provide an excellent, rapid treatment for depression but carry with them the risk of uncomfortable side effects and do not directly address interpersonal problems. A combination of techniques, such as using medication to augment psychotherapy, may confer advantages over a single treatment modality, but it also exposes the patient to the risks of both forms of treatment. It is important that, after a thorough evaluation, Ms. A. and her therapist carefully weigh the options.

In this case, Ms. A. had clear preferences and concerns: her school insurance plan only covered twenty outpatient visits, so she was unable to commit to a longer course of treatment. She also preferred nonpharmacologic interventions because of a history of extreme sensitivity to medication. Furthermore, Ms. A. was troubled by her recent relationship and wanted the opportunity to address the issue in psychotherapy. Ms. A.'s therapist preferred a specifically antidepressant treatment—given Ms. A.'s diagnosis—and agreed that Ms. A.'s depression arose in the context of a recent interpersonal role dispute (the problematic relationship with the professor). So, the therapist recommended IPT, a time-limited, antidepressant psychotherapy that focuses on interpersonal relationships.

Here's what happened next: Ms. A.'s therapist encouraged Ms. A. to discuss her feelings, wishes, and expectations about her relationship with the professor. It became clear that Ms. A.'s disappointment stemmed from her expectation that the relationship would continue, whereas the professor saw it as a "summer thing." Encouraged by her therapist to confront the professor, Ms. A. was able to voice her disappointment about unmet expectations in the relationship. When it became clear that Ms. A. and the professor would be unable to reconcile their differences, the therapist helped Ms. A. grieve the loss of the relationship. By actively attending activities that allowed her to socialize with other students, Ms. A. was subsequently able to find a more appropriate boyfriend. She also enlarged her network of social supports in graduate school. Her grades returned to their usual level of excellence as her depressive symptoms resolved.

In her IPT treatment, Ms. A. was encouraged to focus on her current interpersonal relationships. In particular, she focused on the nonreciprocal, disappointing aspects of her relationship with her professor and eventually confronted him about them. Because she saw that the relationship was unresolvable, she was encouraged to socialize more with her peers (rather than her professors) and was able to enter a new relationship with a man who attended a nearby professional school. Ms. A.'s symptoms remitted as she made active choices to change the nature and scope of her current interpersonal relationships.

THE IPT THERAPIST

IPT therapists are usually experienced psychiatrists, psychiatric social workers, psychologists, therapists, and nurses who have gained additional expertise in this treatment approach. They are necessarily familiar with the signs, symptoms, and treatment of depression and are generally already trained in another kind of psychotherapy, such as supportive psychotherapy or insight-oriented treatment.

Thus far, most IPT therapists have trained in IPT through the use of supervised videotaped cases. Until recently, this training was available only to those therapists treating patients in treatment protocols. During the past several years, however, training courses have been offered to psychiatric clinicians at the annual meeting of the American Psychiatric Association and elsewhere. Training programs have also become available at academic institutions such as Cornell University Medical Center and the University of Pittsburgh.

In contrast to the "neutral" stance of the traditional psychoanalyst, the IPT therapist assumes a warm, non-neutral, supportive position with the patient and may often give advice or even make direct suggestions. An IPT therapist is something akin to a cheerleader for a quarterback: visible, gung ho, and aware of the action despite remaining on the sideline.

The therapist is responsible for maintaining the parameters of the treatment. He or she contracts with the patient to embark on a time-limited treatment (typically meeting weekly for sixteen sessions). After properly assessing the patient, the therapist diagnoses a depression, links the depression to one of four interpersonal problem areas—grief, a role dispute, a role transition, or interpersonal deficits—and plans with the patient to work on the identified problem area. The therapist is also responsible for negotiating fees, schedules, and policies for missed appointments.

THE IPT PATIENT

To be eligible for treatment with IPT, the patient must meet criteria for a depressive disorder, must be ambulatory (both physically able to get to sessions and not in need of immediate hospitalization), and must agree to the parameters of treatment (weekly sessions, appropriate fees, time-limited treatment). Once the patient agrees to treatment, the patient's illness and treatment are conceptualized by using a "medical model." The patient is formally diagnosed with a major depression and is given the "sick role," which brings with it benefits and responsibilities. In the sick role, the patient's "job" becomes taking whatever steps are necessary to get better. Typically, this role provides tremendous initial relief for the patient.

Excused from certain overwhelming social obligations by virtue of being ill, the patient is obliged to take an active role in improving his or her health. These new obligations include attending appointments, explicitly working on the identified interpersonal problem area, and actively participating in treatment. The patient is also encouraged to spend some time socializing or participating in out-of-the-house activities. Although these instructions must be given judiciously to avoid further demoralization in an already pessimistic patient (by pushing the patient too hard), socialization is important both in generating material for the treatment and in helping the patient feel more capable and therefore less depressed.

Patients infected with HIV have been found to be excellent candidates for IPT. Originally, researchers were concerned that HIV-positive patients would be unable to benefit from a time-limited treatment, given their diminished life expectancy and the feeling that HIV infection was "good reason" to be depressed. To the contrary, Markowitz and colleagues are finding that these individuals—precisely because they are facing shortened life spans—are very motivated to effect radical changes in their lives during the course of a brief treatment, and their symptoms respond dramatically as well.

One of our patients, Mr. B., benefited greatly from the hopeful and structured framework provided by IPT. Mr. B., a fifty-four-year-old restaurant owner, became depressed following the loss of his business during a period of economic decline. He was subsequently hired as the manager of another restaurant where, for the first time in his adult life, he answered to a superior. He experienced his boss as critical and demanding and soon dreaded going to work. As he became more depressed, Mr. B.'s decline in sleep and concentration interfered with his job performance, which in turn exacerbated his relationship with his employer. Mr. B.'s symptoms progressed to the point that he awakened each day at 3 A.M., lost all interest in food, and began to ruminatively believe that he was "responsible for his own downfall." His Hamilton Depression score, a score on a rating scale that measures depression, indicated that he was moderately depressed.

Relieved to learn in IPT that his symptoms were attributable to a medical illness (major depression), Mr. B. arranged for some time off from work to address his medical problem. Working with his therapist, Mr. B. came to understand that he was experiencing difficulties related to a role transition. As he explored his feelings related to the loss of his business and the transition to the role of an employee, Mr. B. came to see that he no longer experienced himself as a useful or productive member of his community. Encouraged by his therapist, Mr. B. decided to deepen his commitment to a local Boys' Club by using his expertise in restaurant management to revitalize a failing soup kitchen project. Feeling useful and valued again, Mr. B. began to review with his therapist his goals for himself. Deciding that, in the short run, he needed to keep his current job, Mr. B. arranged to meet with his boss and negotiate a more amicable work relationship. Although he continued to experience his work as demeaning, he was able to find compensatory pleasure in his experiences at the Boys' Club. Toward the end of treatment, he began to consider the possibility of leaving the restaurant business to work full-time in the public sector.

Having been given the sick role, Mr. B. was exempted from work for a period of time because of his illness, but in exchange he was expected to participate in the treatment process. In this case, Mr. B. was encouraged to develop his interest in a volunteer project that would enhance his self-esteem and put him back in charge. Learning that his skills were valued at the Boys' Club gave Mr. B. the courage to resolve his differences with his boss and to actively reassess his career goals. After a sixteen-week treatment with IPT, Mr. B. not only felt less depressed but also had a better sense of his own aspirations.

FIRST PHASE OF TREATMENT

The first phase of IPT, which can take up to three sessions, is devoted to assessing the patient, diagnosing depression, setting the framework for treatment, and instilling hope.

The assessment and diagnosis of the patient include a full evaluation of signs, symptoms, past psychiatric history, family history, medical history, and current mental status. In addition to this comprehensive "medical" evaluation of the patient, the IPT therapist also takes an *interpersonal inventory*. The interpersonal inventory consists of a review of important past and present relationships, a history of patterns in relationships, recent changes in key relationships, and nonreciprocal expectations in current relationships. With the patient, the therapist assesses the significance of each relationship, determines its satisfying and unsatisfying aspects, and targets those areas the patient might wish to alter within the relationship. This crucial first step in the treatment allows the therapist both to diagnose a depression and to define an *interpersonal problem area* that henceforth will serve as the focus of treatment.

The therapist uses the diagnosis and the interpersonal problem area (grief, role dispute, role transition, or interpersonal deficits) to set the framework for treatment. The patient is explicitly informed that he or she has *depression*, a *medical disorder*, thereby assigning the patient the *sick role*. The therapist then offers the patient an *interpersonal formulation:* having emphasized that depression is a medical disorder with a constellation of psychological and physical symptoms, and while avoiding explicit causal statements, the therapist links the patient's current interpersonal problem to the depression and offers IPT as a powerful treatment for both the depression and the interpersonal problem. The therapist can also use outside confirmation (for example, a list of criteria from *DSM-IV* or a Hamilton Depression Rating Scale) to help convince the patient that he or she has an illness.

For example, in Mr. B.'s case, one might offer the following interpersonal formulation:

> The reason you are not sleeping or eating well is that you have a depression. A depression is a medical illness that affects almost 10 percent of Americans. The good news is that depression is a very treatable illness. Doctors think that depression is related to interpersonal stresses, such as the kind of difficulties you have been experiencing recently in your new job. We call that a role transition. Although you may need to take some time off from work in order to get better, I believe that, with psychotherapy, you will soon be feeling like yourself again. IPT works by helping you make the connection between how you feel and what's going on in your life—such

as your problems with your boss and your wish to be running your own business again. During the next sixteen weeks, we'll be meeting to help you figure out how to better handle that situation. I expect that this will both help you feel better and resolve your interpersonal role transition.

As you state the interpersonal formulation, you should also weave in some of the basic elements common to most good psychotherapeutic treatments: (1) offer expertise and understanding, (2) begin psychoeducation about depression, and (3) instill hope. Once the therapist and the patient agree on the formulation and the practical aspects of the treatment are arranged (length of treatment, fees, scheduling), the next phase of treatment begins.

MIDDLE PHASE OF TREATMENT

During the middle sessions (roughly, sessions four through thirteen), the patient and the therapist focus on the identified problem area to bring about change in interpersonal relationships. In the following section, we illustrate and summarize the goals of the four IPT problem areas and the strategies for handling each. These techniques are fully elaborated in the original manual, to which the reader is referred for a more comprehensive description of IPT.

Grief

The loss of a loved one typically produces a set of time-limited symptoms, including sadness, insomnia, and changes in appetite. This normal response to loss is called *uncomplicated bereavement* and is not a psychiatric disorder. Uncomplicated bereavement does not require psychiatric intervention. Some individuals, however, are unable to grieve normally and go on to develop a major depressive disorder, *complicated bereavement*.

The goal of IPT in complicated bereavement is to help the patient mourn appropriately while gradually establishing new activities and relationships to substitute for what has been lost. The patient is encouraged to review the depressive symptoms and to relate the onset of the depression to the death of the loved one. With the therapist, the patient reviews the positive and negative aspects of his or her relationship with the deceased and describes the events and feelings that occurred just prior to, during, and following the death. This process facilitates a release of affect (catharsis), which is an important part of mourning. Sometimes the therapist will recommend grief-related activities, such as reviewing photo albums and home movies, to further facilitate the catharsis. The therapist and the patient then actively consider ways for the patient to become more involved with other people and to find substitutes for what has been lost. This task may take the form of joining organized groups (churches, support groups, team sports), enhancing relationships within an existing support network, or starting new relationships.

Mrs. C., a patient whose problem was formulated as complicated bereavement, benefited from the grief work of IPT. Mrs. C. is a forty-two-year-old white Catholic housewife whose husband died of prostate cancer a year and a half prior to presentation. His death followed a period of protracted illness. After her husband's death, Mrs. C. refused to admit he had died. She would not visit the cemetery, left his belongings undisturbed, and actively avoided the hospital where he had received chemotherapy. Previously an energetic and capable mother, she had become progressively more lethargic and withdrawn, until her teenage daughters insisted she seek medical attention. On evaluation, Mrs. C. reported significant neurovegetative symptoms and had a Hamilton Depression score consistent with a severe depression.

With her therapist, Mrs. C. reconstructed her ambivalent feelings about her relationship with her husband (he had beaten her on more than one occasion) and reviewed the upsetting details of caring for him as he progressively succumbed to metastatic prostate cancer. The process was speeded by the patient's willingness to comply with the therapist's recommendation to visit the hospital where her husband had died, to accompany her daughters to the cemetery, and to give the deceased husband's personal effects to a favorite nephew. Mrs. C. resumed her active participation in church charities and once again became involved with the activities of her family. Although she continued to feel sad when she thought of her husband, her overall mood and level of functioning returned to normal.

Interpersonal Disputes

All relationships involve transient periods of disagreement and conflict. In some relationships, however, these episodes assume seemingly unresolvable proportions and become potentially toxic to one or more of the involved individuals. When depressive symptoms are associated with a conflict in a relationship, IPT defines the problem area as an *interpersonal role dispute*.

The goal of IPT is to identify the dispute, plan a strategy for change, and modify expectations and communication. Treatment strategies include reviewing the depressive symptoms and relating them to the role dispute, looking for parallels in other relationships to determine the role of the patient in perpetuating the behavior, and examining the hidden gains achieved in the dispute. Finally, the therapist must assess the stage of the dispute and (1) calm the patient to facilitate resolution (if negotiations are underway), (2) reopen old battle wounds to reopen negotiation (if the relationship is at an impasse), or (3) assist mourning (if the relationship is clearly dissolving). A role dispute can be with a friend, spouse, co-worker, parent, child, or any other significant person.

Mrs. D. is an example of a patient whose depression was related to conflict with her husband. She is a twenty-eight-year-old housewife whose depressive symptoms emerged as she prepared to take a secretarial job in a doctor's office. This was the first time Mrs. D. had considered employment since marrying her husband two years before. Mrs. D. had been looking forward to the job because she liked being around people and was increasingly bored and restless at home. Her husband, however, disapproved of the plan and hoped instead to begin a family—with the expectation that Mrs. D. would remain at home to care for children. As her husband's anger about the proposed job mounted, Mrs. D. resentfully agreed to delay employment. Their fighting subsided, but Mrs. D. remained at home, angry and frustrated. She slept many hours, had an increased appetite, and at presentation met criteria for an atypical depression.

Mrs. D.'s depression was formulated as a role dispute that had reached an impasse. With her therapist, Mrs. D. acknowledged the anger and frustration she felt with her husband's inflexibility, but she also realized that she felt completely dependent on him and was afraid to displease him for fear of retaliation. When her therapist conducted an interpersonal inventory, Mrs. D. realized that she had a pattern of similar interpersonal experiences: she had had similar controlling relationships with earlier boyfriends, as well as with her father, who had rigidly controlled her dating as an adolescent.

With the help of her therapist, Mrs. D. recognized that she had difficulty verbalizing her needs in relationships, which made it difficult for her to successfully negotiate with her husband. Mrs. D. was encouraged to state her needs directly to her husband—as well as to attempt to better understand his needs. After she did so, the couple agreed that Mrs. D. would go to work part-time—with a plan to stop work when they eventually had children. Her husband continued to voice dissent, but Mrs. D. accepted the job and began employment. Mrs. D. became less depressed as she began to enjoy her new responsibilities and increased autonomy, although she continued to verbalize her disappointment that her husband was unable to fully support this endeavor.

Role Transition

People's lives are punctuated by change: shifts in roles from childhood through adulthood. Most people manage these transitions (for example, going to college, getting married, becoming parents, retiring) without developing overt psychopathology. Similarly, most people navigate the sharpest curves along their path (for example, promotion, demotion, physical illness, bankruptcy) without developing a clinical depression. In individuals prone to depression, however, these expectable and unexpectable changes can precipitate a depressive episode.

The goal of IPT in the treatment of these individuals is to identify the *role transition*—defined as any major life change not specifically related to the death of a loved one—as it relates to the depressive episode. Because these changes are often experienced by the patient as "free fall," simply labeling the chaos as a transition can be therapeutic (compare Mr. B.). Once the transition is identified and labeled, the therapist helps the patient mourn the loss of the old role—recognizing both its positive and negative aspects—and identify positive as well as negative features of the new role. Additionally, the therapist helps the patient acknowledge an emerging mastery of the new role and thereby enhance his or her self-esteem.

Strategies for accomplishing these goals include relating the depressive symptoms to the changes that have occurred, reviewing feelings of loss about the old role, encouraging appropriate expression of affect, realistically assessing the pros and cons of the old and new roles, exploring opportunities in the new role, and encouraging the development of an appropriate set of skills and supports to meet the challenges of the new role.

Mr. E., a twenty-two-year-old unemployed former college student, is an example of a patient who developed a depression in the setting of graduating from college. He was referred for treatment after voicing passive suicidal ideation to a pastoral counselor. Mr. E. had become increasingly frustrated and depressed in the year following his graduation from a small New England college because of his inability to get a job. He had returned to New York City with a poorly formed plan to "become a diplomat" and "facilitate world peace." Because he had no income, he was forced to live with his parents in their small apartment. As the months passed, fighting with his parents escalated as Mr. E.

repeatedly turned down possible job opportunities that he deemed "bourgeois."

Mr. E.'s case was conceptualized as a *role transition.* Treatment initially focused on mourning the loss of idealism of his college days while instilling hope about the increased range of possibilities that awaited Mr. E. in adulthood. While acknowledging the virtue of Mr. E.'s wish to hold a socially responsible job, the therapist encouraged Mr. E. to confront the realities of possible employment for a recent college graduate. Mr. E. was also encouraged to construct a plan that would allow him, over time, to reach his long-term goal of contributing to world peace. As he became more aware that his diminished self-esteem was only further diminished by the ongoing disputes with his parents, Mr. E. decided that it was essential he leave the apartment.

Encouraged by his therapist to widen his list of job possibilities, Mr. E. submitted an application to the Peace Corps, which would result in a two-year stay abroad. Although Mr. E. faced a several-month wait for an opening in the Peace Corps, his mood dramatically improved as he began to anticipate his new job and to plan for its challenges. Similarly, Mr. E.'s relationship with his parents improved as the family anticipated and prepared for his departure.

Interpersonal Deficits

The category of interpersonal deficits is the least studied and least conceptually defined of the four IPT problem areas. It is used when there appears to be no acute interpersonal problem related to the depression (otherwise, we would use one of the other problem areas) and implies a long-standing paucity of interpersonal relationships. Typically, these patients are more difficult to treat because of their underlying character pathology, which has presumably interfered, over time, with their ability to form interpersonal relationships.

The goal of the treatment is to help the patient reduce his or her overall isolation by attempting to form new relationships.

The therapist employs strategies such as relating the depressive symptoms to the patient's isolation, reviewing the history of past relationships, and looking for patterns of problems in relationships. If the patient's interpersonal relationships are so impoverished that there is virtually no material available for the sessions, one can also examine the patient's positive and negative feelings for the therapist in an effort to better understand the difficulties the patient experiences outside the treatment setting.

Ms. F. is an example of a patient who had a long history of impoverished interpersonal relationships. She is a thirty-three-year-old single female who worked intermittently, selling jewelry and auditioning for acting roles. She reported feeling sad and anxious during the past several years as she seemed unable to "find a job and a man and settle down." She initially reported that she had "tons of friends," but when questioned further, she seemed to maintain only superficial relationships with casual acquaintances and could describe no substantive friendships since childhood.

Ms. F.'s case was formulated as *interpersonal deficits*, and the patient and the therapist embarked on the difficult task of restructuring Ms. F.'s interpersonal relationships. Ms. F.'s progress was impeded by her mistrust of the therapist, which was addressed with the patient as an example of the kind of problems she typically experiences in relationships. With a great deal of coaxing, Ms. F. enrolled in a course in a local college because she had always wanted to finish her college degree. Ms. F. attended the course regularly and formed one new relationship with another older student. At the end of treatment, Ms. F.'s symptoms had improved somewhat, with Hamilton Depression scores moving from the severe to moderate range. She was pleased about her new friend and showed more trust with the therapist. She remained unemployed and fairly isolated, however, and was referred for continued psychotherapy.

As is clear from the case of Ms. F., this fourth problem area often implies a poorer prognosis, probably related to the considerable psychopathology extant in this group. Nevertheless, important strides are often made in treatment, allowing for significant reduction in symptoms and improved interpersonal relationships. Whenever possible, however, it is preferable to use one of the first three problem areas.

END OF TREATMENT

During the last few sessions, the patient and the therapist review the progress made in treatment, explicitly discuss termination, and facilitate a mourning process for the loss of the treatment. At this juncture, the therapist must also decide whether the patient's treatment needs have been met completely or further treatment is indicated.

In most instances, IPT works in the time allotted, and treatment ends without need for continuation sessions. In this majority of cases, the end of treatment is framed as a "graduation," and the gains made in treatment are recognized and applauded. The signs and symptoms of depression are also reviewed, and strategies for managing a recurrence are explicitly discussed. A review of interpersonal problem areas alerts the patient to his or her interpersonal weak spots and allows the patient and the therapist to anticipate potential future difficulties. Evidence suggests that the effects of IPT persist beyond termination and that patients continue to effect positive changes in their interpersonal relationships at one-year follow-up.

If the patient's symptoms have not fully resolved, the therapist helps the patient realistically assess what has and has not improved. Typically, the patient has made some gains that can diminish a patient's sense of frustration if the therapist recommends continued treatment. In the event of partial or complete treatment failure, the therapist can elect to continue to treat the patient in a different modality (for example, initiate pharmacotherapy) or refer the patient to a colleague.

Although originally developed as a time-limited, acute therapy, IPT has also been used as a maintenance treatment. In these studies, IPT was administered weekly or even monthly either alone or in combination with medication to prevent relapse in previously depressed individuals. These studies suggest that tricyclic antidepressants and IPT alone each diminish rates of relapse but that combination treatment (IPT plus medication) probably performs somewhat better than either therapy alone. Following a sixteen-week course of IPT, some previously depressed individuals will require a referral for maintenance treatment. Generally, those individuals who have a history of recurrent depression should be referred for maintenance therapy after IPT; those with a history of only a single episode may not require subsequent sessions unless symptoms recur.

Finally, this last phase of treatment is typically the hardest phase for the therapist, who must pass through a "role transition" of sorts as the patient achieves autonomy and separates from the therapist. Although stopping psychotherapy is generally difficult for a psychotherapist, the kind of intense, positive alliance and period of rapid gains fostered in a time-limited treatment (especially when the treatment is successful) intensifies these difficulties for the IPT therapist. Nevertheless, it is essential that the therapist encourage the patient's independence and commend his or her efforts toward separation as the therapy draws to a close.

SPECIAL ISSUES

A variety of issues generally confronts a clinician when implementing a new treatment approach. This section addresses some of the practical matters that are likely to arise for a clinician using IPT for the first time.

Medication

You may wonder whether it is possible to combine IPT with medication because many depressed patients are routinely treated with pharmacotherapy as well as psychotherapy. There are no known contraindications to using pharmacotherapy in combination with IPT. In fact, because of its use of the "medical model," IPT is quite compatible with the concurrent use of medication. In many cases, a combination of antidepressant and psychotherapy will be the treatment of choice for the moderately to severely depressed individual. Results from the NIMH Collaborative Depression Study, however, suggest that, at twelve weeks, IPT alone was as effective as imipramine alone in the reduction of depressive symptoms. It is therefore important to assess each patient individually, to understand his or her treatment preferences, and to tailor the treatment for the individual. In our experience, many depressed patients respond to IPT alone; however, the more severely depressed patients may require concomitant pharmacotherapy to avert hospitalization.

Differential Therapeutics

No single treatment is appropriate for all patients. In general, the more techniques you know, the more options you will have available to you to tailor your treatment strategies for the individual patient. IPT is best suited for a depressed patient who is interested and able to work on the interpersonal issues related to his or her depression in a sixteen-week treatment.

In deciding whether or not to use IPT, you must consider the severity of the depression. On the one hand, a very severely depressed patient (for example, unable to maintain adequate intake of food, marked suicidal ideation, prominent psychotic features) requires hospitalization and is not appropriate for an outpatient treatment of any kind. On the other hand, the traditional "healthy neurotic" patient without a clear depression may not require the focused, symptom-driven approach of IPT and may instead opt for an open-ended exploratory psychotherapy such as psychoanalysis.

Another important consideration when prescribing IPT is whether or not the patient would benefit from a time-limited treatment. We have found that, in many cases, the time limit provides incentive for both therapist and patient and spurs the latter on to quick results. Groups of patients who might particularly benefit from this rapid, intensive approach include individuals with a life-threatening illness, patients with a strong wish to rapidly regain functioning, patients with circumscribed time in a particular location, and those with limited financial resources or insurance coverage. Although this area has not been well studied, a brief psychotherapy may be less appropriate for severely character-disordered patients with comorbid depression if the magnitude of the character pathology would prevent the patient from engaging rapidly in treatment.

Finally, IPT is not indicated for the cognitively impaired depressed patient who cannot talk about his or her relationships in a systematic way. This kind of patient should be referred for a supportive treatment with medication.

Transference

As described in earlier sections, the relationship between the therapist and the patient is warm, supportive, and not neutral. In another theoretical frame, one might say that the IPT therapist attempts to foster and capitalize on a positive transference without ever interpreting it.

In IPT the transference is generally not commented on unless, in the case of interpersonal deficits, the negative transference can be used to demonstrate a problem that is typical of the patient's interpersonal relationships. In this latter case, transference is addressed as an *interpersonal* issue (for example, between patient and therapist) rather than as transference per se.

Managed Care

In an era of increased concern about cost management and allocation of resources, IPT is perhaps uniquely positioned among the psychotherapies to appeal to managed care companies. IPT is a time-limited treatment with defined treatment goals and a discrete focus on a current crisis or episode.

Perhaps most important, IPT is one of only two codified psychotherapies (the other is cognitive behavioral therapy) to have demonstrated efficacy—under research conditions—in a depressed population. With IPT you can substantiate your belief that psychotherapy works with hard data from controlled, randomized, clinical trials.

In our experience, IPT is an effective, time-limited treatment for depression. We have seen patients recover from debilitating depressions while making significant, positive changes in their interpersonal relationships. We have helped depressed HIV-positive men move from hopeless, nihilistic views of the future to productive, focused activity that allows them, in several instances, to live out lifelong dreams and goals. We have worked with demoralized, immobilized individuals who, during a course of IPT, develop new relationships and career plans. We have found that IPT is an excellent treatment that has the added benefit of enabling patients to exercise greater control over their interpersonal relationships.

Although IPT will continue to be an important research tool in the work of rigorously assessing the efficacy of psychotherapy, IPT will soon find its place in the private office. With training centers for IPT developing and more experience with the technique emerging outside a research setting, IPT is now available to the general clinician. IPT, a powerful, focused, time-limited psychotherapy, is a relatively new—and decidedly potent—option for the treatment of ambulatory patients with moderately severe depression.

NOTES

P. 71, *empirically demonstrated link:* Brown, G. W., & Harris, T. (1978). *Social origins of depression: A study of psychiatric disorders in women.* New York: Free Press.

P. 72, *several large controlled clinical trials:* Elkin, I., Shea, M. T., Watkins, J. T., et al. (1989). National Institute of Mental Health Treatment of Depression Collaborative Research Program: General effectiveness of treatments. *Archives of General Psychiatry, 46,* 971–982; Kupfer, D. J., Frank, E., Perel,

J. M., et al. (1992). Three year outcome for maintenance therapies in recurrent depression. *Archives of General Psychiatry, 47,* 1093–1099.

P. 72, *treatment of many other clinical syndromes:* Klerman, G. L., & Weissman, M. M. (1993). *New applications of interpersonal therapy.* Washington, DC: American Psychiatric Press.

P. 72, *The techniques and interventions of IPT are published in a manual:* Klerman, G. L., Weissman, M. M., Rounsaville, B. J., & Chevron, E. S. (1984). *Interpersonal psychotherapy of depression.* New York: Basic Books.

P. 73, *Meyer postulated:* Meyer, A. (1957). *Psychobiology: A science of man.* Springfield, IL: Charles C. Thomas.

P. 73, *Sullivan enlarged this concept:* Sullivan, H. S. (1953). *The interpersonal theory of psychiatry.* New York: Norton.

P. 73, *Bowlby, drawing on the work of ethologists:* Bowlby, J. (1969). *Attachment and loss: Vol. 1. Attachment.* London: Hogarth Press.

P. 73, *Studies of women in the 1970s:* Brown, G. W., & Harris, T. (1978). *Social origins of depression: A study of psychiatric disorders in women.* New York: Free Press.

P. 73, *positive association between marital disputes and major depression:* Weissman, M. M., Klerman, G. L., Paykel, E. S., et al. (1974). Treatment effects on the social adjustment of depressed patients. *Archives of General Psychiatry, 30,* 771–778.

P. 77, *The patient is formally diagnosed:* Parsons, T. (1951). Illness and the role of the physician: A sociological perspective. *American Journal of Orthopsychiatry, 25,* 56–62.

P. 78, *Patients infected with HIV:* Markowitz, J. C., Klerman, G. L., & Perry, S. W. (1992). Interpersonal psychotherapy of depressed HIV-seropositive patients. *Hospital and Community Psychiatry, 43,* 885–890.

P. 78, *His Hamilton Depression score:* Hamilton, M. (1960). A rating scale for depression. *Journal of Neurology, Neurosurgery and Psychiatry, 25,* 56–62.

P. 80, *a list of criteria from* DSM-IV: American Psychiatric Association. (1994). *Diagnostic and statistical manual of mental disorders* (4th ed.). Washington, DC: Author.

P. 81, *for a more comprehensive description of IPT:* Klerman, G. L., Weissman, M. M., Rounsaville, B. J., & Chevron, E. S. (1984). *Interpersonal psychotherapy of depression.* New York: Basic Books.

P. 88, *Evidence suggests that the effects of IPT persist:* Weissman, M. M., Klerman, G. L., Prusoff, B. A., et al. (1981). Results one year after treatment with drugs and/or interpersonal psychotherapy. *Archives of General Psychiatry, 38,* 52–55.

P. 88, *IPT has also been used as a maintenance treatment:* Frank, E., Kupfer, D. J., Perel, J. M., et al. (1990). Three year outcomes for maintenance therapies in recurrent depression. *Archives of General Psychiatry, 47,* 1093–1099; Klerman, G. L., DiMascio, A., Weissman, M. M., et al. (1974). Treatment of depression by drugs and psychotherapy. *American Journal of Psychiatry, 131,* 186–194.

P. 89, *There are no known contraindications:* Frank, E., Kupfer, D. J., Perel, J. M., et al. (1990). Three year outcomes for maintenance therapies in recurrent depression. *Archives of General Psychiatry, 47,* 1093–1099; Manning, D. W., Markowitz, J. C., & Frances, A. J. (1992). A review of combined psychotherapy and pharmacotherapy in the treatment of depression. *Journal of Psychotherapy Practice and Research, 1,* 103–116.

P. 90, *Results from the NIMH Collaborative Depression Study:* Elkin, I., Shea, M. T., Watkins, J. T., et al. (1989). National Institute of Mental Health Treatment of Depression Collaborative Research Program: General effectiveness of treatments. *Archives of General Psychiatry, 46,* 971–982.

INDIVIDUAL PSYCHOTHERAPY

Jules R. Bemporad

Ordinary depression is an exquisitely painful mental state whose major characteristic is a feeling of sadness and despair. Clinical depression, however, regardless of type, exerts its pathological effects on more than mood alone. The individual's cognition is altered so that he feels hopeless and helpless and experiences an unrealistic lack of self-esteem. He may also demonstrate self-punitive intentions or a wish to escape and hide or, not uncommonly, to depart this life altogether.

Vegetative symptoms also occur, depending on the form of depression presented. Some individuals feel drained of energy and appear lethargic and apathetic. They lose their appetite for food or sex and complain of early morning wakening. Others report eating and sleeping too much. Still others suffer from uncontrollable agitation or are plagued by morbid fears and anxiety.

Depression may present in varying forms of symptoms, severity, and chronicity. In fact, most individuals have experienced episodes of extreme sadness or unhappiness, particularly following a significant loss or disappointment. For the healthier individual, however, these painful interludes clear rather rapidly as the individual adjusts to new situations. Also, as noted by Freud as early as 1917, mourning differs from depression by not affecting the individual's sense of self-worth. In grief, one may be in despair over an impoverished environment but retain the usual sense of self. In depression, this very sense of self is often altered so that the external loss is complemented by a sense of inner emptiness or of worthlessness. One study that compared depressed and bereaved individuals found that the bereaved group, though certainly miserable, saw their state as a continuation of their usual existence, whereas the depressed group described an alteration of their very sense of themselves.

Depression, therefore, is more than an escalation of a sad mood. It comprises changes in cognition, volition, and physiology. Furthermore, as alluded to above, it affects individuals in varying forms of severity and chronicity. Some individuals are constantly somewhat depressed or dysphoric no matter how rewarding or punitive their circumstances are at the moment; others succumb after an understandable loss or reversal of their usual modes of finding meaning or gratification in life; and still others experience recurrent episodes of severe depressive reactions, even with minimal provocation, that are complicated by delusions that amplify and express their low self-regard. Each of these forms of depression requires a type of psychotherapy tailored to the particular syndromes that make up the multifaceted disorder of depression.

To convey the logic behind the choice of different forms of psychotherapy, it might be helpful if I resort to an analogy in which the psyche is compared to a computer. According to this analogy, severe, recurrent depression with some psychotic features that may be part of a bipolar disorder or that occurs even without episodes of mania can be seen as representing some alleged defect in the actual mechanical (genetic) structure of the computer itself. Therefore, the clinician attempts to compensate for the inherent damage by a variety of measures that usually include medication as well as psychotherapeutic treatments and, sometimes, hospitalization.

Those depressions that are chronic (characterological) and that appear to result from irrational modes of processing experience may be conceived of as problems with the early programming of an otherwise intact psychic computer. In such cases, the individual's formative years were such that she ascribes meaning to her usual experiences in an aberrant manner, particularly regarding estimations of the self and of significant others. Those forms of depression called *dysthymic disorders* do not present with the striking delusions or vegetative alterations typical of psychotic or bipolar depression, but rather exhibit an almost constant sense of dysphoria that affects and reinforces a patient's negative reaction to everyday life. In my clinical experience, pharmacological agents are not always helpful for such patients, and even when some benefits are seen, pronounced side effects may cause individuals to refuse medication. Needless to say, psychotherapy is not always helpful in these cases either.

Psychotherapy is often the treatment of choice for chronic characterological depression, particularly because this form of therapeutic intervention aims at correcting irrational beliefs about the self and others that perpetrate the depression. At times, these irrational beliefs are acted out in the therapeutic situation toward the therapist (transference) or more commonly may be described toward significant others in the patient's emotional orbit. In either event, the aim of therapy is to "reprogram" the psychic computer to obtain a more accurate and appropriate analysis of the data received in everyday life.

The third form of depressive disorders, adjustment disorders with depressed mood, may account for the majority of depressed individuals seen by clinicians, counselors, or therapists. In keeping with the computer analogy, these individuals have intact mechanical (genetic) structures and have been fortunate enough to have experienced fairly realistic early programming (adequate childhoods) so that the data of experience are adequately processed. The problem is that these individuals have encountered some experience that is so personally horrendous to them that they cannot integrate it into their usual belief systems (data that their computers cannot process normally), and so they recoil with feelings of depression and despair. The particular precipitant varies from individual to individual but reverberates deeply with some vulnerability regarding their estimation of themselves or their immediate environment.

For example, a study of depressed women in England found that the disorder followed some "provoking incident." This incident, however, need not have been an actual material loss or deprivation; rather, it may have resulted in the loss of an idea or ideal that the individual required for a sense of well-being. As an illustration, the researchers cite the case of a woman who succumbed to depression when she learned that her husband had been unfaithful some years earlier. In this case, the woman's material external and interpersonal life did not change, but her opinion of her husband, herself, and their marriage certainly was altered.

Adjustment disorders also require a specific form of therapy. Usually, drugs are not so useful in these generally healthy individuals. The task of therapy is not only symptom remission but also the return of the individuals to their prior adequate state, the de-escalation of the transient disorder to a more permanent disability, and the prevention of their rushing into situations that may offer short-term relief but long-term negative consequences.

In summary, depression may be considered a spectrum of different disorders with different clinical presentations, possibly different etiologies, and different therapeutic requirements.

PSYCHOTHERAPEUTIC INTERVENTION

Perhaps the most important principle to keep in mind when initiating psychotherapy for depression is that one is treating, not a "disorder," but rather a total human being who happens to be depressed at this moment in his or her life. As psychotherapists, we don't simply treat diseases, we treat people. I have found that a thorough history of the patient is needed to assess prior levels of adaptation and functioning. I also assess the particular personality characteristics that may facilitate or impede recovery, the current social context in which the illness occurred, the nature of the precipitant, and prior episodes of psychiatric or physical illness. To highlight the importance of assessing the total situation of a depressed patient, compare the following hypothetical examples.

Mr. A. is a middle-aged single engineer who became depressed after his company forced him into early retirement following a fiscal restructuring. Mr. A. describes a solitary existence with little social support and limited interpersonal skills. He has no friends, dated sporadically in college, and sees his family, with whom he is not close, only on holidays. He has no hobbies and, aside from reading technical journals, no real interests other than his former vocation. He states that he was always a "loner" and feels uncomfortable in social situations. During his previous employment, he kept to himself, working in a lab and making minimal contact with co-workers. He relates that his work was the only thing that gave meaning to his life and that he now finds his existence empty and devoid of any satisfaction.

Mr. A. also says that he always felt somewhat depressed but that since his unemployment, he is overwhelmed by feelings of despair. To add to his misery, he wakes up at about four in the morning and cannot go back to sleep, finds he cannot concentrate sufficiently to read technical literature, has lost his appetite, and feels exhausted all the time. These incapacitating symptoms prevent him from seeking a new position. During the initial evaluation, it is difficult for him to talk, and he barely alters his facial expression of sadness. When he does speak, it is in a monotonous manner with little inflection. He states that he feels hopeless about his future and has had thoughts of killing himself. These profound statements are uttered with almost no emotion.

Miss B. is an attractive seventeen-year-old high school student who comes for evaluation with her parents. Initially, Miss B. appears sociable, almost cheerful, but as she describes the recent course of events, she begins to cry, causing her parents to comfort her. Miss B.'s parents describe their daughter as a happy, normal youngster who never exhibited any psychopathology. Although not a particularly good student, Miss B. is involved in social activities and school clubs and is described as "very popular" and "well liked."

Her depression began when her boyfriend, whom she had dated for the past year, told her he wanted to terminate their relationship. At that time, she broke into tears and seemed inconsolable to her family. Following this rejection, she insisted on staying home from school, spending most of her time sleeping or talking about her sorry state to her girlfriends on the telephone.

Miss B. also describes a strong desire for sweets and says she worries that she might become obese. She talks about her former beau with alternating tenderness and anger. She is also concerned with the loss of social status that might result from this breakup. When she thinks of returning to school, she suffers anxiety about seeing her former boyfriend or about confronting her friends now that she is no longer "his girl." The only reason she agreed to her parents' request that she seek professional help was to obtain some medicine that would quell her "awful" feelings of anxiety and despair.

I would diagnose both Mr. A. and Miss B. as suffering from a depressive disorder following a blow to their self-esteem. In Mr. A.'s case, however, this recent precipitant presented an added burden to an already limited personality. His basic resources for compensating for his loss are definitely restricted. This unfortunate man has few, if any, sources of meaning or gratification that can modify the impact of losing the one aspect of his life that caused him to feel worthy or gave him a sense of satisfaction. His prior circumscribed mode of life made him much more vulnerable to a severe loss, so he could be diagnosed as manifesting a major depressive disorder. His psychological condition and the paucity of social supports would alert me to consider the possibility of his committing suicide and the need for hospitalization. Also, his depression is so advanced, with marked vegetative symptoms, that verbal therapy alone would have slight effects at this stage. Therefore, initially, I would try (or refer) Mr. A. for medication (see Chapter Six in this volume for details) to alleviate his considerable suffering and to bring him to a state where he can respond to psychotherapeutic modes of treatment. Given his lifelong history of schizoid functioning, the poverty of his social supports, and his reliance on work as a means of obtaining a sense of worth, I would also consider group therapy and employment counseling, in addition to individual therapy and medication.

In contrast, Miss B.'s dysphoria can be seen as her experiencing a severe blow to her self-esteem and a deprivation of age-appropriate gratification, possibly for the first time in her young life. Her disappointment, though acutely painful, may not be very enduring because she seems to have the innate capability and external social supports to overcome her sense of rejection. Although her dysphoria is considerable, I would diagnose her condition as an adjustment disorder with depressed mood on the basis of her prior healthy functioning, the absence of neurovegetative symptoms, her developmental stage in the life cycle, and the magnitude of the precipitant for someone of her age. Therefore, I would attempt supportive therapy, allowing her to ventilate her feelings while concentrating on her strengths. I would also encourage her to resume her normal activities. If her depression proved more incapacitating or intensified, I would consider the addition of antidepressant medication on a short-term basis to help her readjust to her normal gratifying mode of life. As her depression cleared, it would be profitable for her, if she so desired, to explore why this rejection and its concomitant loss of social status affected her so greatly.

These two disparate instances of clinical depression are presented to emphasize the need to appreciate the social context in which the disorder occurs, as well as the characteristics of the individual afflicted. We as therapists have to keep in mind that depression is part of our humanity that, at one time or another, may affect all of us. People's ability to overcome this most painful state of being depends largely on the magnitude of the loss they have endured, its particular meaning for them, and their prior capability to find satisfaction in their everyday lives and their opinions of their basic self-worth. In addition, social supports—for example, friends or family who can buffer the sense of aloneness that usually accompanies an episode of depression—can help in decreasing the intensity and duration of the disorder. Finally, some inborn vulnerabilities that may have escaped detection to date can effect the spectrum of response to loss found in our patients. With these factors in mind, I next consider the psychotherapeutic indication for the variety of depressive states according to their severity and chronicity.

Severe or Psychotic Depression

The form of affective illness called severe or psychotic depression is classified as a major depressive disorder in the *DSM-IV*. In addition to a gross mood disturbance, physiological and cognitive symptoms are a significant part of the clinical presentation. At times these latter manifestations may be so prominent as to obscure the basic feeling of sadness or anhedonia, and so the individual complains of inability to eat, sleep, or concentrate or may fill the consultation with grossly irrational beliefs of personal worthlessness or evil. The symptom cluster resembles an organic illness, with marked neurovegetative and cognitive alterations, even in those instances where a clear psychological precipitant can be identified.

The immediate task is to relieve the patient's extreme suffering. Indeed, severe depression has been described by its victims, on recovery, as the worst experience that a human being can be made to endure. The initial treatment is threefold:

1. To institute appropriate antidepressant medication, dispensed by a psychiatrist skilled in use of medication, to lessen the marked dysphoria and to eliminate or at least reduce the neurovegetative symptoms that add to the patient's misery

2. To initiate a supportive relationship with the patient so as to allow a sense of trust to develop, thereby permitting the sharing of personal suffering and the insurance of compliance with medical treatment

3. To protect the patient from self-harm either through the enlistment of family members or by hospitalization

This last treatment goal is especially relevant because most antidepressant medications exert their effect one or two weeks after initiation. During this "lag time," I normally see a patient frequently and sometimes keep in touch by phone between visits. I also communicate to the patient's family her exquisite vulnerability, instructing them to stay with the patient and to attempt to involve her in activities that will interrupt her preoccupation with guilt or sense of impoverishment.

Severely depressed individuals experience a discontinuity with their former sense of themselves. Some may interpret this altered state of consciousness as a punishment from God, a deserved torment that proves their worthlessness, or as an unjust disaster that has befallen them for no perceptible reason. Whatever the patient's rationalizations for her painful state, I try to point out that severe depression is an abnormal state similar to a painful toothache or high fever. It should be understood that the patient is not her usual self and that the initial task of treatment is to return the patient to her premorbid state of self. Without giving unrealistic reassurances, I describe the depression as a temporary phenomenon that will clear in time.

Meanwhile, the patient is in a debilitated state and incapable of judging accurately certain aspects of her everyday existence. Some patients, for example, will say they are too sick to be helped or do not deserve to be helped and so refuse to take medication. In such instances, the therapist has to insist strongly that medical treatments must be complied with, again making the significant point that the patient's judgment is impaired by the illness to such a degree that decisions about treatment are best left to others. Usually, the patient's family has to be instructed to make sure the patient is taking the required anti-depressants.

The certainty of compliance, however, usually depends on the patient's trust in the therapist and the nature of the therapeutic relationship. The psychological meaning ascribed to taking medication is an important factor in the treatment of most patients. Some depressed patients ascribe magical powers to medication when it is dispensed by an idealized therapist and report relief before the medication can have exerted its physiological effect (usually four to six weeks). Depressed patients who are so in need of nurturance and support may view the medication as a sign of being cared for by someone who is concerned about their well-being. In contrast, paranoid patients, even when they are depressed, may believe that the prescribed medication is a covert attempt to control or secretly change them against their will, so they rarely comply with a treatment plan. Here again is an example of the need to consider the patient's total personality and not simply symptoms in any form of therapy.

Once compliance with medical treatment is achieved, psychotherapy should focus on building an alliance aimed at an honest expression of thoughts and feelings between therapist and patient. Most depressed individuals can be helped by regular contact with an empathic listener who takes their suffering seriously and appreciates their psychological predicament. I have found that the patient's friends, family, or spouse, though well intended, grow impatient with the depressive's unrealistic self-recriminations or repeated litany of despair and pessimism. Most severely depressed individuals drive other people away with the very symptoms of their illness, thereby becoming more isolated, feeling more abandoned and hopeless, and escalating their sense of worthlessness. So, being a consistent figure in the depressed patient's life can be a signal that one is not entirely hopeless or totally without personal worth.

This empathic relatedness should not include unrealistic reassurances on the part of the therapist. Limits to the extent of contact should be set at the onset of therapy. While in the midst of a depressive episode, the patient's dependency needs may be so great that he or she will want to continue a session beyond the stated time for termination or to call the therapist frequently, ostensibly with complaints but actually to feel in psychological contact. Although certainly sympathetic to the suffering that the severely depressed patient is forced to endure, I have found it best to state emphatically, at the beginning of treatment, what my own particular preferences are in terms of phone calls, extra sessions, and other practical aspects of practice.

I've also found it particularly helpful to explore possible activities a patient can pursue on his own that can reduce or distract him from the feelings of depression. These activities will obviously vary with each individual, but in general, the patient's difficulty in concentrating on complex tasks limits the choices to relatively simple activities that do not require too much intellectual effort. Some patients find exercise (jogging, tennis) beneficial; others are helped by more sedentary pursuits (reading, sewing); still others feel better when engaging with others in conversation or more social situations. The point is for the patient to develop ways to combat the painful feeling of depression on his own, so that he doesn't see himself totally at the mercy of his illness.

As the patient improves, sessions may be devoted to (1) seeking out the particular vulnerabilities and provoking factors that caused the individual's decompensation and (2) rebuilding one's psychological life after having suffered a severe illness and the effect of this experience on one's future life.

For example, a middle-aged housewife presented with a severe depression after her husband of twenty-six years told her he was leaving her for another woman. At first this patient reacted with anger at her husband's rejection. After a few days, however, she became increasingly convinced that the breakup of her marriage was all her fault. She began remembering instances in which she had been inconsiderate of her husband and decided she had driven him away. Together with this fault finding, she sensed herself as basically an unworthy, selfish person with whom no one would ever want to live.

As these symptoms increased, she stayed home alone, refusing to answer her phone, being too embarrassed to divulge to anyone, her grown children included, that she had been abandoned. Despite this aspect of pridefulness, she was convincing herself that she really deserved to be abandoned because of a whole list of personal limitations. Soon these recriminations were transformed into repetitive intrusive thoughts that kept telling her how mean, ugly, and ungrateful she was. At this point, one of her children came to her home and discovered her in a dishevelled state, preoccupied with her own thoughts as her face betrayed a sense of inner agony. She was taken to a local physician, who admitted her to a psychiatric inpatient service.

This woman's depression responded partially to medical treatment in the hospital. She could now sleep through the night, had more energy, had a return of her appetite, and was appropriately concerned about her appearance. She no longer felt as if she were surrounded by "a lead overcoat," and the accusatory intrusive thoughts were gone. She still believed, however, that she was an unworthy human being who had been a neglectful and nagging wife who deserved to be deserted. She could not conceive of her future without him and doubted her ability to enjoy life again now that he was gone. In fact, she was not certain that she wanted to go on living and often thought her best option would be to take her own life.

In contrast with her description of herself, this woman's children and friends described her as an especially caring and giving person who tried to please her husband and make a happy home for him. This view was confirmed by the patient's own telling of her history without her being aware of it. It became apparent that she had consistently sacrificed her own desires in order to make her husband and children comfortable and content. As she relinquished more and more of her psychological independence, she relied increasingly on her family's well-being for her sense of worth and meaning in life. It seemed that her husband's rejection of her as a spouse was also rejection of her whole existence and of her values. Her years of working at being a successful housewife and mother were viewed as a colossal failure because she was unable to hold her family together.

In response to these beliefs, therapy focused on the patient's limiting her sources of meaning or worth to the response of a few others in her social orbit and her tendency to blame herself if she did not receive feedback from others. As the patient continued to describe her past history, she became aware that her self-accusations were quite similar to judgments she had received from her mother as she was growing up. This mother had been consistently critical of the patient and never seemed satisfied, much less proud, of any of the patient's endeavors.

The patient gradually realized that she had formed a very negative self-image in childhood that she carried forward into adult life without conscious awareness. In considering the patient's condition as a result of prior experiences and in proposing that these modes of relating are repeated in adult life, psychodynamic therapy differs from cognitive or behavioral therapies. Psychodynamic theorists consider the symptoms of depression to be the reemergence of a childhood state of self that the patient had repressed but that the narcissistic blow associated with the precipitant brings into consciousness. The patient is thought to resume the child-parent relationship, although in an exaggerated and distorted manner.

Often, the therapist unwittingly takes the place of the feared yet needed parent, through transference, as the patient reexperiences the rejections and humiliations of childhood. In many cases, the painstaking analysis of this transferential distortion, either toward the therapist or to others in the patient's adult life, forms the bulk of the therapeutic process.

For example, this woman recalled that she had believed she would grow up to be a spinster because no man would want her. Consequently, she felt deep gratitude toward her former husband for saving her from this fate. So, therapy revealed a poor sense of self that was consolidated in childhood. Later, she was able to overcome that sense of self through devotion to her family and limitations on possibly self-enhancing activities that might threaten these defenses. Her husband's rejection was a blow to her narcissistic equilibrium and caused a reemergence of older, childhood judgments of herself.

At this point in therapy, I sought to replace these irrational views of herself and others with a more reasonable appraisal by repeatedly pointing out the unrealistic nature of her judgments of herself and her husband. Gradually she realized that her husband had replaced her critical mother as the person able to determine her sense of worth. Because he was demystified and shorn of his transferential power, the patient was able to obtain an equitable divorce settlement, found she could still enjoy being with her children in the absence of her estranged spouse, contacted friends to combat feelings of loneliness, and started to think of finding a job. Although expressing bitterness about her marriage and husband, she was no longer as depressed and could look to the future with some optimism.

This case demonstrates the synergistic result of medication and psychotherapy in a patient who experienced a major depressive disorder. The course of tricyclic antidepressants that was started during her hospital stay and continued into psychotherapy did much to diminish the degree of dysphoria, reduce the neurovegetative symptoms, and make the patient more available to cooperate in psychotherapy. The psychotherapy allowed her to view her recent loss in the context of life experience and to understand the meaning of her depression as stemming from abusive relationships during a most unhappy childhood. In addition, psychotherapy helped ease this woman's sense of loneliness and abandonment, permitted the building of a more realistic sense of self, and aided in planning for the future.

Large-scale studies have shown that medication is useful in the suppression of depressive symptoms, whereas psychotherapy helps in social adjustment. Patients who received both treatments did better than those who received either pharmacotherapy or psychotherapy alone. Individuals who have experienced a severe depressive episode have also experienced a shattering of their habitual modes of gaining satisfaction from their everyday activities. They require physical treatment to reduce their depressive symptoms, but they also require psychotherapy to put this experience into perspective, to understand what they have been through, and to be able to go on with their lives.

Dysthymic Disorder

Dysthymic forms of depression are not characterized by one or repeated episodes that alternate with longer periods of relatively normal functioning. Rather, a dysthymic disorder might be seen as a chronic, stable form of milder depression that may, in part, be perpetuated by the individual's mode of life. As such, it could be assumed that this form of disorder is part of the patient's personality, and indeed some clinicians and researchers have offered the term *depressive personality* as a more accurate diagnostic label. The concept of personality refers to deeply entrenched characteristics that pervade the individual's everyday behavior, including attitudes, values, beliefs, and behaviors. These traits are relatively stable and persist with little change throughout the lifespan.

Pathological personalities are distinguished from their more normal counterparts by their inflexibility and lack of adaptive functioning in the face of the usual demands or expectations of adult experience. Therefore, a depressive personality may be defined as the persistent constellation of psychological characteristics that result in a chronic feeling of depression that is present consistently, though its intensity may vary with environmental changes. This chronic sense of depression is thought to be the result of aberrant childhood experiences that have caused the individual to develop inappropriate and unrealistic modes of appreciating reality. In my former computer analogy, these disorders represent a malfunction in the integrating centers so that later input data are not correctly processed.

John Bowlby, one major theorist on the antecedents of adult depression, believed that chronic depression usually results from one or more of three forms of childhood environments:

1. Where the child never formed a safe, satisfying relationship with adults despite numerous efforts to do so
2. Where the child is told repeatedly by the parents how unlovable, incompetent, or inadequate he or she is
3. Where the child suffers a significant loss without appropriate substitution

These childhood experiences, according to Bowlby, create irrational belief systems that distort the way experience is processed in adult life and lead to constant feelings of unworthiness, a conviction that one is unlovable, a fear of impending loss, and a lack of the ability to derive enjoyment from one's everyday existence.

Psychotherapy with such patients involves clarification of these underlying themes, which the individual is usually unaware of. These basic beliefs commonly were formed in childhood in the patient's interchange with needed loved ones but are carried forward into adult life, where they are no longer appropriate or valid.

The therapeutic process aims to make the here and now experience between patient and therapist reveal how these beliefs of the past continue to influence the patient's current life and to show how the present is different from the past in terms of the patient's greater autonomy and control of his or her life.

These older beliefs are manifested in dreams and fantasies, but most blatantly in relationships with significant others. These relationships can be characterized as replaying or transferring the childhood relationship toward the parent into adult life and are termed *transference distortions.*

As mentioned above, the consideration of childhood experience continuing to affect adult life, the belief that these childhood beliefs are largely out of awareness and are defended against by the rest of the personality, and the use of therapy to analyze these older beliefs about oneself and others differentiate psychodynamic psychotherapy from other forms of verbal inter- actions. Psychodynamic psychotherapy fosters the emergence of these beliefs in the therapeutic situation by being less directive, confrontational, or prescriptive than cognitive or behavioral therapies.

The transferential relationships usually found in depressed individuals demonstrate how the individuals continue as adults to attempt to win the love they never obtained as a child or to avoid the pain of abandonment or punishment received as a child. For example, a young scientist sought out psychotherapy when her supervisor hired an additional researcher in his lab. The patient was convinced that the senior man would prefer the new employee, whom she perceived as abler, prettier, and wit- tier than herself. As this patient related her past history, she described herself as always melancholy and never really happy. She had no real hobbies and only a few friends. Although earn- ing a decent living, she could not spend money on herself with- out feeling guilty or being certain that some misfortune would befall her. She only felt secure when she was working, although she did not particularly enjoy the kind of work she did. Work represented a way to please important others or, at least, to pre- vent their criticism or abandonment.

This young woman had worked very hard, hoping to impress this supervisor with her industry and dedication. When he seemed pleased, she felt safe. But if she failed to please him, she would chastise herself for not trying hard enough and being lazy. In the latter instances, her depression would increase, and she imagined she would be fired and never able to work again.

When the new researcher appeared and her boss showed an appropriate professional interest in her, the patient became increasingly anxious and depressed. She was certain that this new employee had been hired to replace her, despite the clear need for additional help in the lab. She concluded that she deserved to be fired because she was basically unworthy. To justify these conclusions, she remembered and magnified every instance when her work was not of the highest quality or when she imagined she had failed to do her job properly. These thoughts and feelings escalated until she could think of nothing else. She came to work every day in a state of agitation, waiting to hear that she was fired. She was sure she would be let go, after which she thought she would kill herself.

This patient described a childhood without nurturance or care. Her parents were constantly critical of her and made her feel like a burden on the family. She was not allowed to play with other children but had to do household chores from an early age. She was told repeatedly how inferior she was, compared with her brother (who was told the same about himself in relation to her). At dinner the parents would complain about their stressed financial situation and often remarked that they could have been rich if they didn't have children to support. She was made to understand that her only chance at redemption in her parents' eyes was to bring honor to the family. Therefore, she was expected to exhibit model behavior, excel at school, and never dare to express any desire or want of her own. This woman did excel in her studies, eventually obtaining a scholarship to graduate school and gaining employment in the prestigious laboratory where she now worked. Despite these accomplishments, her parents were not satisfied and commented that none of her achievements would have been possible without their financial support.

As the patient related her history, I assumed that she had reinstated or transferred her relationship to her father in her relationship to her boss. There had been earlier indicators of this transference behavior in her idealization of college professors whom she would try to please by doing well on exams and volunteering for extra projects. In her present position, however, there were no report cards or exams on which an outstanding grade would prove her industriousness. She felt uneasy without regular concrete proof of her dedication and so was never sure that she was trying sufficiently hard.

As we worked together in therapy, the underlying themes that dominated her behavior and feelings were made explicit and brought to awareness. I used instances of her past to demonstrate how she had formed an irrationally low opinion of her abilities, how she feared punishment for having needs or desires, and how she allowed others to manipulate her self-esteem. She eventually grasped the psychological connection between her father and her boss. She began to understand how she had projected her father's attributes onto the latter transference object. Simultaneously, we discussed how her fear of her father's judgment had shaped her whole existence and thus limited her range of interest and activities.

These discussions also elicited a memory of her being on a car trip with her parents as a young child. She had wanted an ice-cream cone and insisted that they stop and buy her one. Suddenly, her father pulled the car off the road, dragged her out of the car, and then left her stranded on the highway as he and his wife proceeded on their trip. She remembered feeling terrified at being left alone on a deserted highway. She prayed that if her parents returned, she would never ask for anything again. After what must have seemed an eternity to her, her parents did return to pick her up and spent the next twenty minutes or so berating her for her inordinate desires.

This memory and others like it allowed her to appreciate how her deprived childhood had permeated all aspects of her psychological being. With each revelation, she began to alter her beliefs and her behavior. She no longer feared that she would lose her job and was even able to buy some fashionable clothes and an expensive sound system that she had long wanted. Sometimes when she bought herself something or spent an enjoyable time with friends, she would come to therapy afraid I'd be angry at her and would no longer want her as a patient.

These irrational beliefs were interpreted as transference reactions to myself, wherein I became the feared father who would punish her for daring to indulge her needs. These instances of transference were interpreted as further evidence of the strength of her irrational fears. These beliefs were also manifested in dreams in which she would come to therapy sessions during which I would be transformed into her father while she watched in horror. Part of her believed that I was only pretending to want to help her, that really I saw her, as did her father, as an evil and lazy person, which was her true self. These dreams helped affirm her distorted view of herself as evil and of others as hating her. It might be valuable to indicate that another unique aspect of psychodynamic therapy is its emphasis on dreams, fantasies, memories, and other aspects of the inner life of the individual and not only manifest behavior. These representations of psychic reality, which is the private province of each individual, are most helpful in demonstrating to the therapist and the patient the irrational judgments that continue to perpetuate the illness.

As we corrected some of her basic childhood beliefs, the patient ventured more and more to lead a more gratifying life that was less impeded by her fear of losing loved ones or increasing their wrath for living a free existence. With each step, she found that she was not punished or abandoned for going against the tenets that were instilled in her as a child. In this manner, she began to approximate a healthy, relatively accurate perception of herself and others as therapy progressed toward termination.

In summary, the psychotherapy of dysthymic disorder (or depressive personality) involves:

The identification and acknowledgement of irrational beliefs

The appreciation of how these beliefs continue to direct adult behavior, particularly regarding the distortion of the self and others in relationships

The tracing back of these beliefs to childhood experiences and their transferential persistence in the present

The understanding that such beliefs are maladaptive and perpetuate inappropriate limitations on behavior, as well as painful affects

The determination to behave in an adult manner that often is in contradiction to the instilled beliefs

This therapeutic endeavor involves making radical changes in personality functioning and not simply symptom suppression, so this cannot be accomplished too rapidly. In the past, therapists would allow the patient to arrive at past material via nondirective free association, which often took months or years. Then they would interpret transference manifestations only to themselves, waiting for it to emerge directly at a much later date. I believe that this lengthy process may be shortened greatly by directing the patient by specific questions, or by the therapist, rather than the patient, bringing up significant areas of psychopathological functioning.

In addition, transference to significant others in the patient's life may illuminate the patient's distortions about self and others. I usually don't wait for transference to become manifest toward myself. This more active role on my part in focusing on problem issues and the use of relationships outside the office can do much to reduce the length of therapy without compromising eventual effectiveness.

Medication may also shorten the length of exploratory therapy. Not infrequently, patients with depressive personalities will avoid recollections of their past because of the painful feelings evoked by these memories. The discovery that one's parents were abusive or neglectful or that the sought-after love or approval can never be obtained may cause an intensification of the usual baseline depression and result in the continued repression or suppression of such material. The use of antidepressants helps decrease the degree of depression evoked by these memories and allows for a more rapid emergence of significant events from the past. I've found that covering such patients with antidepressants, while not greatly affecting the chronic baseline depressive state, does facilitate treatment by preventing the depressive effects that accompany painful realizations that emerge in the course of therapy.

Adjustment Disorder with Depressed Mood

Adjustment disorders with depressed mood occur in basically healthy individuals who encounter traumatic situations that temporarily cause the emergence of a depressive mood, together with milder doubts about one's ability to function adequately or about one's self-worth. In continuing the computer analogy described above, these individuals are blessed with a healthy basic mechanism and an adequate early programming, so data are accurately processed. The difficulty resides in the encounter with data that cannot be computed easily and that therefore cause a self-limited breakdown of the psychic machine. Therefore, these disorders follow clear precipitants of such magnitude to alter significantly the life experience of the individual. Prior to the reactive disorder, the individual usually describes a premorbid history of relatively normal functioning with adequate relationships and interests, as well as appropriate self-regard.

Adjustment disorders will usually clear on their own with sufficient time as the individual devises methods to overcome the difficulties that he or she has encountered. It might be questioned, therefore, whether psychotherapy is justified for these essentially healthy individuals, who will get better in any case.

In my experience, therapeutic intervention is warranted in these cases

To reduce suffering, which is often considerable

To prevent the individual from grasping at poor solutions in order to reduce the pain

To minimize the duration of the disorder or its transformation into a more chronic illness

To help the individual discover some unknown vulnerability that caused somewhat excessive reaction to life's vicissitudes

One clinical illustration of an adjustment disorder may be seen in the following case history.

A young woman presented with persistent depression, decreased interest in former activities, a sense of worthlessness, and a questioning of the meaning of her life. These symptoms had appeared gradually after she returned to her city of origin some six months earlier. She moved back home because her husband had been accepted for a fellowship at a hospital in that locale. Prior to their move, the patient had been a schoolteacher, a profession she enjoyed greatly, had had a satisfying group of friends, and was happily married to a young doctor in specialty training. Shortly before their departure, she had given birth to her first child, an event she and her husband had anticipated with great excitement.

After they moved back to her hometown, they settled into a small apartment and the husband began his fellowship. Then a series of disappointments ensued: the fellowship proved more demanding than expected, so her husband spent most evenings and many nights at the hospital. Her old friends moved away, so she found herself essentially alone all day with a newborn. Costs in their new location were higher than anticipated, precluding their getting household help.

In addition, the patient had to renew her relationship with her parents. This was a particularly painful prospect because her mother had been controlling, intrusive, and critical in the past, and the patient always felt infantilized and demeaned in her presence. The mother took advantage of having a new grandchild to see the patient often, and after each visit the patient felt demoralized and criticized. On more than one occasion, the mother asked the patient and her family to move in with her because this arrangement would ameliorate their financial problems and also allow the mother to help with the baby. The patient dreaded this eventuality but admitted that, from a fiscal point of view, it made sense.

She could see only two options for herself: (1) to remain in a small apartment all alone with an infant for days at a time, scrimping on money or (2) to move in with her mother, lose her autonomy, and be subject to the mother's control and criticism. Neither choice was particularly appealing. Feeling trapped in her situation increased her sense of hopelessness and helplessness. She missed her former life in which she saw her husband frequently and had a gratifying career and a stimulating social life.

The first task of therapy with this patient was to allow her to express her frustration and despair openly and fully. She had kept these feelings to herself because she did not want to burden her husband, who was working so hard to ensure them a comfortable future. The patient could not describe her condition to her mother because she believed the latter would use the patient's misery as a further source of criticism and an added inducement to move in.

The mere fact of having a sympathetic listener did much to alleviate her sense of isolation. I encouraged her not to be so protective of others and to share these feelings with her husband. When she did so, the husband showed appropriate concern and asked to accompany her to her next therapy session. During this hour, the three of us spoke realistically about possible plans to allow the patient a more gratifying existence. He volunteered to come home for dinner more regularly and to donate more of his weekend time to his family. He also insisted on securing a loan to help them through this particularly difficult year. The patient felt tremendous relief at having others try to share her burden and became noticeably more animated during the session. She suggested the idea of investigating "mothers' groups" to initiate a new circle of friends and to share baby-sitting with other young mothers.

In a short time, the patient was able to hire a part-time nanny and to find part-time work in a local school. Her depression passed, and she saw more of her husband, was relieved of continuous child care, resumed a professional role, and began to make new friends with common interests and problems. We continued therapy awhile longer to investigate the particularly marked effect the mother had on her. Through a discussion of her past, the patient realized that she had always desired to be free of her mother and to prove to her mother that she could be a success on her own. The recent position of dependency and self-perceived "weakness" made her see herself as a shameful failure. Her childhood reactions to her mother's controlling behavior coalesced into a protective and defensive self-image of hyperindependence, and she insisted that she should never be in need of help from others and should be able to handle any situation. The patient understood the irrational and maladaptive nature of her compensatory idealized self and became more comfortable with herself as an ordinary person with human limitations and needs.

As with other individuals with adjustment disorder with depressed mood, psychotherapy with this patient

- Allowed for the expression of feelings surrounding the particular life situation at that moment
- Sought out realistic options and the prevention of maladaptive solutions (in this instance, moving in with mother)
- Explored specific personality vulnerabilities (in this case, the patient's compensatory idealized self) that may have contributed to the illness

Psychotherapy can play a significant role in the treatment of depressive disorders. I have found that most individuals, whatever form their depression may take, respond most favorably and are greatly helped by regular contact with an empathic and caring therapist. Depressed individuals are victimized by intense suffering and require the support that psychotherapy can supply. I believe that these individuals, who have so often been abused, rejected, or mistreated in myriad ways for so much of their prior lives, benefit immeasurably from a therapeutic relationship characterized by respect, humanity, and genuine concern.

Beyond this basic yet all-important sense of mutuality that therapy affords, different forms of depression present indications for variations in treatment. For some forms of severe depression, psychotherapy can ameliorate particular facets of the depressive syndrome, such as social adjustment, that are relatively untouched by medical treatments. For more chronic forms of depression, psychotherapy may be the treatment of choice in restructuring maladaptive aspects of the personality. Milder forms of depression that are seen with adjustment disorders also can be helped by psychotherapy in supporting and guiding the individual through a difficult period of his or her life.

The type of psychotherapy should be tailored to the severity and form of the presenting depression. However, of equal if not greater importance in selecting a psychotherapeutic approach are the individual characteristics of each patient, for ultimately, psychotherapy exerts its effects on the person, rather than on the disease.

NOTES

P. 95 *as noted by Freud:* Freud, S. (1917). Mourning and melancholia. *Standard Edition, 15,* 151–169.

P. 96, *an alteration of their very sense of themselves:* Clayton, P. J., Herjanic, M., Murphy, G. R., et al. (1974). Mourning and depression: Their similarities and differences. *Canadian Journal of Psychiatry, 19,* 309–312.

P. 98, *a study of depressed women in England:* Brown, G. W., & Harris, T. V. (1978). *Social origins of depression.* London: Tavistock.

P. 104, *who are so in need of nurturance:* Salzman, C., & Bemporad, J. (1990). Combined psychotherapeutic and psychopharmacological treatment of depressed patients: Clinical observations. In D. W. Manning & A. J. Francis (Eds.), *Combined pharmacotherapy and psychotherapy for depression* (pp. 153–181). Washington, DC: American Psychiatric Press.

P. 108, *Large-scale studies have shown:* Klerman, G., & Schecter, C. (1982). Drugs and psychotherapy. In E. S. Paykel (Ed.), *Handbook of affective disorders* (pp. 465–474). New York: Guilford Press.

P. 109, *they also require psychotherapy:* Frank, E., Kupfer, D. J., & Levenson, J. (1990). Continued therapy for unipolar depression: The case for combined treatment. In D. W. Manning & A. J. Frances (Eds.), *Combined pharmacotherapy and psychotherapy for depression* (pp. 133–150). Washington, DC: American Psychiatric Press.

P. 109, *The concept of personality refers:* Millon, T., & Katik, D. (1985). The relationship of depression to disorders of personality. In E. E. Beckham & W. R. Leber (Eds.), *Handbook of depression: Treatment, assessment, and research* (pp. 700–745). Homewood, IL: Dorsey Press.

P. 110, *John Bowlby, one major theorist:* Bowlby, J. (1980). *Loss.* New York: Basic Books.

5

GROUP THERAPY

Joan L. Luby

Group psychotherapy as a general term refers only to the central objective of treating multiple patients simultaneously. Within this category are various therapeutic approaches that share little common philosophy. Among them one finds support groups, self-help groups, crisis groups, cognitive behavioral groups, interpersonal groups, and analytically oriented groups.

Many of these treatment modalities have been applied to patients with depression. Meaningful differences in therapeutic technique and objectives can be found when comparing the role of the depressed patient in these various settings. In this chapter, I review the use of specialized cognitive-behavioral groups for depression but focus primarily on the practical use of interpersonal group therapy for depressed adults.

INTERPERSONAL
GROUP THERAPY

The analysis of adaptive and maladaptive patterns of social and interpersonal interactions within the "here and now" context provide the central focus and therapeutic substrate for the interpersonal psychotherapy group. Given this highly social and interactive base, the success of such a group is dependent on appropriate patient selection and resultant group composition.

Group Selection

A heterogeneous group of balanced gender and with a mixture of diagnoses and personality styles is the most effective combination. Yalom has shown that the ideal size for an interpersonal group, when considering both critical mass and the opportunity for individual participation, is seven or eight patients (with a lower limit of five and an upper limit of ten). Therefore, ideally two or three depressed patients should be included in a group of individuals with a variety of other emotional problems.

More important than mixed composition, however, is the prerequisite that all patients value interpersonal relationships; that is, patients must have a conscious desire to engage in satisfying relationships with other human beings. This prerequisite is a very important one to consider when screening the depressed patient for group participation.

For example, on one occasion when prescreening patients for such a group, my co-leader and I were initially enthusiastic about a patient who had the perfect "CV" for psychotherapy: intelligence, insight, and psychological mindedness. On further interview, however, the patient more clearly emerged as a subtly angry and guarded individual with motivation to change in many ways but who overtly expressed that she had little interest or motivation to form intimate relationships. Despite characteristics that made her suited for more general psychotherapeutic work, my co-leader and I decided that she would not be an appropriate group candidate. This important exclusion should be kept in mind when therapists are considering referring depressed patients to interpersonal groups.

Another important exclusionary criterion is the severely depressed patient characterized by social apathy and withdrawal. These patients will not be appropriate candidates for outpatient groups. They will, in general, lack the necessary interest and relational capacity to engage in the group meaningfully and will be better served by other treatment modalities, at least initially. Severity itself, however, and particularly its association with impaired patterns of interpersonal relating, should not be the basis of exclusion because these are the very symptoms that group treatment is designed to address. As is true of most psychotherapeutic modalities, the capacity for insight and self-evaluation is also a necessary quality for useful group participation and as such should be evaluated by the outpatient therapist prior to referral to group.

Therapeutic Factors

Yalom has defined eleven therapeutic factors that characterize the healing process in group psychotherapy: (1) instillation of hope, (2) universality, (3) imparting of information, (4) altruism, (5) corrective recapitulation of the primary family group, (6) development of socializing techniques, (7) imitative behavior, (8) interpersonal learning, (9) group cohesiveness, (10) catharsis, and (11) existential factors. Many of these factors also operate in other forms of psychotherapy; some are specific to or operate more powerfully in a group format. The therapeutic importance of these factors for individual patients in a group depends on characteristics of both patient (diagnosis and personality style) and group process (content, purpose, and phase of treatment).

Several of these therapeutic factors seem particularly relevant to the treatment of depressed patients. Universality, for example, is a potentially immediate and activating factor for the depressed patient entering a therapy group. The recognition that one's distress is similar to that experienced by others could be a revelation to an isolated and lonely patient. This may be particularly true when depressed patients observe one another and is one primary reason for including more than one depressed patient in mixed interpersonal groups.

Universality can also have a liberating impact on depressed patients, who typically enter a group feeling stigmatized. The awareness of the similarity of others' emotional experiences may serve to break down an entrenched sense of shame and hopelessness and perhaps to draw these patients out of their shells. Furthermore, patients learn that vulnerability to depression and mental illness in general cuts across personal and social boundaries. For those who blame themselves for becoming depressed, this insight may promote more realistic explanations about how and why depression occurs. I can recall one such moment in an outpatient group when a depressed patient expressed her amazement and sense of disbelief that another patient who was attractive and professionally successful could be suffering from depression as well.

Altruism, the sense of fulfillment gained from the act of helping others, is a potentially powerful experience for the depressed patient in group. Because depressed individuals suffer from doubts about their self-worth and competence in the interpersonal realm, they often are reluctant to engage or offer feedback to peers. This behavior, which is prevalent in social interactions, is generally recapitulated in the group setting. In fact, depressed patients may fear that their contributions will have a detrimental effect on others. By supporting these patients and by encouraging them to reveal their thoughts, the leader can help them rediscover their ability to contribute positively to others' lives. The belief and experience that one has something valuable to offer others is an important building block in the reestablishment of self-esteem.

Another therapeutic factor—the instillation of hope—is similarly pertinent to depressed patients. Hopelessness is a disabling symptom of depression that can be difficult to approach therapeutically and that is often resistant to individual treatment strategies. In a group setting, a patient has an opportunity to witness the progress of peers, both depressed and others. This experience emphasizes the plasticity of the depressive state and the fact that recovery is an attainable goal. An important turning point in the treatment of depression may occur with this experience. Outpatient therapists should be aware of these therapeutic factors because they will likely constitute an important part of the patient's reaction to group treatment. It will be helpful to interpret and further process the patient's experiences along these lines in individual treatment when it occurs simultaneously in group.

Importance of Interpersonal Learning

As previously discussed, interpersonal learning provides the foundation for therapeutic change in this form of group treatment. For several reasons, it may also be uniquely important for depressed patients. An interpersonal emphasis in the group addresses an individual's maladaptive social behaviors and is based on the notion that open and intimate human relationships are essential to psychological well-being. The process of interpersonal learning involves exploration of the underlying intrapsychic distortions and false assumptions that operate in an interactional context to cause relationship failures. This factor is, of course, also at play in the transference relationship of individual psychotherapy, but it is stimulated and facilitated to a greater degree in the social climate of the group.

Virtually every psychiatric disorder affects a patient's interpersonal functioning. The depressive disorders, however, are thought by some to be etiologically tied to interpersonal pathology. Depressed patients are known to be withdrawn, isolated, and avoidant of social contacts. Clinical observations also suggest that the important interpersonal relationships of these patients are characterized by distortions and conflict.

One pattern of interpersonal difficulty has been described by Bemporad. He has emphasized the characteristic need for an idealized, dominant other in the relationships of depressed individuals. The depressive has deep ambivalent feelings toward this idealized other—a mixture of intense dependency and secondary anger and resentment—when these needs go unmet. Arieti has also discussed this key interpersonal component of depressive psychodynamics. He stresses the importance of the "dominant other" in the modulation of the depressed patient's self-esteem: "[This] dominant other has provided the patient with the evidence, real or illusory, or at least the hope that acceptance, love, respect, and recognition of his human worth were acknowledged." Any threat to this relationship can precipitate an exacerbation of illness; loss may cause decompensation. These interpersonal dynamics may be intimately connected to the course of the illness and, in some cases, to its origins.

An example of just such a dynamic emerged between a young female depressed patient and another group member in a sixteen-week outpatient group. The patient was a highly intelligent and professionally successful woman whose depression was precipitated by a breakup with a boyfriend months prior to entering the group. Although she offered useful feedback to other group members, she kept her own intrapsychic conflicts well concealed. This patient quickly made a strong alliance with a forceful and attractive female member. The patient participated when an issue involved this chosen "partner," and she became her ally in all interpersonal conflicts. This behavior was done at the expense of her own stated goals and, perhaps, as a means of avoiding them.

This behavior also prevented the patient from establishing an independent identity in the group. As Arieti predicts, the "dominant other" played the vital role of verifying the esteem and well-being of this depressed patient. Thus, this patient was driven to protect and please her partner even at great personal expense. The pair became an accepted alliance, serving the depressed patient's dependency and her partner's grandiosity.

As the group developed, peers began to question and challenge the alliance, and the pair gained insight into the dynamics of their relationship. The depressed patient's commitment to the compromise was so powerful that she chose to defend and maintain it even in the face of her partner's willingness to give it up. Although the depressed woman was not yet able to change, she became aware of her problem and its maladaptive social solution. In the open structure of this group, the complex interactive pathology was manifest in a clear and workable way.

Beck's extensive work on depression also emphasizes the disordered interpersonal experience of depressed patients. He points to the devaluation of intimacy and attachment relationships that are associated with depression. Loss of pleasure and satisfaction in pursuing such close relationships seems to follow from weakened attachments and may progress to feelings of apathy or indifference toward previous love objects. Paradoxically, these same patients often have heightened and unrealistic dependency needs. These symptoms, along with the depressed patient's characteristic negative expectations and cognitive distortions, profoundly affect their interpersonal lives.

Interpersonal psychotherapy (IPT) for depression is a technique of individual treatment (described in Chapter Three) that is based on and aims to specifically target the interpersonal pathology of depression. This short-term, individual psychotherapeutic treatment focusing on the role of dysfunctional interpersonal relationships in the onset and perpetuation of depression is thought to facilitate recovery from acute episodes and possibly to have positive long-term effects on the risk of relapse.

HOW IT WORKS

It seems clear that interpersonal group psychotherapy is suited to the treatment of depressed patients for a number of theoretical reasons. The practical matter of how to be therapeutic to the depressed individual in such a group, however, is less straightforward. Although a comprehensive review of the theory and techniques of interpersonal group psychotherapy is beyond the scope of this chapter (see Yalom's 1985 book for these details), I address some of the fundamental points and touch on their unique application to depression.

Staying in the Here and Now

As I mentioned above, the inclusion of two or three depressed patients in a mixed group is preferable. Two therapists, one of each gender, is optimal. Such inclusion recapitulates a family group and addresses interpersonal issues relating to gender. The need for two therapists is also important to keep each other open, honest, and on track and to offer perspective on each other's interpersonal dynamics within the group.

It's recommended that co-therapists meet to "debrief" after each group, to discuss the process and direction of the group, and to engage in treatment planning. I have found in my own experience co-leading interpersonal groups that this postgroup analysis is invaluable toward understanding the group process and gaining insight into one's own interactions with patients. My co-leader and I have even made written progress notes that we then sent to patients. This procedure added another opportunity for therapist participation and group analysis that contributed to the depth of the group process.

The interactive group is, by design, a relatively unstructured setting. An open format in which the therapists take a relatively nondirective stance allows the group to develop freely into a social microcosm. This evolution is necessary to facilitate the therapeutic process. To preserve the integrity of the microcosm within the group setting, extra group contacts among members are generally discouraged. Over time, the members will become a unique social system with complex lines of power, intimacy, alliance, and animosity. Interactions in the group are thought to recapitulate outside relationship patterns. The manifestation of these patterns within the supportive and protected environment of the group enables the therapeutic work to take place.

As group therapists, we work within the here and now by focusing on intragroup dynamics as they unfold and by de-emphasizing historical or genetic material; that is, the emphasis is on the way patients are relating to each other in the group, rather than on dissatisfaction or frustrations in a patient's outside relationships.

I can recall, for example, a patient in a group I co-led who constantly brought up problems in his relationship with his wife. This insertion had the effect of distancing him from other group members who were unfamiliar with his wife and unable to make an objective assessment. One of the challenges for the group therapist, then, was to identify the broader psychological pertinence of outside relationship problems as they related to group behavior. In this case, the task was twofold. The first goal was to look at how the patient's preoccupation with his wife allowed him to avoid engaging with other members. The second goal, and perhaps more challenging, involved looking for interactions between the patient and other group members with similar dynamics to those with his wife. This technique enhances the experiential potency of the group through a use of material immediately at hand and thus emotionally charged. A loop of experience and processing of experience within the group is established and becomes the basis of therapeutic change.

Engaging the Depressed Member in the Group

Several inherent problems arise when attempting to apply theory to practice, not the least of which is getting a depressed patient to enter a therapy group. Consider the fundamental psychological characteristics of depression: pessimism, hopelessness, withdrawal, and lack of motivation. With these qualities, the depressed patient is not prone to be self-directed and treatment-seeking and can remain unidentified by mental health professionals altogether. Furthermore, some depressed patients resist the prescription of group treatment because of an expectation that they will be negatively evaluated and ultimately rejected by a group. These impediments are best addressed in a supportive fashion in individual sessions, preferably with the referring therapist, or as screening visits to the group therapist. When such obstacles are overcome, the interpersonal group is the ideal therapeutic arena to address many of these socially maladaptive behaviors.

Given these reservations, the depressed patient may also be seen as "at risk" both for nonparticipation in the group and ultimately for group dropout. Given the mixed composition of the group, the more socially comfortable and extroverted members will tend to dominate. It is likely that the depressed patient will passively allow the agendas of other patients to supersede his or her own, thereby missing important opportunities. This pattern should be identified and addressed in the group. It is incumbent on the therapist, and should be encouraged of other group members, to encourage and actively seek out the participation of depressed patients. Such attempts are likely to succeed only if they capture in the depressed patient a thread of underlying awareness and dissatisfaction with the social isolation and deprivation he or she experiences.

We as therapists should look for subtle and perhaps unconscious indications that this pattern of isolative behavior is unpleasant or in other ways ego-dystonic to the patient. Further, we should confront head-on any presumed underlying feelings of alienation or isolation as they occur in the here and now. Direct but empathic statements to the depressed patient, such as, "I have the feeling that you are wishing you weren't here today; can you tell us anything about that?" may catalyze a more therapeutic exchange between the depressed patient and other group members.

The clinical symptoms of depression are often associated with an underlying experience of impoverishment. Social withdrawal and inertia may be, in part, a reaction to this sense of emptiness. This withdrawn demeanor, however, is likely to be perceived by others as off-putting, helping to bring about the social rejection that these patients fear. Rage may also be an overt or covert characteristic of depressed patients that significantly impairs their interactive success. The rageful, depressed patient repels others but is typically perplexed as to why this occurs. The unmasking of such interactive group dynamics is a good example of the kind of "process" material that the leader aims to call to the group's attention.

These kinds of difficulties engaging in group treatment might also be anticipated and addressed by the outpatient therapist. In this way, the therapist can then serve as an important scaffold and catalyst to the patient's group participation.

An individual in a short-term (sixteen-week) outpatient group stands out as an example of the process described above. This chronically dysphoric, isolated patient was highly desirous of social engagement. Although he participated diligently in the group, he expressed himself in an overly detailed, monotonous, and emotionless fashion, without sensitivity to listeners' responses. During the course of therapy, through feedback initially from the leaders and later from peers, he learned that his interpersonal style bored and distanced others. Gradually, after many sessions and continuous reenactment of this process, he came to understand his own active role in his social isolation.

Guidelines for the use of interactive group treatment of major depression can be given, but there is no formulaic approach. Although there are common behavioral features of major depression, the individual expression of depressive symptoms will be determined by a patient's underlying character traits. A depressed patient's behavior in group, then, will be a function of this more complex equation, and such individual differences defy the use of a standardized method.

In other words, one does not treat depression itself in these groups, but rather its individual interpersonal manifestations. These manifestations, rather than being mere concomitants of depression, may be vital to the maintenance and inception of the illness. The treatment of depression, from this perspective, intervenes in an individual's interpersonal world, rather than in his or her symptom state.

Measuring Outcome

Interpersonal group therapy is less conducive to controlled outcome research than more standardized forms of group treatment. Systematic studies of interactive or psychodynamic groups for depression are scarce. These kinds of groups are less amenable to study than cognitive groups, for example, because of difficulties in the control and replication of the therapeutic techniques. Such variables as the leader's therapeutic technique, as well as group composition and the frequent co-occurrence of other treatment modalities, make this kind of research difficult.

The few studies that have been conducted have looked at different group compositions and comparison groups and have yielded a conflicting array of results. One study by Covi and Lipman reported interpersonal group treatment to be less effective than cognitive-behavioral groups for depression. Similarly, Steuer and colleagues found psychodynamic groups for elderly depressives to be inferior to cognitive-behavioral groups on the basis of the Beck Depression Inventory (BDI) but equal by several other measures. The use of the BDI may be a biased measure because the symptoms that it rates are specifically those that cognitive-behavioral groups focus on. Other studies have found interpersonal groups equal in efficacy to cognitive-behavioral group treatment for depressed college students. In a more recent review of several studies of this issue, the conclusion that "psychodynamic" group psychotherapy for depressed patients is as effective as individual treatment modalities has also been suggested.

INPATIENT INTERPERSONAL GROUPS

Some patients may require brief or intermittent hospitalizations during the course of outpatient treatment for major depression. Such a circumstance may provide an opportunity for group participation of a different nature. Thus, it is important to be aware of the uses and goals of an inpatient group within comprehensive inpatient treatment planning.

Inpatient groups may be a standard component of the treatment plan of the hospitalized depressed patient. Even though a patient in the throes of a severe neurovegetative depression will not be accessible to interpersonal learning, he or she may profit from other therapeutic factors. The simple immersion of a depressive into a social environment has therapeutic impact: breaking the habitual isolative pattern. The patient grows more aware of the outside world and is, at least temporarily, diverted from ruminative self-preoccupations. In addition, the therapeutic factors of universality and instillation of hope can also be active in the beginning phases of the inpatient group treatment of depression, just as they are operative in outpatient settings. In general, these benefits warrant the inclusion of even severely ill patients in an inpatient group; later, as they improve, they'll be able to make use of other therapeutic factors.

Special Issues

The inpatient setting itself presents unique challenges to the group psychotherapist. Many of the problems peculiar to the inpatient unit will affect the functioning of any group in this setting independent of diagnostic composition. A very basic and significant difficulty that the group faces is the challenge of co-existing with other, possibly competing treatment modalities on the unit. The success of the group rests on a strong commitment by group members, and this base, in turn, requires that the milieu and individual therapists be strongly supportive of group participation.

If the group is not fully accepted and valued by the staff, patients will not engage in treatment in a serious way. Milieu support is established through the education of staff about the mechanisms and proven effectiveness of group treatment. Thus, it is imperative that group therapists work closely with inpatient staff to ensure unified staff support for the group.

The frequent discharges that are characteristic of current inpatient units pose another challenge to the group process. Groups are subjected to rapidly changing membership and must tolerate repeated additions and losses. This is a difficult situation for most patients, but the depressive is particularly vulnerable. The adaptation to new members and, more significantly, the loss of existing relationships will be stressful for depressed patients. The experience may reenact previous traumatic losses, heightening the affective responses from these patients. Although this can be a disturbing rather than soothing process, it stimulates important material for therapeutic work. The focus on processing actual group events in combination with reality testing from peers helps the patient identify internally driven distortions in his or her current emotional reactions. The group format provides the patient the opportunity to reexperience painful emotions of loss in a supportive therapeutic environment.

One might expect this rapid patient turnover to pose an obstacle to the development of the necessary degree of cohesion among inpatient group members. Cohesion is a therapeutic factor that has been repeatedly associated with positive treatment outcome. Maxmen has shown, however, that members of a diagnostically mixed inpatient group experiencing such rapid turnover still rate cohesion as a highly valued therapeutic component. Although group composition may change daily, the fact that inpatients live together in a specialized treatment milieu may be ample compensation. As Betcher points out, extra group contacts on the unit occur in such an intense and personal context that they serve as a catalyst to relationship development. Thus, despite the fleeting nature of these relationships, the level of intimacy achieved may be profound.

Another challenge for the leaders of inpatient groups is that the severity of psychopathology in hospitalized patients is likely to be high. Depressed patients in particular may be some of the most despairing and hopeless group members. Their tendency toward rumination and negative self-absorption poses obvious impediments to participation in and acceptance by the group.

The initial goal with these patients is to help them gain insight into the way their interactive style perpetuates the loneliness and isolation they feel. Patients can be encouraged to examine how their behavior alienates and repels those around them. They can learn from group feedback, for example, that ruminative preoccupation is interpreted by peers as a lack of interest. In this way, the interactive pathology of depression is identified and mobilized in group psychotherapy.

Role of the Therapist

The inpatient therapist must take a very directive role because of the severity of members' interpersonal impairment. Thus, the therapist must actively facilitate and support patient participation and interaction. Group leaders must be attuned to the existing ego strengths of different members and encourage their application to group process. A severely depressed patient, for example, despite outward withdrawal and apathy, may have the capacity for important insights and empathic listening in the group. Contributions of this nature may require delicate prompting by the leader, but once elicited, are often far more valuable to peers than those offered by therapists. The objective of the group therapist, more challenging in the inpatient setting, is to facilitate the members' ability to initiate and ultimately play a part in directing the group process.

Similarly, the creation of an atmosphere of mutual support and acceptance has been shown to be of particular value in outcome studies of group therapy. Such an environment cannot be fostered when patients remain withdrawn or apathetic. Therapists must encourage active participation both for the unique value of its content and for the subtler ways in which it becomes the framework for trust and acceptance in the group. The therapeutic effectiveness of a group depends on actively contributing members who can learn to both process psychological material and express support of and interest in peers. The creation and maintenance of this specialized environment with severely impaired patients in a short time frame is the major challenge of the inpatient therapist.

Not uncommonly, leaders will be frustrated with the slow progress of the inpatient group in general, but particularly of its depressed members. Group leaders can become overwhelmed by the excessive needs, demands, and immobility of these patients, especially in the time-limited treatment setting, and can themselves experience demoralization and hopelessness.

Setting Goals: The Agenda Group

Therapists can take several important measures to enhance patients' motivation and progress and, accordingly, to prevent their own discouragement. Appropriate goal setting is fundamental to the maintenance of patients' desire and commitment to work in the group. Goals beyond the capacity of the patient can be overwhelming and serve only to reinforce negative self-evaluations. Accordingly, assistance in setting more reasonable goals and acknowledgment of these smaller but progressive steps will aid in maintaining a patient's morale. This aid, in turn, can contribute to group morale and group integrity in general. For group leaders as well, this method provides markers of recovery, in what may, at times, feel like a sea of pathology.

The "agenda group," as described by Yalom, provides a useful framework for accomplishing appropriate goal setting. An agenda is required of each member at the outset of the daily group. This agenda is a short-term interactional treatment goal chosen by the patient: it is timely, circumscribed, and thus realizable, affectively significant, and pertinent to current group dynamics. Ideally, the agenda is based on the wish to change an interactional problem that is recognized by the patient and manifested in the group. Group leaders often assist in the formulation of an appropriate agenda, but the idea should arise out of a grain of motivation and self-awareness in the patient. This kind of agenda secures the patient's investment in and responsibility for treatment and change. It is a tool used to focus on a treatment objective that is achievable within the limited time period of a single group session.

The agenda is of particular relevance to depressed patients who require tangible goals to enter meaningfully and participate in a group. Typically, they are not proactive patients and have trouble with social initiative secondary to a poor self-concept and ruminative preoccupation. Slife suggests further that depressed patients have diminished cognitive processing abilities, which may interfere with their spontaneous group participation. The agenda is a contract between the group and the patient that encourages the depressed patient's active group involvement and earnest pursuit of a meaningful treatment goal.

Consider, for example, a female depressed patient who is often cold and sharp in interactions with men. She finds herself unable to form desired relationships in this area. An appropriate agenda for such a patient might be to become aware of the impact of her approach on the men in the group. This assignment could be achieved by her requesting that male patients give her direct feedback if they experience her as distant and off-putting. The stated agenda encourages the patient to seek and consider valuable (although at times negative) feedback from others. Such an agenda can also be accomplished within a sixty- to ninety-minute group session.

Therapists and peers can refer to an agenda to remind a patient of the originally stated goals when behaviors, perhaps unconscious, seem to contradict these intentions. Patients can act to avoid facing their problems at times despite a desire on another level to deal with them. The agenda also serves as a guide in pursuing a manageable treatment goal within a single group session. This guidance is crucial in the inpatient setting, where the length of an individual's involvement in the group is unclear at the outset and, unfortunately, often brief.

COGNITIVE-BEHAVIORAL GROUP THERAPY

A widely used approach to the outpatient group treatment of depression is modeled on Beck's cognitive theory of depression. This theory is based on the notion that depression arises out of a series of negative self-image distortions that become self-perpetuating. In effect, the patient develops a negative self-concept and a pessimistic worldview based on past experiences. The illness evolves and escalates by a process of habitual negative misinterpretations of new life situations. Effective therapy must interrupt the process of cognitive distortion and modify maladaptive belief systems.

Beck's theory is easily adapted to a diagnostically homogeneous group format. Cognitive distortions are readily identified in groups, standing out because of their lack of external verification by others. For example, a patient who inaccurately experiences another as rejecting and aloof will find that his or her perceptions are not borne out by observers. In this way, dysfunctional beliefs and misperceptions are made more accessible to treatment. Further, the social dynamics of a group will stimulate a depressed patient's underlying negative self-comparisons and bring core esteem issues to the fore. The homogeneous quality of the group allows these common themes to be the central focus and principal group agenda.

The techniques of cognitive-behavioral group therapy (CBG) differ markedly from those used in interpersonal groups. Cognitive-behavioral groups are highly structured, homogeneous, and virtually always time limited (so-called closed-ended). They rely more heavily on a well-defined set of treatment goals, in contrast with the open format and heterogeneous composition of interpersonal groups. The duration of treatment of the CBG varies from weekly to twice-weekly sessions occurring over sixteen to twenty weeks. A clear commitment to the entire treatment process is required of all patients, and some clinicians have recommended assessing a flat fee for the entire treatment process at the outset to help ensure compliance at this level.

Setting Goals

As in interpersonal groups, the use of two leaders and a patient group of six to ten is recommended in cognitive-behavioral groups. Similar to the agenda method used in inpatient interpersonal groups, reasonable and circumscribed goals are emphasized. Goal setting and treatment pace are somewhat more regulated, depending on the phase of the group. Associated homework assignments are also an essential part of the process.

The sequential administration of the Beck Depression Inventory (BDI) is not an uncommon practice. This inventory allows the leaders to assess and provide a visual record of the patients' progress during the course of the group by charting scores. Educating patients about the definition of depression and the mechanisms of cognitive-behavioral treatment are addressed at the beginning phases of treatment. Subsequently, more specific goals surrounding negative cognitive and behavioral processes and suggestions for alternative, more adaptive, and less depressogenic processes are taught.

Some group clinicians outline three major phases to time-limited (closed-ended) cognitive groups. The first is an educative one in which the theory and rationale of cognitive-behavioral therapy are explained and practiced. Then, "graded task assignments" are used in an effort to help patients recognize negative self-conceptualizations in daily life and modify behavior accordingly. Therapeutic tasks are carried out in a formal way, usually with the use of specific written assignments.

During the second phase, tools learned in the first phase are implemented within the interactive group context. Here, one's negative self-perceptions are checked against those of group peers. The third phase centers on an examination of termination issues and a reframing of the concept of cure. The primary goal is to encourage acceptance of the idea that future treatment needs do not imply failure. Therapists emphasize the fact that recovery from depression may be a lifelong process likely to require periodic return to some form of treatment.

It seems clear that some aspects of cognitive-behavioral group treatment involve the use of interactional group techniques and group process to facilitate cognitive treatment goals. A basic example is the importance of group feedback. Reality testing and, more specifically, the checking of one's self-perceptions and interpretations against the observations of a peer group are a primary step in the interruption of the depressive cognitive construct.

Furthermore, the group, by its social and interactional nature, will cause a patient's underlying negative self-comparisons to surface and be available for therapeutic change. Altruism, in addition to its therapeutic function discussed earlier, might have another benefit in a cognitive group. Beyond the increase in self-esteem that is gained by making useful contributions to others, the depressed patient's role in correcting the cognitive distortions of a peer may facilitate the undoing of his or her own negative misperceptions. "Thus, the members of the group reality-test assumptions, and in so doing, increase their skills in correcting their own maladaptive reactions."

Cognitive group psychotherapy offers a short-term, cost-effective treatment alternative to patients suffering from this disorder. Unlike psychodynamic or, more specifically, interactive group approaches, it has an advantage of being readily testable in the experimental setting, and several studies have supported its use for symptom reduction in major depressive disorders.

Measuring Outcome

Many of the techniques of CBG described were derived from systematic study of efficacy. Early support for a cognitive group approach has been reported by Gioe, who compared cognitive and group experiences both individually and in combination and found the latter to be superior. Covi and Lipman compared cognitive-behavioral therapy both alone and in combination with antidepressant medication to interpersonal groups and concluded that CBGs are superior.

OTHER SPECIAL CONSIDERATIONS

Several other issues arise when considering group therapy for your depressed patient. These are described below.

Managed Care Concerns

In many ways, group treatment modalities are well suited to survive in the emerging wave of health care reform. The widespread use of time-limited, short-term group treatment (generally of sixteen to twenty sessions) should fit in well with the objectives of managed care plans to offer limited and circumscribed care. Although individual plans vary widely, many regard one group session as the equivalent of half a session, and thus a course of group treatment will use only eight to ten out of a typical twenty-visit limit, for example.

Difficulties may emerge when obtaining authorization for the entire course of treatment; many plans have specified caps on the number of sessions they will authorize at any given time. Clearly, therapists need to have assurance that all of the sessions are authorized because participation in the full course of treatment course is required in order for the intervention to be meaningful. It may be necessary, therefore, to request special authorization and to speak directly to an insurance company's administrative officials about such issues to obtain the necessary authorization.

Medication

The issue of medication will invariably arise in the group treatment of depressed patients. Those patients requiring medication as an adjunct to psychotherapy may request that physician group therapists administer this treatment. For several reasons, and these are more specifically pertinent to mixed interpersonal groups, pharmacological management should be sought outside the group.

First, the mental status exam necessary for psychopharmacological assessment and maintenance cannot be obtained during typical group sessions unless it is a specific goal of the group as a whole. Unless this is the case, extra group contacts between the therapist and the patient would be required to perform the task. But, as previously mentioned, extra group contacts with select patients have a detrimental effect on group transference dynamics by introducing the appearance of favoritism. It's important to preserve the tangible equality of the treatment relationship for all group members.

Additional issues arise simply from the act of giving medication: depressed patients who receive medication may tend to define their disease as primarily biochemical, taking less responsibility for the interpersonal elements of the illness. The task of encouraging a patient's awareness of the interpersonal components of his or her depression can be accomplished with greater ease when the group therapist is operationally removed from that biochemical definition. The adjunctive use of pharmacotherapy prescribed by an outside physician, however, is a good example of the need to pursue collateral but complementary treatments for the depressed patient.

Suicidality

In working with patients with major depression, suicidality is likely to surface in at least some patients, thus presenting a challenging issue for a therapy group. The suicidal patient absorbs significant amounts of energy from the group and requires that attention be shifted from other ongoing issues. When ideation or gestures occur, anxiety is aroused in group leaders and members alike. Peers may feel compelled to come to the aid of the distressed patient despite being overwhelmed by this task and distracted from their own therapeutic issues. When not appropriately addressed, suicidality is a prohibitive stress for the group. For this reason, many therapists may unnecessarily exclude suicidal patients from group treatment.

When an acute suicide risk or threat does arise during an ongoing group, it can be processed in a way that is meaningful for the group as a whole. The suicidal patient's problem must take precedence, but despite its obvious urgency, members may harbor feelings of resentment about the shift in focus. It is important, therefore, to go back and explore these feelings once the crisis is resolved.

A determination of the seriousness of the risk by the leaders, however, is the first order of business and may warrant individual sessions with one or both of the therapists. If hospitalization is not indicated but additional measures are required, group members can be recruited to participate in a temporary support network of frequent extra group checks with the patient in crisis. This technique can serve not only to aid a suicidal patient through difficult times but also to increase dramatically the sense of cohesion and trust in the group.

The crisis can stimulate myriad important interpersonal issues that should be processed once the immediate dangers are settled. For the nonsuicidal group members, feelings of helplessness or betrayal may arise. Group members will be shocked about the intensity of a peer's distress if it was not previously evident. Reactions are as diverse as a loss of faith in group treatment to personal guilt about their inability to provide adequate support to the patient. Additionally, suicidal ideation may be interpreted by more intimate peers as a disavowal of the importance of the relationship; it is seen as a betrayal of commitment.

Other practitioners have specifically treated suicidality by forming a homogeneous group of suicidal patients. Such groups may offer advantages to suicidally preoccupied patients unavailable in heterogeneous groups. In a widely cited paper, Frederick and Farberow discuss this issue and elaborate on the unique focus and format of the suicidality group. These authors alter fundamental aspects of the group framework. For example, they encourage supportive extra group contacts between members, in contrast with the standard position taken by most interpersonal group leaders prohibiting extra group contact during the treatment process. Additionally, fixed time limitations are not recommended; rather, a flexible termination date is suggested, depending on the needs of the members.

Other authors go farther to suggest that regular attendance should not be a requirement of this type of group. The commitment to weekly group meetings is entirely voluntary. Patients are presented with the concept that they are "welcome to attend." The objective is to make the group a nonjudgmental, open environment that is available, safe, and appealing to the suicidal patient.

The leaders of suicidality groups describe rapid cohesion and a marked absence of resistance: "[T]he person is exposed by the flagrancy of his symptom from the moment he enters such a group. The pathology of a suicide attempter . . . cannot be easily hidden by defensive measures." The authors concluded that patients in these circumstances have such exposed psychopathology that resistance is not an obstacle in the treatment process. Another important advantage to this format is that the suicidal act loses much of its interpersonal power in these settings. "The experience is openly discussed and seen not as unique but as an area of common experience." Further, suicidal patients are expected to play an active, supportive role in steering peers away from suicidal solutions. This role is therapeutic for both the patient in crisis and to group members offering help.

The course and direction of this type of group is largely dependent on whether patients are immersed in or past the acute crisis. Obviously, a strongly supportive and practical approach is taken during times of crisis. These episodes may demand the input of outside sources, such as individual therapists, friends, or family; involvement and availability of external resources are important components of the crisis management. After the suicidal crisis resolves, more self-reflective and probing work should be encouraged. Some group therapists suggest that the short-term suicidality group should be used for patients in acute crisis and that long-term groups are indicated for stabilized patients wishing to pursue a more insight-oriented path.

Frederick and Farberow also describe a decrease in the intensity of therapist-patient transference as another appealing element of the homogeneous group for suicidal patients. They regard this as an advantage in the treatment process in that it "reduces the projection of blame by widening the base of the transference phenomenon." These authors suggest that the group situation, by its very nature, diffuses the intensity of the patient's expressed feelings toward the therapist. A patient's affects are shared and absorbed by the group as a whole, rather than by the therapist alone. In this way, the group format is well suited to cope with the intense and difficult negative emotions, sometimes overwhelming to the individual therapist, that occur in suicidal patients.

Moving beyond suicidal ideation, what is the impact of a completed suicide on a therapy group? This is experienced as a trauma of no small magnitude to the group and its leaders, and it stimulates powerful and painful issues. Few case reports in the literature depict the impact of a suicide on a therapy group, and clinical experience with the phenomenon may be sparse. Kibel shares his account of a patient's suicide during an ongoing group and its effect on group process and content. He describes several stages that the group collectively moved through in reaction to the trauma. Initially, the response was one of shock and sadness; this phase was rapidly followed by attempts to deny the loss by diminishing the importance of the deceased patient to the group. Regression was evident: members showed increased dependence on the leader and reverted back to previous problematic behaviors. Some members withdrew emotionally from the group, and a few dropped out.

As the slow process of working through the trauma continued, Kibel observed that some members reacted with guilt that the group had been unable to detect the patient's level of distress. Underlying anger and blame of the therapist also surfaced. It is notable that several patients were highly motivated toward intrapsychic change after this event. They accepted confrontation with increased openness and seemed to have a newfound fervor to participate in therapeutic work.

Group therapists who have lost a group member through suicide experience many complex and painful emotions. Kibel writes, "Typically there is a tremendous loss of self-esteem. The suicide is seen as both a personal failure and a sign of professional inadequacy." The therapist wonders, had he or she done enough? Kibel reminds us that, compounding this burden, "the therapist must cope with his or her own embarrassment in front of the other patients while at the same time engaging in the formidable task of trying to mitigate their reactions to the suicide." The therapist must cope with his or her own countertransference reactions and genuine despair and sorrow over the event and distinguish these feelings from the group's projections and distortions about his or her role or responsibility. Although this kind of trauma is a relatively rare event, the group therapist who undertakes the treatment of depressed and suicidal individuals must be prepared to deal with it.

Obviously, the use of a co-therapist is invaluable in such difficult circumstances. The task of supporting and comforting frightened or guilty patients and keeping the group essentially intact through the crisis period is a substantial one. Maintaining group norms of open and honest disclosure while respecting the privacy of the deceased patient is also a challenge. The co-therapy model is useful in this process because leaders will be struggling with their own strong reactions and may be compromised. Co-leaders not only share this burden but, more important, also provide each other with an objective perspective when processing the powerful transference that arises in these circumstances. Sharing leadership responsibility helps maintain perspective and steer the course in a therapeutically effective way.

The primary focus of this chapter has been on the theories and techniques of group treatments for depression. Although these principles are most useful to those interested in the direct practice of group therapy, they are important for individual therapists as well, for several reasons.

Most important, understanding group process and content helps the individual therapist identify depressed patients who are in need of and who are likely to be capable of group treatment. Once such a referral is successful, the individual therapist may play a more facilitative role when well informed about the nature of the treatment. In addition, regular communication between the individual and group therapists about a patient's process and progress in each modality is likely to benefit both forms of treatment.

NOTES

P. 124, *the ideal size for an interpersonal group:* Yalom, I. D. (1985). *The theory and practice of group psychotherapy* (3rd ed.). New York: Basic Books.

P. 125, *eleven therapeutic factors:* Yalom, I. D. (1985). *The theory and practice of group psychotherapy* (3rd ed.). New York: Basic Books.

P. 127, *etiologically tied to interpersonal pathology:* Klerman, G. L., Weissman, M. M., Rounsaville, B. J., & Chevron, E. S. (1984). *Interpersonal psychotherapy of depression.* New York: Basic Books.

P. 127, *dominant other in the relationships of depressed individuals:* Bemporad, J. R. (1977). Resistances encountered in the psychotherapy of depressed individuals. *American Journal of Psychoanalysis, 37,* 207–214.

P. 127, *human worth were acknowledged:* Arieti, S. (1978). *On schizophrenia, phobias, depression, psychotherapy, and the farther shores of psychiatry.* New York: Brunner/Mazel, p. 230.

P. 129, *affect their interpersonal lives:* Beck, A. T. (1967). *Depression: Causes and treatment.* Philadelphia: University of Pennsylvania Press.

P. 129, *Yalom's 1985 book for these details:* Yalom, I. D. (1985). *The theory and practice of group psychotherapy* (3rd ed.). New York: Basic Books.

P. 134, *One study by Covi and Lipman:* Covi, L., & Lipman, R. S. (1987). Cognitive-behavioral group psychotherapy combined with imipramine in major depression. *Psychopharmacology Bulletin, 23,* 173–176.

P. 134, *Similarly, Steuer and colleagues:* Steuer, J. L., Mintz, J., Hammen, C. L., et al. (1984). Cognitive-behavioral and psychodynamic group psychotherapy in treatment of geriatric depression. *Journal of Consulting and Clinical Psychology, 52,* 180–189.

P. 134, *group treatment for depressed college students:* Hogg, J. A., & Deffenbacher, J. L. (1988). A comparison of cognitive and interpersonal-process group therapies in the treatment of depression among college students. *Journal of Counseling Psychology, 35,* 304–310.

P. 136, *Maxmen has shown:* Maxmen, J. S. (1973). Group therapy as viewed by hospitalized patients. *Archives of General Psychiatry, 28,* 404–408.

P. 136, *Betcher points out:* Betcher, R. W. (1983). The treatment of depression in brief inpatient group psychotherapy. *International Journal of Group Psychotherapy, 33,* 365.

P. 138, *The "agenda group," as described by Yalom:* Yalom, I. D. (1983). *Inpatient group psychotherapy.* New York: Basic Books.

P. 138, *Slife suggests:* Slife, B. D., Sasscer-Burgos, J., Froberg, W., & Ellington, S.

(1989). Effect of depression on processing interactions in group psychotherapy. *International Journal of Group Psychotherapy, 39,* 79–104.

P. 139, *Beck's cognitive theory of depression:* Beck, A. T. (1967). *Depression: Causes and treatment.* Philadelphia: University of Pennsylvania Press.

P. 141, *three major phases:* Covi, L., Roth, D., & Lipman, R. S. (1982). Cognitive group psychotherapy of depression: The close-ended group. *American Journal of Psychotherapy, 36,* 459–460.

P. 142, *correcting their own maladaptive reactions:* Hollon, S. T., & Shaw, B. F. (1979). Group cognitive therapy for depressed patients. In A. T. Beck, A. J. Rush, B. F. Shaw, & G. Emery (Eds.), *Cognitive therapy of depression.* New York: Guilford Press, p. 335.

P. 142, *has been reported by Gioe:* Gioe, V. J. (1975). Cognitive modification and positive group experience as a treatment for depression (Doctoral dissertation, Temple University, 1975). *Dissertation Abstracts International, 36,* 3039B–3040B. (University Microfilms No. 75–28, 219).

P. 142, *CBGs are superior:* Covi, L., & Lipman, R. S. (1987). Cognitive behavioral group psychotherapy combined with imipramine in major depression. *Psychopharmacology Bulletin, 23,* 173–176.

P. 145, *unique focus and format of the suicidality group:* Frederick, C. J., & Farberow, N. L. (1970). Group psychotherapy with suicidal persons: A comparison with standard group methods. *International Journal of Social Psychiatry, 16,* 103–111.

P. 146, *cannot be easily hidden by defensive measures:* Frederick, C. J., & Farberow, N. L. (1970). Group psychotherapy with suicidal persons: A comparison with standard group methods. *International Journal of Social Psychiatry, 16,* 103–111.

P. 146, *not as unique but as an area of common experience:* Asimos, C. T., & Rosen, D. H. (1978). Group treatment of suicidal and depressed persons: Indications for an open-ended group therapy program. *Bulletin of the Menninger Clinic, 42,* p. 517.

P. 146, *to pursue a more insight-oriented path:* Comstock, B. S., & McDermott, M. (1975). Group therapy for patients who attempt suicide. *International Journal of Group Psychotherapy, 25,* 44–49.

P. 146, *widening the base of the transference phenomenon:* Frederick, C. J., & Farberow, N. L. (1970). Group psychotherapy with suicidal persons: A comparison with standard group methods. *International Journal of Social Psychiatry, 16,* 103–111.

P. 147, *Kibel shares his account of a patient's suicide:* Kibel, H. D. (1973). A group member's suicide: Treating collective trauma. *International Journal of Group Psychotherapy, 23,* 42–53.

P. 147, *personal failure and a sign of professional inadequacy:* Kibel, H. D. (1973). A group member's suicide: Treating collective trauma. *International Journal of Group Psychotherapy, 23*, 42–53.

P. 147, *formidable task of trying to mitigate their reactions to the suicide:* Kibel, H. D. (1973). A group member's suicide: Treating collective trauma. *International Journal of Group Psychotherapy, 23*, 42–53.

6

SOMATIC THERAPY

Charles DeBattista and Alan F. Schatzberg

It is rare for a week to go by without running across an article on the virtues or vices associated with the latest antidepressant medications. Popular books such as *Listening to Prozac*, by Peter Kramer, have also sparked the public's imagination about the utility of these medications. Depending on what you read, these medications are either completely safe miracle cures that can eliminate any case of depression or dangerous psychotropic drugs that turn ordinary people into murderers and nymphomaniacs.

The truth, of course, is somewhere in between these extreme positions. All medications, including antidepressants, carry the potential for therapeutic benefit as well as problematic side effects, and it is increasingly imperative for all of us who treat major depression to be aware of these, for three major reasons. First, just as we as therapists struggle to keep abreast of the current developments in antidepressant therapy, so do our patients. On the one hand, if you treat depression, you probably have encountered a number of patients who have read about a particular antidepressant and ask for it specifically. On the other hand, you may have had patients who are quite scared of trying any "mood-altering drug." So it's important that you be in a position to advise your patients on what the treatment options are and what they might expect with each option.

Second, third-party payers, HMOs, and managed care companies are increasingly involved in clinical decision making on a given patient. It is not unusual these days for an insurance company to "suggest" drug therapy or other interventions for your depressed patients regardless of whether or not you believe it's a good idea.

Finally, there may be legal considerations. We know of at least one incident of a patient successfully suing his psychiatrist after being treated long term with psychotherapy alone for a depressive episode. The litigant did not improve substantially, switched psychiatrists, and was then treated successfully and rapidly with an antidepressant. He sued the former psychiatrist, arguing that he should have at least been informed about drug therapy as an option to avoid years of psychotherapy. It is an increasingly complicated world we clinicians must operate in, and if you treat depressed patients, knowing something about antidepressants is a necessity even for nonpsychiatrists.

THE BIOLOGY OF DEPRESSION

In the past thirty years, we have moved from regarding depression as an almost purely psychological disorder to one with important biological underpinnings. It is known, for example, that depression can run in families; if one parent has a problem with major depression, the chance that the children will have a similar problem is much higher than would be expected by chance alone. Likewise, if one identical twin develops a problem with recurrent depression, the chance that the other will is very high, even if the twins are reared apart from birth. Hormonal factors, too, are known to play a part in some depressive episodes. Abnormalities in the pituitary and thyroid systems are being studied intensively in patients with major depression.

In the science of antidepressant drug development, a major focus of research has been to understand the chemistry of the brain and how abnormalities may result in depression. Researchers are just beginning to learn how important a relatively small number of brain chemicals are in the cause and treatment of depression. The brain is an intricate electrical meshwork of billions of nerve cells, or neurons. For the brain to carry out any of its infinite functions—as diverse as initiating voluntary movements and daydreaming about that recent trip to the Bahamas—these neurons have to communicate with each other is some way. They transmit messages to each other by releasing chemicals, appropriately called *neurotransmitters*, that can be read by neighboring cells. Once this information is received, the neurons can pass the information on to other appropriate neurons in a specific pathway of cells to get a specific job done. These chemicals cross a gap, called a *synapse*, between the cells.

Neurotransmitters are of many types, but several seem to be particularly important in major depression. These include a chemically similar group of compounds called *monoamines*, such as serotonin, norepinephrine, and dopamine. The neurotransmitters act on specific sites, called *receptors*, in the neighboring cells and fit into these receptors like a key in a lock (see Figure 6.1). Once a lock is opened, the message can be transmitted to the appropriate neuron. All known effective antidepressants seem to affect the balance of neurotransmitters and receptors in the brain.

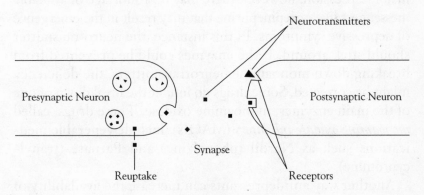

Figure 6.1
Action of Neurotransmitters

Evidence suggests that some depressive episodes are caused by a relative deficiency of monoamine neurotransmitters or a problem in their receptors. First, drugs that deplete these neurotransmitters in the brain seem to induce depression in many people. Thus, old blood pressure drugs, such as reserpine, depleted norepinephrine and dopamine, resulting in clinical depressions in many people. Second, all known effective antidepressants seem to work by enhancing the level of monoamine transmitters in the brain. Drugs that don't increase the availability of serotonin, norepinephrine, or dopamine don't seem to be effective antidepressants. Drugs like Prozac (fluoxetine), Elavil (amitriptyline), and Nardil (phenelzine), however, are adept at increasing the availability of monoamine neurotransmitters, although they produce this increase by different mechanisms.

Some drugs prevent the breakdown of the neurotransmitters, thereby increasing their availability. The nervous system has a method of clearing neurochemicals so that they don't stick around too long. If they did, the neurons might be stuck with one particular message, and new messages might not be able to get through to the brain cells. So the nervous system employs other chemicals, called *enzymes,* whose job is to break down the neurotransmitters after they have relayed their messages. In major depression, however, there may be a shortage of available messengers like norepinephrine that may result in the emergence of depressive symptoms. In this instance, the neurotransmitter should stick around. If the enzymes could be prevented from breaking down monoamine neurotransmitters, the deficiency might be corrected. Some drugs do inhibit the breakdown of one of the main enzymes, monoamine oxidase. These drugs, called *monoamine oxidase inhibitors* (MAOIs), include venerable medications such as Nardil (phenelzine) and Parnate (tranylcypromine).

Another way antidepressants can increase the availability of monoamine transmitters is to prevent them from being recycled back into the cells that release neurotransmitters. This recycling, or reuptake, is another important way that the nervous system keeps neurotransmitters from staying around too long after they've finished their job. The reuptake process also provides the material to make more neurotransmitter that can be released again. Many antidepressants block the reuptake of serotonin, norepinephrine, or dopamine, so the neurotransmitters act for longer periods of time before they are broken down or recycled. These antidepressants include the aptly named selective serotonin reuptake inhibitors (SSRIs), such as Prozac, which act selectively on serotonin (see Table 6.1); and the tricyclic antidepressants (TCAs), such as Elavil (amitriptyline), which act on both serotonin and norepinephrine.

Indications for Antidepressant Drug Therapy

Major depression is an extremely common disorder in outpatient practice. It is not true, however, that all cases of major depression require treatment with medications.

For example, many milder cases of major depression respond adequately to psychotherapy alone, and some patients prefer to avoid drug therapy at all costs. So how do you decide whether a

Table 6.1
Selective Serotonin Reuptake Inhibitors (SSRIs)

Drug	Dosage Range (mg/day)	Comments
Prozac (fluoxetine)	20–60 mg	Activating, insomnia; oldest and best studied
Paxil (paroxetine)	20–50 mg	Constipation
Zoloft (sertraline)	50–200 mg	GI upset, few drug interactions
Luvox (fluvoxamine)	100–300 mg	GI upset, fewest drug interactions

given episode of major depression warrants a trial of anti-depressants?

A number of factors should tip the scale in favor of using anti-depressants. Among these factors is the severity of symptoms. As a rule, the more severe the depressive episode, the more likely an antidepressant trial is indicated. In fact, it is probably unwise to treat someone with severe vegetative symptoms, such as loss of appetite with a more than 10 percent weight loss or unrelenting insomnia, with psychotherapy alone. Early treatment with antidepressants may help the patient improve faster and relieve much needless suffering.

Likewise, a patient in whom the suicide risk is high should receive the most intensive and aggressive treatment available. Although some patients actually have used the older classes of antidepressants to kill themselves, antidepressants have doubtless saved many lives by treating the underlying depression.

Depressed patients who have significant impairment in social or occupational functioning are also candidates for a trial of anti-depressants. We have seen many patients who are so depressed that they are on the verge of losing jobs or relationships that they have maintained for thirty years. These losses could prove catastrophic, so it makes sense to employ antidepressants early in such cases to minimize the risk of additional losses.

A history of recurrent depression in the moderate to severe range should be a red flag to you that this patient needs as much help as he or she can get. Recurrent depressive episodes are severely disruptive at best and life ending at worst. Substantial evidence suggests that maintenance treatment with antidepressants can substantially decrease the risk of recurrence and should be considered in anyone with two or more depressive episodes in the past five years or three severe episodes in a lifetime.

Naturally, if someone has a history of a good response to anti-depressants in the past or is not responding to psychotherapy, a medication trial warrants serious consideration. Finally, some subtypes of depression may be particularly responsive to antidepressants or other biological therapies but less responsive to other interventions. These subtypes are discussed at the end of this chapter.

Working with a Medication Consultant

Once it is clear that the patient is a candidate for an antidepressant, the next step may be finding a consultant to manage the medications. (This issue is discussed in the next chapter, on combining therapies, but we include some comments here from the point of view of the psychopharmacologist.) In health maintenance organizations, managed care settings, and small communities, available options may be limited. Ideally, however, the consultant should be a psychiatrist with broad psychopharmacology expertise who is willing and able to communicate openly with the therapist, as well as with the patient. An important role for the consultant is educating the patient-referring therapist about treatment options and the risks and benefits of one approach over another. A consultant who is unable to take the time necessary to keep both patient and therapist informed is inadequate. It is generally advisable for you to call or meet with the potential consultant, review the case, and decide whether the match between consultant and therapist is a reasonable one.

Dividing the treatment between psychotherapy and medication management is increasingly common and offers several advantages and disadvantages. Among the advantages are that two heads are frequently better than one in managing difficult cases. Different clinicians will have differing perspectives that, in combination, can improve diagnosis and treatment. In addition, the use of a medication consultant may actually save the patient money. Instead of seeing a more expensive psychiatrist on a weekly basis, it may be possible for the patient to meet much less frequently with the psychiatrist for medication management while meeting on a weekly basis with the psychotherapist. Finally, dividing the medication management and psychotherapy may allow the therapy to focus on psychological issues. Patients on medications frequently have concerns about side effects or other medical issues that can be a significant distraction for the flow of therapy.

The primary disadvantage of splitting treatment responsibility is that it means more work. Because the psychotherapist and the psychiatric consultant are presumably seeing the patient at different times, they need to coordinate the care. This arrangement means frequent phone contacts, mailing of records, and so on. The therapist is generally meeting with the patient more frequently and may have a greater burden informing the medication consultant about the patient's progress or problems that arise. The patient may discuss his or her concerns about a given medication to the psychotherapist and, in this case, should be encouraged to call the medication consultant directly.

Another potential difficulty with dividing the treatment is that disagreement may arise between consultant and therapist about diagnosis or treatment. This friction can significantly undermine care when the psychotherapist suggests to the patient that he or she probably should not be on a given medication. Similarly, patient care suffers when the medication consultant reports to the patient that he or she does not believe in the diagnosis or particular treatment provided by the therapist. These disagreements are best settled in a face-to-face meeting between therapist and consultant, rather than through the patient. If the lines of communication remain open, disagreements can frequently be settled to the patient's benefit.

Types of Antidepressant Medications

The antidepressants are chemically unique but do share some common features. They all have at least two names—a generic name, such as buproprion, and a trade name, such as Wellbutrin. The trade name is the name a drug is given by the manufacturing company to market the drug to the public. Physicians, as well as the public, may be more likely to remember a drug that makes one "well," such as Wellbutrin, or that elevates one's mood, such as Elavil, than the more nondescript, generic names buproprion or amitriptyline. A drug has only one generic name, but a drug produced by many companies may have many trade names.

As described above, all antidepressants seem to work primarily the serotonin and norepinephrine systems. Likewise, all antidepressants seem to take three to six weeks or longer to really kick in. This may be how long it takes to cause important changes in the receptors. None of the antidepressants marketed are addictive or produce a "buzz," so they're not likely to be sold on the streets.

Antidepressants are all about 70 percent effective in relieving symptoms of depression, although some may be more effective for some subtypes than others. Also, people who do not respond to one antidepressant have a reasonable chance of responding to another. The choice of which antidepressant to start with often depends on the side effect profile of the drug more than other factors. Drugs within a given class may be chemically related or tend to work the same way and to have similar side effects.

Selective Serotonin Reuptake Inhibitors (SSRIs)

The SSRIs are the dominant class of antidepressants in the United States and currently include Prozac (fluoxetine), Zoloft (sertraline), Paxil (paroxetine), and the soon-to-be-released Luvox (fluvoxamine). Since the introduction of Prozac to the American market in 1988, the SSRIs have been prescribed to several million people. Their popularity can be attributed to several simple facts: they work, have few side effects, are simple to use, and are quite safe, even in overdose. We believe that the SSRIs work by blocking the reuptake of serotonin, thereby making more serotonin available between nerve cells to the job it was meant to do.

Indications. The SSRIs have been studied in most subtypes of depression, but most studies have focused on outpatients with mild to moderate major depression. Even though there are fewer studies of hospitalized patients with more severe depression, evidence suggests that the drugs may be just as effective as their older counterparts. At least compared with a placebo, the SSRIs seem very capable of improving the symptoms of hospitalized patients with serious depressive subtypes. So far, the SSRIs have been studied in atypical depression, melancholia, psychotic depression, and dysthymia. An additional factor in the popularity of the drugs is that they seem to be useful for many other disorders besides depression. Unlike most other antidepressants, for example, the SSRIs all seem to be useful in treating obsessive-compulsive disorder. Other, somewhat less studied uses include the treatment of eating disorders such as bulimia, panic disorder, and certain pain problems.

Side Effects. As a rule, the SSRIs have fewer side effects than the other classes. However, that doesn't mean you will not come across an occasional patient who takes one dose of Prozac, feels terrible, and resents you for ever recommending such a nasty medication.

Although the side effects vary somewhat from drug to drug in this class, the drugs do share some common toxic effects. For instance, all of the serotonin drugs have the potential for some gastrointestinal (GI) upset early in the course of treatment, and this is the most common reason patients stop taking them. About 20 percent to 40 percent of patients develop GI problems, which can range from mild stomach upset to nausea, vomiting, and diarrhea. In our experience, Zoloft may be slightly more likely to cause GI upset than the other SSRIs, but people seem to adapt to this side effect within a few weeks, as they do with all the serotonin drugs. Taking the SSRIs with food seems to help.

Problems with insomnia can also develop in some patients, particularly with Prozac. That is why we advise that our patients take the medication in the morning. Conversely, if somnolence becomes a problem, the dose should be taken before bedtime. Restlessness has been described by patients, particularly with

Prozac and Paxil. This can be a difficult side effect to contend with, but decreasing the dose often helps. Another fairly common complaint with patients on these drugs is sexual difficulties, including inability to achieve an orgasm or delayed ejaculation. About 10 percent to 20 percent of patients complain about sexual difficulties. Anecdotal evidence suggests that cyproheptadine in doses of 4 to 8 milligrams per day alleviates this side effect. Another strategy that has some anecdotal success is to have the patient withhold the morning dose on days of anticipated sexual activity. Obviously, this strategy may not be feasible in your most sexually active patients.

Other, more common side effects reported with these drugs include headaches, excessive sweating, dry mouth, and decreased appetite. A general approach for dealing with any of these side effects is to decrease the dose and then increase it gradually, rather than stop the medication. Also, reassuring the patient that he or she will adapt to many of these symptoms over a few weeks along with gentle dosing is frequently all that is required to keep patients on the medication.

Dosing. There seems to be significant confusion about the proper doses of the various selective serotonin agents. We have seen patients with doses exceeding 200 milligrams per day of Prozac walk into the clinic for evaluation of their depression. If these patients were not particularly depressed to begin with, the severe restlessness, insomnia, and financial hardship that goes along with these high doses would surely take their toll.

No evidence suggests that megadoses of any of the SSRIs is helpful. In fact, the dose response curve for Prozac is fairly flat. Doses in the range of 60 milligrams or more per day seem somewhat less likely to be helpful for depression than doses in the 20- to 40-milligram-per-day range. Higher doses may be of less utility, in part, because they are associated with more side effects.

Therefore, we suggest that patients start out at 20 milligrams per day of Prozac. If they are unable to tolerate this dose, they may drop down to the 10-milligram capsules or even 5 milligrams per day in the Prozac suspension. The dosage may be increased by 20 milligrams every two weeks as tolerated until a maximum dose of 60 milligrams per day is achieved. For Paxil, the dosing is similar with a starting dose of 20 milligrams per day and the maximum effective dose of 50 milligrams per day.

Sertraline may be the exception to the flat dose response curve, with higher doses being associated with increased efficacy. We recommend starting at 50 milligrams for Zoloft. If no response is seen at two weeks, the dose may be doubled to 100 milligrams and then gradually titrated up to a dose of 200 milligrams over the next two weeks. A number of case reports have described withdrawal symptoms associated with these drugs, particularly Paxil. The symptoms reported include malaise, nausea, and headaches. Therefore, it is a good idea to taper these drugs with a decreasing dose over the course of two weeks, rather than stop them suddenly.

Cyclic Antidepressants

Until the advent of Prozac in 1988, the cyclic antidepressants (so named because of their cyclic chemical structure) were the dominant group of agents used to treat depression. Since the discovery that imipramine (Tofranil) was an effective antidepressant in 1958, about a dozen cyclic antidepressants have found their way into the American market (see Table 6.2). They were initially popular for a number of reasons.

The cyclic antidepressants were easier to use than the other major class of antidepressants of the day, the MAOIs. They did not require the dietary restrictions or have the same type of potentially lethal interactions with other drugs. In addition, they were and still are the best-studied group of all antidepressants. For example, there have been more inpatient studies of cyclic antidepressants for seriously ill depressed patients than studies of other drugs.

Table 6.2
Cyclic Antidepressants

Drug	Starting Dose	Therapeutic Dose
amitriptyline (Elavil)	25 mg	150–300 mg
amoxapine (Asendin)	50 mg	200–400 mg
clomipramine (Anafranil)	25 mg	100–250 mg
desipramine (Norpramine)	25 mg	150–300 mg
doxepin (Sinequan)	25 mg	150–300 mg
imipramine (Tofranil)	25 mg	150–300 mg
nortriptyline (Pamelor)	10–25 mg	50–150 mg
potriptyline (Vivactil)	10 mg	15–50 mg
trimipramine (Surmontil)	25 mg	150–300 mg

But the cyclic antidepressants have serious drawbacks, including the fact that every year, many depressed patients kill themselves by taking an overdose of these medications. It doesn't take much. About a one-week supply of imipramine at therapeutic doses is sufficient to do most patients in. The side effects, particularly at higher doses, are also a significant burden for many patients, such as the elderly.

Indications. The cyclic antidepressants have been studied in most subtypes of depression and have shown significant utility for treating both unipolar and bipolar types. These drugs seem to be useful in the treatment of psychotic depression when used in combination with an antipsychotic drug. As discussed below, amoxapine may be useful even without the help of an antipsychotic drug. The cyclic drugs are the most studied drugs in melancholic depression, and some investigators think the drugs may be more effective than the newer agents. However, this remains to be seen. Drugs such as imipramine seem to be less effective than MAOIs in treating the atypical depression described below. Since the 1960s, these drugs have been a mainstay for the treatment of panic disorder. Although most of the cyclics don't seem to help obsessive-compulsive disorder, clomipramine shows clear efficacy in the treatment of this disorder. Other, less common uses for these drugs include the treatment of bulimia, PTSD, chronic pain syndromes, attention deficit disorder, and cocaine abuse.

Side Effects. The list of side effects associated with the cyclic antidepressants is fairly long. Most patients will have some of them if they receive therapeutic doses. In drug studies, up to 40 percent of patients drop out because of side effects from the drugs. The most common of these are so-called anticholinergic side effects. All of the cyclic antidepressants block acetylcholine receptors, and this results in such side effects as dry mouth, urinary retention, constipation, and blurred vision. The biggest culprits in the class are Elavil (amitriptyline) and Vivactyl (protriptyline); Norpramine (desipramine) and Pamelor (nortriptyline) are less likely to cause anticholinergic side effects.

As with the selective serotonin drugs, the body does adapt to some of these side effects over time. Sometimes, very simple maneuvers such as a sugarless gum for the dry mouth or a bulk laxative for constipation is all that is needed. At other times, the drug will have to be decreased or discontinued completely. Sedation is also a common side effect and may be a welcome one for the majority of patients with insomnia as part of their depression. For this reason, the cyclic drugs are perhaps best given at night, when sedation is therapeutic. Drugs such as protriptyline, however, may be experienced by patients as activating and should be given earlier in the day.

A potentially more serious side effect is a significant drop in blood pressure when standing up suddenly—orthostasis. The result is that patients may faint or fall and seriously injure themselves. Older patients, in particular, should have their sitting and standing blood pressures checked regularly while on the cyclic drugs and should be asked about dizziness or lightheadedness when standing.

Perhaps the most serious potential side effect of the cyclic drugs is their effect on the heart. The drugs can interfere with the electrical conduction of the heart, particularly at high doses. In fact, the most common cause of death in overdose is an abnormal heart rhythm or *arrythmia*. Any patient who may go on these drugs should have an electrocardiogram done first to rule out serious conduction problems first.

Dosing. Although all of the cyclic antidepressants may be equally beneficial in treating depression (except perhaps amoxapine in psychotic depression), we tend to recommend agents such as Pamelor (nortriptyline) and Norpramine (desipramine) before other drugs in the class. The rationale for this advice is that nortriptyline and desipramine have fewer anticholinergic side effects and that they can be monitored with blood serum levels rather reliably. If the level is too low, there is little chance that the drug will be effective in treating depression, whereas a high drug level could suggest more potential problems with side effects. Desipramine is dosed just like imipramine, but nortriptyline has a smaller starting dose of 10 to 25 milligrams per day. The dose may be increased by 25 milligrams every three days until a dose of 75 to 100 milligrams per day is achieved. After three days on this dose, a serum level of the drug can be drawn and the dose adjusted accordingly.

Drugs such as desipramine and nortriptyline tend to be more activating than other members of the class and may have more utility in patients with slowed down, "retarded" depressions, as opposed to depressions with more prominent agitation. Drugs such as Elavil and Sinequan (doxepin), however, which can be very sedating, may be a plus in more agitated patients.

It is our experience that the cyclic drugs should be started at fairly low doses to avoid potential problems such as orthostasis. Most of the cyclic antidepressants, such as imipramine and desipramine, are best started at 25 to 50 milligrams for three days and then increased by 50 milligrams every three days until a dose of 150 milligrams is reached. If no response is seen on 150 milligrams for two weeks, then the dose can be increased by 50 milligrams every four days until side effects become a problem or a dose of 300 milligrams per day is achieved. Nortriptyline is usually initiated at 10 to 25 milligrams per day and titrated gradually to doses in the 50 to 150 milligrams-per-day range. Trials of less than six weeks on a therapeutic dose (~ 150 milligrams per day) may be inadequate to see a response.

Monoamine Oxidase Inhibitors (MAOIs)

The first reports of successful treatment with antidepressants were of the MAOI iproniazid in 1956. That makes the MAOIs arguably the oldest class of antidepressants in use. The MAOIs are also the least commonly used class today because of potentially lethal drug interactions and side effects. These risks are unfortunate because the drugs may have significant utility in treating depression and other disorders if used carefully. In the near future, MAOIs will be released that do not have the same problems as the older agents with diet and drug interactions. Currently, the MAOIs include Nardil (phenelzine) Parnate (tranylcypromine), and Deprenyl (selegiline) (see Table 6.3).

Indications. MAOIs are used in the treatment of major depression. As discussed below, the MAOIs may have particular utility for the subtype of atypical depression characterized by mood reactivity, heaviness in the limbs, as well as eating and sleeping too much. The MAOIs may also have special utility for the up to 30 percent of all depressive episodes that have a significant anxiety component or associated panic attacks. These drugs also can be very valuable in treating depressions that have not responded to other classes of antidepressants.

Many patients who have failed other trials swear by the MAOIs. Other indications for the MAOIs include panic disorder and agoraphobia, for which these drugs have long been used.

Table 6.3
Monoamine Oxidase Inhibitors (MAOIs)

Drug	Starting Dose	Therapeutic Dose
phenelzine (Nardil)	15–30 mg	45–90 mg
tranylcypromine (Parnate)	10 mg	20–40 mg
selegiline (Deprenyl)	5–10 mg	20–60 mg

Deprenyl is used at low doses to treat Parkinson's disease because it can help boost the availability of dopamine and ameliorate the underlying problem of the disorder.

Side Effects. The most common difficulty that patients have with these drugs is a problem with blood pressure. At therapeutic doses, patients can develop orthostasis and fall. As you can imagine, this is a particularly serious problem in the elderly. Often, this problem can be circumvented by simple maneuvers such as warning the patient not to get up too quickly from a sitting or lying position, drinking about eight glasses of water a day, or wearing support stockings.

The side effect that most therapists worry about is a dangerous increase in blood pressure called a *hypertensive crisis*. This side effect usually occurs when the patient inadvertently eats foods that contain high amounts of tyramine, such as aged cheeses, salami, and red wines. When a hypertensive crisis occurs, the patient will typically experience a significant headache and occasionally develop strokes. A related serious side effect is a dangerous increase in body temperature, or *hyperpyrexia*, that may lead to coma and death. This may happen when other drugs, such as demerol, selective serotonin antidepressants, Bupropion, or even over-the-counter decongestants are used concomitantly. For this reason, MAOIs should only be given to patients who can be compliant with the list of dietary and concomitant medication restrictions. Much less serious but fairly common side effects include excessive stimulation, insomnia, and sexual dysfunction such as anorgasmia. Cutting back the dose may help in the case of stimulation or sexual dysfunction, but these can be side effects to get around. We sometimes end up switching to another class of antidepressants.

Dosing. Phenelzine can be started at 30 milligrams per day and increased to 45 milligrams per day after three days. Then the dose can be increased by 15 milligrams per week to a maximum dose of 90 to 120 milligrams per day. The higher doses may be needed in patients who can tolerate the side effects and have severe or refractory depressions. Tranylcypromine needs to be started at a lower dose; 10 to 20 milligrams per day is what is recommended. The dose can be increased at a rate of 10 milligrams per week until doses in the range of 50 to 60 milligrams per day are reached. Selegiline can be started at 5 to 10 milligrams per day and also increased by 10 milligrams per week until a dose range of about 30 to 50 milligrams per day is reached.

Atypical Antidepressants

Atypical antidepressant drugs (see Table 6.4) are "atypical" because they work a little differently or are chemically distinct from drugs in the other three classes we have described. These drugs include Effexor (venlafaxine), Wellbutrin (bupropion), and Desyrel (trazodone).

Effexor is the newest antidepressant released to the American market and differs from the standard SSRIs in that it not only blocks the reuptake of serotonin but also blocks the reuptake of norepinephrine much like the tricyclic drugs. It is chemically unrelated to the cyclic drugs, however, and doesn't seem to have the side effects of agents such as Elavil and Tofranil. Wellbutrin was released in 1989 and seems to work by blocking the reuptake of dopamine, although it is not known how it works. Desyrel has been around since 1981 and blocks the reuptake of serotonin like the selective serotonin drugs. It differs in that it

Table 6.4
Atypical Antidepressants

Drug	Starting Dose	Therapeutic Dose
venlafaxine (Effexor)	25–75 mg	75–400 mg
bupropion (Wellbutrin)	100–200 mg	300–450 mg
trazodone (Desyrel)	50–100 mg	300–400 mg

also gets broken down into chemicals that may directly stimulate the serotonin receptors to help alleviate depression.

Indications. All of these drugs have been proven useful in the treatment of major depression. Effexor has been studied in inpatients with serious depressions, including those who have not responded to trials of other antidepressants. It may be useful in 30 percent to 40 percent of patients who have not responded to other treatments. Wellbutrin has been studied in atypical depression and may be as useful as MAOIs for this subtype. Early suggestions were that Wellbutrin was less likely to induce mania in patients so predisposed, but this assertion has not stood the test of time. Wellbutrin also can be fairly activating, particularly at high doses, so it may be used in patients who have more slowed down, "retarded" depressions.

Conversely, Desyrel is very sedating and has been used as an antidepressant in depressive episodes with disturbing insomnia and anxiety to augment the effect of other antidepressants and as a sleeper even in nondepressed patients. It has been criticized as being a less robust antidepressant than most others.

Side Effects. Because these drugs differ in chemical classes and in how they work, their side-effect profiles differ from one another. The most common side effects of Effexor are nausea, insomnia, somnolence, and sexual problems. This profile is much like that of the SSRIs and can be handled the same way. Most people adapt to these side effects (except to the sexual dysfunction) in the first three or four weeks. At high doses, Effexor may also cause an increase in blood pressure, so blood pressure should be checked at every medication visit. The most serious side effect with Wellbutrin has been a dose-related increase in seizures. It should be used with caution in patients who have a history of seizures or head trauma. Otherwise, Wellbutrin has been well tolerated, with occasional insomnia, restlessness, nausea, and headaches being reported. The most common side effect of Desyrel is sedation. If the dose is given before sleep, it is not usually a problem, but some people can still feel drowsy when awakening. Sometimes, taking the medication with food slows the absorption and decreases the sedation. Desyrel can also cause orthostasis, and blood pressure should be checked in the sitting and standing positions, especially at higher doses in the elderly.

Dosing. The usual starting dose of Effexor is 37.5 milligrams twice a day, but older patients may need to start on half this dose. The dose can be increased to 75 milligrams twice a day in the second week. Most outpatients appear to respond to doses in the 150- to 225-milligrams-per-day range. If no response is seen at these doses, the dose can be increased by 75 milligrams per week to a dose in the 300- to 400-milligrams-per-day range.

Wellbutrin is typically started at a dose of 100 milligrams twice a day and can be increased at a rate of 100 milligrams per week until a dose in the optimal divided 300- to 400-milligrams-per-day dose range is achieved. We tend to start trazodone at 50 milligrams per day, rather than the higher doses of 150 milligrams per day that the manufacturer advises. The higher doses seem to be too sedating for most people and may represent a problem for blood pressure in the elderly. The dose can be increased by 50 milligrams every three days until a dose in the range of 150 to 300 milligrams per day is achieved. This seems to be an optimal dose range for trazodone, and higher doses may be less efficacious.

ELECTROCONVULSIVE THERAPY

Electroconvulsive therapy (ECT) is one of the oldest and most controversial treatments in all of psychiatry. It has been used since the 1930s, and studies during the past 15 years would suggest it is perhaps the most effective treatment available for major depression. So what's the controversy all about?

ECT involves passing an electric current through a patient's brain for the purposes of inducing a series of generalized seizures. This technique may not sound very therapeutic, but repetitive seizures seem to induce change in neurotransmitters and receptors that parallels those seen with long-term anti-depressant medication use. Unfortunately, nobody really knows how ECT works. The fact is that we use it because it often works when nothing else does.

ECT has a jaded history. For many years, ECT was applied indiscriminately and without careful studies to support its use. In addition, popular media presentations, such as the ECT scenes in the movie *One Flew Over the Cuckoo's Nest*, did much to cement public opinion against this procedure. ECT almost faded away in the 1950s and 1960s, with the advent of effective antidepressants. Now, however, ECT is used primarily in the treatment of major depression. Since the 1970s, ECT has had a resurgence because of good studies showing its effectiveness and the failure of antidepressant drugs to help up to 30 percent of those who take them. The procedure is also substantially more benign than it was in the 1940s and 1950s, with the development of better machines to administer the treatments and the involvement of anesthesia to induce sleep and relax the muscles. Currently, patients almost don't move at all during an ECT induction.

On the down side, patients do experience some confusion and memory loss around the time of treatments, and some patients complain of memory loss for several months after a typical series of six to twelve ECT treatments for depression given every other day. But for many patients, ECT may be safer, quicker, and more effective than numerous antidepressant trials.

We employ specific criteria for the use of ECT in depression that are similar to those used at other university centers. One criterion is that ECT may be used when antidepressant drugs have not been tolerated or pose a major medical risk. For example, a patient who has not tolerated the nausea associated with the SSRIs and cannot take a tricyclic because of a cardiac conduction problem may be a candidate for ECT. A second criterion is that ECT may be used with patients who have had adequate antidepressant trials but failed them. A patient with a serious depressive episode and who has failed two reasonable antidepressant trials should be considered for ECT. A third criterion is that ECT may be used when a rapid response is required because of imminent suicide risk or serious risk to the patient's health by the depression. A patient who is so depressed that he or she is unable to eat and has dropped a dangerous amount of weight may fall into this category. The presence of catatonia in depression, mania, or schizophrenia can also be very serious, and we frequently advise the use of ECT in these cases. Finally, if a patient has responded to ECT in the past, it is likely to be successful again.

SUBTYPES OF MAJOR DEPRESSION

During the past forty years, several subtypes of major depression have been defined that appear to be more responsive to some treatment regimens than others. These include psychotic depression, atypical depression, melancholic depression, and seasonal depression.

Psychotic Depression

Psychotic depressions are those in which patients meet criteria for major depression but also have psychotic symptoms, such as delusions and hallucinations. The delusions often involve issues such as guilt, personal inadequacy, nihilism, or somatic concerns and are referred to as *mood congruent symptoms* when they go along with feeling depressed.

For example, an elderly patient we consulted on became increasingly depressed during a period of six weeks to the point that she was bedridden and required a feeding tube to eat. She believed that she did not deserve to live because she had severely mistreated all of her (six) children when they were growing up. The grown children had no recollection of ever being mistreated and, to the contrary, described her as a loving and doting mother. Try as they might, however, the puzzled and very concerned children could not convince this unfortunate woman that she had done them no wrong.

Common hallucinations include derogatory voices telling the patients they are worthless, culpable, or deserve to die. Sometimes patients can have psychotic symptoms that don't seem to be related to the depression, such as feeling they are being persecuted or controlled by some external force. These are referred to as *mood incongruent psychotic symptoms.*

Depression with psychotic features is obviously a very serious condition that, like all serious cases of major depression, should be medically evaluated to rule out potentially treatable causes such as thyroid problems or brain tumors. This is not the kind of depression for which psychotherapy alone is a good idea.

First, no evidence suggests that psychotherapy alone helps psychotic depression. Second, a high incidence of suicide and other morbidity is associated with depressive episodes that have psychotic features. Finally, much evidence supports the assertion that certain medical treatments help. It turns out that antidepressants in combination with antipsychotic drugs such as Haldol or Prolixen are helpful in the majority of patients.

Unlike other types of depression, psychotic depressions do not appear likely to respond to antidepressants alone. An exception may be a cyclic drug called amoxapine, which is chemically somewhere between an antidepressant and an antipsychotic. In one study, it was found to be about as effective as the combination of antidepressant and standard antipsychotic drug in treating psychotic depression.

An approach that is gaining increasing acceptance in many hospitals as first-line therapy for psychotic depression is ECT.

This very old treatment approach, previously discussed, offers several advantages to drug therapy. Many investigators think it is more effective than drug therapy, works faster, and in many cases is better tolerated than the combination of drugs.

If the patient meets the criteria for ECT described above, it may be used as a first-line treatment for psychotic depression. Otherwise, we recommend that patients with psychotic depression be tried first on a trial of a combination of a standard antidepressant and an antipsychotic because this is the best-studied approach. If this fails, then amoxapine can be tried. Failure to respond to two medication trials may warrant a series of electroconvulsive treatments.

Melancholic Depression

Melancholic depression is another subtype of major depression that historically has been thought to be biologically driven and more responsive to biological treatments than other approaches. In fact, the diagnostic criteria of melancholic depression included past good response to biological therapies such as ECT or antidepressants, prominent vegetative symptoms such as early morning awakening, feeling much worse in the mornings (diurnal variation), significant loss of appetite and weight loss, and loss of interest or pleasure in almost all activities.

The problem is that most studies have not supported the assertion that melancholic depression responds more favorably to somatic therapy than to other approaches. What is known is that melancholic depression, like psychotic depression, is a little different from the garden variety major depressive episode. Around 30 percent of depressed patients will show marked improvement when treated with a sugar pill or placebo alone. A much lower percentage of patients with melancholic depression appear to respond to placebo, and this proportion may reflect the fact that these depressions tend to be more severe. In a similar vein, patients with melancholic depressions do not tend to respond to hospitalization alone, unlike many patients with major depression. And last, although very few studies compare antidepressants and psychotherapy for these patients, some studies suggest that melancholics respond less favorably to psychotherapy alone than do other types of depression.

Given this information, we suggest that patients who meet criteria for melancholic depressions not be treated with psychotherapy alone if possible. Although the tricyclic antidepressants are the best-studied drugs in treating melancholic depression, evidence suggests that other antidepressants, including the SSRIs and Effexor (venlafaxine), may be just as good. Because these drugs tend to be better tolerated than the cyclic drugs, it may be reasonable to start with them first. If the patient fails to respond to these drugs, a cyclic drug may be tried. If the patient fails two different classes of antidepressants or meets criteria for ECT, then ECT becomes an important treatment option.

Atypical Depression

Atypical depression is a subtype that grew out of early observations with antidepressants that some patients respond better to the MAOIs than to tricyclics. This has been confirmed in many studies during the past thirty years, and the criteria for atypical depression were included for the first time in *DSM-IV.*

The criteria include a reactive mood, meaning that, unlike in melancholic depression, a patient's mood can be temporarily lifted by something positive that happens. Other symptoms are so-called reverse vegetative symptoms: eating too much instead of loss of appetite, and sleeping too much instead of insomnia. It turns out that these symptoms are not too "atypical" at all, but their presence may suggest using one class of antidepressants over another. Although many studies suggest that MAOIs are useful for treating this type of depression, they are among the most difficult antidepressants to use because of the problems described above.

The good news is that drugs like Prozac and Wellbutrin (buproprion) may be just as good. These have been less well studied than the MAOIs, but a few studies have suggested good efficacy for the atypical subtype of depression. Because these drugs are less toxic than the MAOIs, we recommend starting the treatment with an SSRI or Wellbutrin if the patient meets the criteria for an atypical depression. If the patient fails a reasonable trial, then the drug can be stopped and an MAOI started after a suitable washout period. Drugs such as Prozac can react fatally with medications such as Nardil, and unfortunately, there may have to be as much as a five-week washout before an MAOI can be started.

Seasonal Depressions

Seasonal depressions have been described for hundreds of years but have only been studied in detail during the past fifteen years or so. These depressions, now called *specifiers* in major depressive disorders, are characterized by depressions that usually begin between October and November as hours of daylight substantially shorten. As the hours of daylight lengthen between February and April, patients may experience a remission of their depression and even become manic or hypomanic. A patient has to have at least three episodes related to the seasons in three separate years in order to be diagnosed with a seasonal affective disorder.

Increasing the amount of time people are exposed to full spectrum light in the winter months may help some people with recurrent winter depressions. Most of these patients will also require an antidepressant or a mood-stabilizing agent as well. Like any other procedure, light therapy or phototherapy should be performed by someone experienced with the procedure.

We suggest using phototherapy alone in patients with milder winter depressions. If no response is noted to two weeks of light therapy in the 2,500 to 10,000 lux range for thirty minutes in the morning, then a standard antidepressant should be added. More serious seasonal depressions should be treated right away with an antidepressant or, occasionally, even ECT. Phototherapy may be used to augment the effect of antidepressants in some cases.

Somatic therapy represents an important and potent option in the arsenal against major depression. Treatment planning for the depressed patient must consider the risks and benefits of various somatic treatments available. Through careful assessment of the patient and consultation with an expert in the somatic therapy of psychiatric disorders, a treatment plan can be developed that offers the maximum opportunity for your patient to be relieved of the burden of depression.

REFERENCES

American Psychiatric Association. (1993). *Practice guidelines for major depressive disorder in adults.* Washington, DC: APA Press.

Anton, R. F., & Sexauer, J. D. (1983). Efficacy of amoxapine in psychotic depression. *American Journal of Psychiatry, 140,* 1344–1347.

Avery, D., & Winokur, G. (1977). The efficacy of electroconvulsive therapy and antidepressants in depression. *Biological Psychiatry, 12,* 507–523.

Baldessarini, R. J. (1985). *Chemotherapy in psychiatry.* Cambridge, MA: Harvard University Press.

Chan, C. H., Janicak, P. G., Davis, J. M., et al. (1987). Response of psychotic and nonpsychotic depressed patients to tricyclic antidepressants. *Journal of Clinical Psychiatry, 48,* 197–200.

DeBattista, C., & Schatzberg A. F. (1994). An algorithm for major depression and its subtypes. *Psychiatric Annals, 24*(7), 341–347.

Dimascio, A., Klerman, G. L., & Prusoff, B. A. (1975). Relative safety of amitriptyline in maintenance treatment of major depression. *Archives of General Psychiatry, 160,* 34–41.

Doogan, D. P., & Callard, V. (1992). Sertraline in the prevention of depression. *British Journal of Psychiatry, 160,* 217–222.

Fairchild, C. J., Rush, A. J., Beck, A. T., et al. (1986). Which depression responds to placebo? *Psychiatry Research, 18,* 217–226.

Feighner, J. P., & Cohn, J. B. (1985). Double blind comparative trial of fluoxetine and doxepin in geriatric patients with major depression. *Journal of Clinical Psychiatry, 46*(3), 20–25.

Georgotas, A., McCrue, R. E., & Cooper, T. B. (1989). A placebo controlled comparison of nortriptyline and phenelzine in maintenance therapy of elderly depressed patients. *Archives of General Psychiatry, 46,* 783–786.

Glen, A. M., Johnson, A. L., & Shapeard, M. A. (1984). Continuation therapy with lithium and amitriptyline in unipolar depressive illness: A randomized, double-blind, controlled trial. *Psychological Medicine, 14*(1), 37–50.

Heldigenstein, J. H., Tollefson, G. D., & Fanes, D. E. (1993). A double blind trial of fluoxetine, 20 mg, and placebo in outpatients with *DSM-III-R* major depression and melancholia. *International Journal of Clinical Psychopharmacology, 8*(4), 247–51.

Klerman, G. L. (1990). The psychiatric patient's right to effective treatment: Implications of Osheroff v. Chestnut Lodge. *American Journal of Psychiatry, 147*(4), 409–418.

Liebowitz, M. R., Quitkin, F. M., Stewart, J. W., et al. (1984). Phenelzine and imipramine in atypical depression: A preliminary report. *Archives of General Psychiatry, 41,* 669–677.

Liebowitz, M. R., Quitkin, F. M., Stewart, J. W., et al. (1988). Antidepressant specificity in atypical depression. *Archives of General Psychiatry, 45,* 129–137.

Lykouras, E., Malliaras, G. N., Christodoulou, G. N., et al. (1986). Delusional depression: Phenomenology and response to treatment. *Psychopathology, 18,* 157–164.

Minter, R. E., & Mandel, M. R. (1979). The treatment of psychotic major depressive disorders with drugs and electroconvulsive therapy. *Journal of Nervous Mental Disorders, 167,* 726–733.

Montgomery, S. A. (1993). Venlafaxine. *Journal of Clinical Psychiatry, 54*(3), 119–126.

Montgomery, S. A., & Dunbar, G. C. (1991, December). *Paroxetine and placebo in the long-term maintenance of depressed patients.* Paper presented to the American College of Neuropsychopharmacology, San Juan, Puerto Rico.

Nelson, C. J., Mazure, C. M., & Jatlow, P. I. (1990). Does melancholia predict response in major depression? *Journal of Affective Disorders, 18,* 157–165.

Prien, R. F., Balter, M. F., & Caffey, E. M. (1973). Lithium and imipramine in the prevention of affective episodes. *Archives of General Psychiatry, 29,* 420–425.

Prien, R. F., Kupfer, D. J., Mansky, P. A., et al. (1984). Drug therapy in the prevention of recurrences in unipolar and bipolar affective illness: A report of the NIMH Collaborative Study Group. *Archives of General Psychiatry, 41,* 1096–1104.

Prusoff, B. A., Weissman, M. M., Klerman, G. L., et al. (1980). Research diagnostic criteria subtypes of depression: Their roles as predictors of differential response to psychotherapy and drug treatment. *Archives of General Psychiatry, 37,* 796–801.

Quitkin, F. M., McGrath, P. J., Stewart, J. W., et al. (1989). Phenelzine and imipramine in mood reactive depression: Further delineation of the syndrome of atypical depression. *Archives of General Psychiatry, 46,* 787–793.

Quitkin, F. M., Stewart, J. W., McGrath, P., et al. (1988). Phenelzine vs. imipramine in probable atypical depression: Defining the boundaries of MAOI responders. *American Journal of Psychiatry, 145,* 306–312.

Rosenthal, N. E., Sack, D. A., Carpenter, C. J., et al. (1985). Antidepressant effects of light in seasonal affective disorder. *American Journal of Psychiatry, 142*(2), 163–170.

Rosenthal, N. E., Sack, D. A., Gillin, J. C., et al. (1984). Seasonal affective disorder: A description of the syndrome and preliminary findings with light treatment. *Archives of General Psychiatry, 41,* 72–80.

Sargent, W. (1961). Drugs in the treatment of depression. *British Medical Journal of Clinical Research, 1,* 226–227.

Schatzberg, A. F. (1992). Recent developments in the acute somatic treatment of major depression. *Journal of Clinical Psychiatry, 53*(Suppl. 3).

Schatzberg, A. F., & Cole, J. O. (1991). *Manual of clinical psychopharmacology* (2nd ed.). Washington, DC: American Psychiatric Press.

Spiker, D. G., Weiss, J. C., Dealy, R. S., et al. (1985). The pharmacological treatment of delusional depression. *American Journal of Psychiatry, 142,* 430–436.

Stewart, J. W., Quitkin, F. M., Terman, M., & Terman, J. S. (1990). Is seasonal affective disorder a variant of atypical depression? Differential response to light therapy. *Psychiatry Research, 33,* 121–128.

Stratta, P., Bolino, F., & Cupilllari, M. (1991). A double blind parallel study comparing fluoxetine with imipramine in the treatment of atypical depression. *International Clinical Psychopharmacology, 6*(3), 193–196.

Thase, M. E. (1989). Comparison between SAD and other forms of recurrent depression. In M. E. Rosenthal & M. C. Bleher (Eds.), *Seasonal affecting disorders and phototherapy* (pp. 64–78). New York: Guilford Press.

Tignol, J., Stoker, M. J., & Dunber, G. C. (1992). Paraoxetine in the treatment of melancholia and severe depression. *International Clinical Psychopharmacology, 7*(2), 91–94.

U.S. Department of Health and Human Services. (1993). *Depression in primary care: Vol. 2. Treatment* (AHCPR No. 93–0550). Washington, DC: U.S. Department of Health and Human Services.

Zimmerman, M., & Spitzer, R. L. (1989). Melancholia: From *DSM-III* to *DSM-III-R. American Journal of Psychiatry, 146*(1), 20–28.

C H A P T E R

7

COMBINED TREATMENT

Michael E. Thase and Ira D. Glick

Major depression is often treated with a combination of psychotherapy and antidepressant pharmacotherapy. In fact, the American Psychiatric Association's "Practice Guideline for Treatment of Major Depression" recommends this combination for most patients. In this chapter, the rationale and modes of providing the combination of antidepressants and psychotherapy are considered. The effectiveness of combined treatment is examined in relation to single modalities.

Because cost containment and managed care now dominate mental health practice, questions relating to cost-effectiveness and sequential application of treatment modalities are also considered. The point is that practitioners now must be aware of indications and contraindications of prescribing drugs alone, psychotherapy alone, or combining the two.

METHODS OF DELIVERY

The combined treatment strategy generally is provided by one of three methods of delivery: (1) a psychiatrist conducting both treatments, (2) a nonmedical psychotherapist working in tandem

Note: Completion of this manuscript was supported, in part, by grants MH–41884 and MH–30915 (MHCRC) from the National Institute of Mental Health and grants DA–07673 and DA–08541 from the National Institute on Drug Abuse. We wish to thank Leslie Vasey and Andrea Emling for their assistance in the preparation of this manuscript.

with a psychiatrist, and (3) a nonmedical psychotherapist working with a nonpsychiatric physician. Although exact data are lacking, it would appear that all three methods are widely practiced.

The psychiatrist as sole provider has several major advantages. A single provider streamlines communication and concentrates the therapeutic relationship on a single dyad. Careful monitoring of medication effects and side effects is almost ensured because weekly visits are scheduled for psychotherapy. Combined treatment as provided by psychiatrists has several drawbacks, however. First, not all depressed patients require treatment with antidepressant medications, and for these patients the specific expertise of the psychiatrist in psychopharmacology may be wasted. Second, there are too few psychiatrists to treat all of the patients who warrant a combined approach. Third, because psychiatrists tend to be the most highly reimbursed mental health professional, this method of combined treatment may be the most expensive.

An additional concern pertains to the psychotherapy training that a minority of psychiatrists receive. Specifically, some psychiatrists are trained in predominantly biomedical models, whereas others (at least in the past) have only received training in more traditional, longer-term models of insight-oriented psychotherapy. In the former case, the psychiatrist may be disinclined to provide psychotherapy; in the latter, the psychiatrist may not be able to provide the more directive, time-limited therapies shown to be effective in depression.

The collaboration of a nonmedical psychotherapist and psychiatrist addresses several of the limitations noted above. Perhaps most important, this model permits both practitioners to focus on areas of specific expertise, with, ideally, a clear division of labor. With the psychiatrist functioning exclusively as the pharmacotherapist, he or she may see many more patients for acute phase therapy.

The psychotherapist-pharmacotherapist collaboration also has several drawbacks. For example, the triadic therapeutic relationship permits the possibility of miscommunication, both "innocently" and via splitting between therapists. On occasion, highly skilled clinicians may blunder into competitive, noncollaborative interactions. The availability and expense of the psychiatrist also remains a consideration. Further, there is no guarantee that the nonmedical psychotherapist is well versed in one of the empirically validated therapies, such as the interpersonal psychotherapy of Gerald Klerman and Myrna Weissman or Aaron Beck's model of cognitive therapy.

The treatment team consisting of a nonmedical therapist and a general medical physician (for example, an internist or a family practitioner) obviates the limited availability and expense of the psychiatrist. It also may lessen problems related to professional competition, although at the expense of losing the psychiatrist's expertise and experience in treating depression as well as in psychopharmacology. This is, of course, the major drawback of the collaboration of the general medical physician and the nonmedical psychotherapist: it is likely that subtleties involved in clinical diagnosis will be missed and the myriad of antidepressant options will not be used.

THEORETICAL JUSTIFICATION

Antidepressant pharmacotherapy and the newer time-limited psychotherapies address the pathophysiology of depression via different mechanisms. Of course, both treatment modalities capitalize on the so-called nonspecific aspects of therapy (expectancy, motivation, and the placebo response), as well as the tendency for many depressive episodes to remit spontaneously. Because we do not consider placebo treatment to be an ethically acceptable option in clinical practice situations, this nonspecific component of the therapeutic process is more properly "rolled into" the active model of treatment.

The pathophysiology of clinical depression is best understood as an interactive, biopsychosocial process. This is an encompassing explanatory model that necessitates consideration of genetic, state-dependent biomedical, cognitive, personality, interpersonal, social support, and life stress factors. The obvious heterogeneity of depressive syndromes is thus viewed as resulting from different combinations and permutations of these biopsychosocial factors.

Monotherapy strategies, whether psychotherapeutic or pharmacological, are heuristically purer treatments directed at simpler models of illness pathology. For example, if depression is viewed as the result of a stress-related activation of distorted attitudes and beliefs, then cognitive therapy may be the most appropriate treatment. Conversely, if the critical pathophysiological event is a stress-induced dysregulation of monoamine neurotransmission, then an antidepressant that stabilizes such dysregulation would suffice. Curiously, despite the intuitive appeal of this approach, clinical methods to permit a more parsimonious matching of treatments to pathologies are not yet well developed.

Without such matching strategies, the following limitations of each monotherapy strategy must be recognized. For example, pharmacotherapy can be expected, at best, to help the patient recover back to his or her premorbid level of adjustment (which may or may not be satisfactory). The message of *Listening to Prozac* aside, most patients who respond to antidepressants do not experience a Pygmalionlike transformation in personality after treatment of a depressive episode. Rather, pharmacotherapy is intended to correct or restabilize state-dependent abnormalities in central nervous system function as reflected by improvements in mood, energy, libido, sleep, and appetite.

The process of antidepressant use requires both pharmacokinetic (absorption, distribution, and metabolism of the drug) and pharmacodynamic (the effects of the drug on presynaptic, synaptic, and postsynaptic mechanisms) actions because clinical response typically lags at least several weeks beyond achieving an optimal dosage. Response to a particular medication should be apparent within six to eight weeks of initiating treatment. Not surprisingly, considerable variation occurs in pharmacotherapy responses and on average a patient has about a 50 percent to 70 percent chance of responding to an initial trial of medication. Moreover, a patient who does not respond to one common antidepressant still has a 25 percent to 50 percent chance of responding to an alternative medication. Key issues limiting effectiveness include tolerability of side effects and compliance with prescribed dosages.

The pharmacotherapist thus presents to the patient a model of illness built on the presumption that medication is necessary to stabilize and, eventually, resolve an abnormality of brain function. Genetic and developmental vulnerability factors may be invoked, as might an exaggerated or sustained reaction to stress and/or a disturbance of circadian rhythms. In any event, when effective, a minimum course of six to nine months of pharmacotherapy is routinely recommended.

The psychotherapist typically works with the patient on models of intervention intended to enhance management of stressful symptoms, improve problem-solving skills, strengthen available social supports, and address issues of loss or unresolved grief. Therapy may involve only the identified patient or draw on couples, family, or group treatment formats. Key issues pertaining to effectiveness include the perceived relevance of the model to the patient and the patient's ability to use the model's interventions to effect meaningful change.

THE BENEFITS OF COMPLEMENTARY EFFECTS

With respect to mechanisms of action, the combination of psychotherapy and pharmacotherapy is at its best when there are complementary effects. For example, a complementary effect is observed when psychotherapy is used to help the patient deal with interpersonal problems that cannot be altered by effective antidepressant treatment. Similarly, a behavioral approach such as social skills training might be used to complement an antidepressant in a patient with long-standing problems with underassertiveness or excessive dependency. More effective interpersonal skills, in turn, might be expected to help the patient avoid future stresses or tolerate stress with fewer symptoms. Because both of these factors have been linked to vulnerability to relapse, such a complementary effect would be expected to have an enduring benefit.

When compared with psychotherapy, pharmacotherapy effects tend to be more rapid and, on occasion, more apparent on somatic symptoms such as energy, sleep, or appetite. Some more severely depressed patients may be too distressed by their somatic symptoms to engage in the psychotherapeutic process. Thus, the earlier-emerging benefits of pharmacotherapy may permit the patient to engage in psychotherapy, more quickly lessening the risk that the patient will drop out because of a discouraging lack of improvement.

Another type of complementary effect is possible when psychotherapy is used to address issues of medication compliance. Beyond concerns about side effects, depressed individuals often are noncompliant with medication for a number of reasons that may be addressed through cognitive, interpersonal, or psychodynamic approaches. Common issues include a fear of loss of control, reactions to criticisms (perceived or actual) from family members or significant others, and difficulties interacting with the pharmacotherapist. In particular, patients may perceive the prescribing physician as authoritarian or uncaring, a perception unintentionally reinforced by the brevity of many pharmacotherapy visits.

At a theoretical level, complementary effects may be understood as resulting from either additive or interactive effects. *Additive effects* are the result of combining interventions that exert unique, specific effects. For example, in the watershed 1979 study of combined treatment by Myrna Weissman and associates, interpersonal psychotherapy exerted effects on guilt and suicidal ideation that added to pharmacotherapy's effects on sleep and appetite. The additive effect of combined treatment may be viewed as resulting from the broader scope of treatment interventions. An *interactive* or *synergistic effect* would describe an outcome that is not explained by the broader spectrum of combined pharmacotherapy and psychotherapy. A patient with a state-dependent loss of abstraction may not be able to use cognitive therapy to modify dysfunctional attitudes unless first benefiting from pharmacotherapy. Through either additive or synergistic effects, combined treatment should result in a greater probability of response, as well as a greater level of symptom reduction when compared with the component monotherapies, when cases are appropriately selected and adequately treated.

Negative Interactions

In an earlier era, concerns about the possibility of negative interactions between psychotherapy and antidepressant pharmacotherapy were commonplace. Specifically, psychodynamically trained psychotherapists often voiced concerns that pharmacotherapy might reduce the patient's motivation for psychotherapy. To date, scant empirical evidence has emerged in support of the notion of a negative treatment interaction of this sort. We note that some patients who begin treatment with a combined approach lose enthusiasm for weekly psychotherapy visits after achieving a rapid response (presumably to the antidepressant). However, we have observed a similar loss of enthusiasm for pharmacotherapy visits after a rapid symptomatic response to cognitive or marital therapy!

It also is not uncommon for a patient to "act out" a conflict in therapy by discontinuing or reducing medication. Thus, the patient's anger at the therapist is displaced at his or her representation, the medication. Similarly, medication noncompliance may be the means by which patients express hostility toward significant others or projections about their own self-hatred for having a mental disorder. Would a Sergeant Friday–like "just the facts, ma'am" approach to pharmacotherapy really sidestep these issues? We sincerely doubt it. Rather, such misadventures would be reflected by high dropout or nonresponse rates, as well as the pharmacotherapist's frustration with "bad patients." A well-functioning model of combined treatment, whether a simple dyad or triad, is most likely the best suited for recognition of the psychosocial factors underpinning noncompliance and initiating appropriately thoughtful interventions.

Another, subtler type of a negative interaction may result when psychotherapy somehow affects the intensity of the pharmacotherapy. One example of this effect was observed in the 1984 study by Michael Hersen and colleagues examining social skills training and the tricyclic antidepressant amitriptyline singly and in combination. Specifically, no additive antidepressant effect was found, but patients receiving amitriptyline alone received a significantly higher dose of medication than those receiving the combined regimen. In retrospect, it appears that the pharmacotherapists were more vigorous in their treatment when they knew they had sole responsibility for the patients. Likewise, a negative interaction may result when the pharmacotherapist and the psychotherapist are not able to collaborate effectively. In this latter case, the difficulties experienced by the treatment team may undermine either form of therapy, including noncompliance with medication or therapeutic homework assignments.

A final issue concerning the theory of combined treatment concerns the clinicians' and patient's attributions of the "active ingredients" of treatment. When treatments are used in combination, it is scientifically impossible to determine which mode of intervention is effective for what symptom. Of course, even when monotherapies are used, it's not possible to tease apart the specific activity of a particular treatment from spontaneous remission or the more general elements of remoralization and positive expectancy. As we discuss later, it is useful to specify target symptoms for both pharmacotherapy and psychotherapy so that, at the least, changes in target symptoms can be attributed to the matching treatment.

THEORETICAL JUSTIFICATION FOR COMBINING MEDICATIONS WITH FAMILY PSYCHOTHERAPY

At times treatment should focus on the obvious and explicit psychiatric symptoms of the identified patient (as in the acute phase of bereavement). When the identified patient has a specific major psychiatric diagnosis, treatment of the individual may, at first, be relatively conventional. For example, a combination of antidepressant and antipsychotic medications will probably be used as a first line of intervention to treat delusional depression.

In most instances, however, treatment will be indicated for both the specific symptoms of the individual family member and the family problems and interactions that accompany these conditions. Some of the family problems may be related to the etiology of the individual illness; some may be secondary to it; others may adversely affect the future course of the illness; and others may not be connected at all. For example, if a recurrent mood disorder has developed in a spouse early in his or her marriage, the therapist's attention must be directed both to treatment of the mental illness and to the nature of the marital interaction, including its possible role in exacerbating the illness. If one family member has a major depressive disorder, consideration must be given to the family's ability to cope with the illness, as well as the manifestations of the disorder that are interfering with the family's other problems in living.

In summary, family intervention is just one component of a multimodal prescription. But that intervention may be crucial to success. Why? Because medications will not only make the patient less vulnerable to marital or family problems but also (in an indirect way) decrease the family's excessive reactions to the patient (see below).

MAXIMIZING COLLABORATION AND TEAMWORK

The triad consisting of the patient, a nonmedical psychotherapist, and a pharmacotherapist permits much variability in the strength of alliances and the clarity of communication. At one level are likely to be disparities in the power of treatment team members. In some settings, the pharmacotherapy is conducted by a psychiatrist who is also the supervisor or team leader. In the most extreme example of this type of professional alliance, the therapist is an employee of the psychiatrist. At the other extreme, the therapist is the employer or director of the treatment team, and the physician sees patients as a contractor. More often, both clinicians are independent practitioners working in tandem. At another level, the intensity of the therapist-patient dyad will generally be stronger than that of the pharmacotherapist and the patient. Regardless, the psychotherapist and the pharmacotherapist must develop an effective method of collaboration to achieve the best possible outcomes.

Effective collaboration requires some work by both clinicians. Most important, things work best when the clinicians explicitly collaborate via direct communication. Although face-to-face treatment team meetings are usually not feasible, regular telephone contact and rapid exchange of impressions via fax or electronic mail are quite possible. Ideally, both professionals will have implicit respect for each other's expertise and contribution. Indeed, a lack of respect will often undermine the collaboration, for example, through offhand comments or other, subtler expressions of affect. Once such a destructive interaction pattern has developed, it may be better for one team member to withdraw by arranging an alternative referral.

Another important aspect of effective collaboration is a clear division of labor. No matter how skillful a psychotherapist or psychiatrist might be, he or she should limit interventions about each other's treatments to only those that support the therapy triad. Here is an example from both psychotherapy and phar-macotherapy perspectives.

> *Patient:* I'm getting pretty fed-up with the side effects of this medications. I've even reduced the dose, and they don't seem much better.
>
> *Psychotherapist (Mr. Jones):* Have you talked with Dr. Smith about this?
>
> *Patient:* Well, . . . a little bit at my last visit, . . . but she didn't do anything about it.
>
> *Mr. Jones:* How did you feel about that?
>
> *Patient:* It didn't bother me much at the time. But as the side effects kept getting worse, especially the constipation, I got madder and madder. More at the medicine than at Dr. Smith. She's so busy. I had to wait three weeks for an appointment, and even then, it's in and out . . . fifteen minutes at the most!
>
> *Mr. Jones:* What do you think Dr. Smith would say . . . how would she react . . . if she knew you were unhappy with your medication treatment?
>
> *Patient:* I'm not sure she'd care much . . . I'd hope so . . . but I just don't think she would. She doesn't understand me the way you do.
>
> *Mr. Jones:* And, if that were true?
>
> *Patient:* It's like I'm alone in this . . . like usual.
>
> *Mr. Jones:* That's a theme we've talked about before, and an important one with respect to your depression. Can we use this as an opportunity to test out your belief, as well as to try to solve your side-effect problem? (Patient nods in agreement.) Okay, . . . you have a belief that Dr. Smith, like many other people in your life, doesn't care enough about you to be helpful, and because of this, you have to take a medicine with very annoying side effects that may also prove to be ineffective. Does this sound true?

Patient: Well . . . yes . . . but maybe a little extreme.

Mr. Jones: And if it's true, how do you feel?

Patient: Lousy! And angry.

Mr. Jones: And if it's not true?

Patient: Well . . . it could be another example of a distorted prediction causing me trouble.

Mr. Jones: Do you have any suggestions to test this out?

Patient: I can call Dr. Smith and tell her how severe my side effects are.

Mr. Jones: I think that's a great idea. Let's plan this out as an "official" homework assignment. By the way, would you mind if I also sent Dr. Smith a note updating her on your overall progress?

Dr. Smith: I was sorry to hear that your medication had so many side effects. How have you felt since we stopped it?

Patient: Better. . . . The constipation, dry mouth, and blurry vision are gone . . . but I'm still very tired, and nervous, and easy to tears, and my sleep is too bad.

Dr. Smith: So it sounds like the depression is unchanged. (Patient nods.) Are you up to trying another type of medication, one that has a different profile and, hopefully, fewer side effects?

Patient: I guess so. . . . But why didn't you chose this first?

Dr. Smith: I picked nortriptyline first because I'm more familiar with it and because I could prescribe it in generic form. As you know, generic medicines can be significantly less expensive. The next medicine, Zoloft, is newer and more expensive. By the way, when Mr. Jones called about your treatment, he mentioned that you expressed some concern about my availability. Would you like to talk about it?

Patient: Well, . . . I guess I overreacted. Mr. Jones thinks I

have a tendency to jump to conclusions, especially when
it comes to things that make me feel uncared for.
Dr. Smith: Does that ring true to you?
Patient: Yes, . . . I think it does. In this case, I went from having bad side effects and worrying about bothering you to
thinking that you wouldn't care anyway. That was pretty
stupid (interrupted in midsentence) . . .
Dr. Smith: I know Mr. Jones wouldn't let you get into calling
yourself names. In any case, although I *am* busy, I do
return my patients' calls, particularly when they're not
doing well. So, if you have trouble with this new medications, will you please call?
Patient: Okay.

THE FAMILY AND DEPRESSION

The association between marital/family conflict and depressive
disorders can be understood in a number of ways. Marital/
family stressors may elicit or precipitate depressive symptoms in
a biologically vulnerable individual; marital/family stress or the
lack of a sufficiently supportive intimate relationship may potentiate the effects of other environmental stressors; depressive
symptoms may trigger maladaptive behaviors and negative
responses from family members, thus acting to elicit marital/
family conflict; or subclinical depression or characterological
traits, behavior patterns, and so on may potentiate marital/
family discord, which, in turn, tends to trigger the onset of a
depressive episode.

For some people with more "autonomous" depressions, social
dysfunction does not appear to antedate the onset of depressive
symptoms. Instead, certain chronic forms of personality change
and social maladjustment appear to develop during the course of
repeated depressive episodes. For most patients with a major
depressive disorder, however, the chronic baseline impairment

of social functioning is antecedent to, or coincident with, the expression of the depressive symptoms. In a longitudinal study of depressed women, Myrna Weissman and Eugene Paykel found that clinically recovered depressives continued to experience problems functioning in their parental and spousal roles several months after recovery from the depressive symptoms. Moreover, the differential benefits of an interpersonally oriented psychotherapy combined with drugs over drugs alone in a sample of depressed women were shown to be specifically in the area of social functioning. These findings manifest at six- and eight-month follow-up and several months after patients experienced relief from the depressive symptoms. Hence, the presence of depressive symptoms is not a necessary precondition to marital/familial distress in these patients, but interpersonal dysfunction is viewed as one of several components of a depressive personality disorder and a relatively constant background to the effective episodes.

There is also a growing body of literature on the marital interaction between a depressed spouse and his mate. The depressive's tendency to be aversive to others in social situations is associated with his tendency to receive aversive responses from others; the depressed individual tends to give and receive aversive stimulation at higher rates than evidenced by other members of the family. Similarly, some evidence suggests that a depressed partner and his mate tend to engage in negative (aversive) exchanges more frequently than do nondistressed, "normal" couples. Furthermore, "distressed" couples are more reactive to recent events, positive or negative, than are their nondistressed counterpart.

The temporal and functional relationships between depression and aspects of marital/family interaction have important implications for the development of treatment plans emphasizing both pharmacotherapy and marital/family treatment. In cases of depression, marital/family conflict is often reported as the primary precipitant in episodes of clinical depression. In such cases, marital or family therapy would be indicated for treatment of the interpersonal problems, often directed to (1) reducing the frequency of aversive communications between partners and (2) inducing more frequent mutual reinforcement, as well as modification of distorted cognitive and perceptual responses to the behavior of the partner. Antidepressant medication can be combined with these therapies for symptom relief without risk of compromising their effectiveness.

In cases in which marital or family conflict appears not to be a contributing factor in the depressive episode, the identified patient should be treated with appropriate medication and then reevaluated for psychotherapy. The addition of short-term supportive marital and/or family therapies may be useful in helping engage the patient in the recommended medication regimen. Similarly, involving the spouse in the treatment may help clarify his or her own reservations about depression or its treatment. For example, it is not uncommon for the spouse to have concerns about his or her partner taking "happy pills" or "drugs" or seeing a "headshrinker." It is easy to underestimate the negative effect that such attitudes may have on the identified patient's adherence with treatment.

The stress of intimate relations by significant others with the depressed patient and the negative impact of the patient's symptoms on these people suggest the need for a biphasic program of marital or family intervention. During the initial phase, psychopharmacological treatments are begun and short-term supportive marital or family therapy is introduced to ameliorate the family's negative reactions to the symptoms (thus reducing secondary stress reactions) and to educate the patient and family as to the nature of the disorder, the recommended treatment, strategies for coping with residual symptoms, and possible relapse. The family can be helpful either directly to the patient or indirectly in maintaining its own homeostasis by early recognition of symptoms, by monitoring the patient's mood, by being aware of early signs of medication side effects, and by encouraging medication compliance. Another objective of family therapy is to help the family develop new patterns necessary as a result of the patient's changes in role and function stemming from both the illness and the medication.

Only after the more severe symptoms have diminished and the patient and family have reached a relatively stable stage of adjustment can a second phase of therapy be initiated. Efforts to modify maladaptive communication patterns and problem-solving strategies, to deal with resistances, and to effect structural changes are best reserved for this second phase of intervention.

Case Illustration

One of us (IDG) recently treated a couple, both members of which suffered from recurrent depressive disorder. Mr. A. was a forty-six-year-old lawyer; his wife, Dr. A., was a forty-five-year-old physician. They had three children, aged twelve, nine, and six. The couple was referred for marital treatment (as a last resort) because of dissatisfaction with the marriage. Divorce was seen as the only solution. During the previous year, there had been an intensification of fighting (and mutual blaming) between the couple that dated back to the beginning of the marriage some twenty years earlier. Areas of conflict included money and child rearing. Dr. A.'s need for control of the relationship was evident in financial and parenting issues, whereas Mr. A. was attempting unsuccessfully to combat her domination. To accomplish this, he would criticize his wife's attempts in both areas. For example, she would discipline the children; he would say she should not have been so tough on them. When she did not discipline them, he would proclaim that she was negligent. Their past history revealed that both had been brought up in Europe in what they described as chaotic households, with parents who fought more than their peers' parents. Each of them had a parent who had experienced depressive episodes. The history of past treatment attempts revealed that both husband and wife had had separate, classical psychoanalyses, which they described as "helpful but not enough to end the marital fighting." Both met criteria for a diagnosis of major depressive disorder, recurrent type.

When the couples treatment started, both were extremely depressed and manifested symptoms of loss of interest and pleasure, low self-esteem, and lack of energy. Hence, treatment sessions centered around mutual blaming for each partner's symptoms. Three sessions led to no improvement. At that point, antidepressant medication was instituted. After six weeks, both experienced considerable improvement in mood and activity level. This change afforded the therapist two tactical advantages. First, with their mood and cognition improvements, the couple could now conceivably begin to deal with examining and altering behavioral interactions that might build a viable relationship. Second, the therapist was now viewed as an expert who could prescribe tasks (for example, taking the right medication) that were effective and thus was in a position to prescribe interpersonal tasks to change the previously described negative feedback systems, such as Dr. A.'s control, Mr. A.'s criticism, and their resulting morass of further depression and lowered self-esteem. At this point, the therapist took advantage of this position by guiding the couple to interpersonal changes that led to further marital improvement.

This case illustrates how the role of psychopharmacology may enhance the efficacy of marital therapy. We also believe that couples therapy is likely to enhance psychopharmacotherapy in many depressive patients.

TREATMENT GOALS

Assessing the cost-effectiveness of combined therapy requires specification of the goals for each modality. Of course, the most important goal is remission of the depressive episode. Treatment effectiveness may be monitored in terms of amelioration of the depressive syndrome (does the patient no longer meet criteria for a major depressive episode), as well as the relative reduction of depressive symptoms. The latter area is particularly important because even persistent low-grade symptoms appear to convey a significantly increased relapse risk following either pharmacotherapy or psychotherapy. By bringing the full potential for combined treatment to bear on residual symptoms, patients should have a better chance to achieve more complete remissions at both syndromal and symptomatic levels.

A second set of important goals stems logically from the assumptions and methods of the psychotherapy. For interpersonal psychotherapy, specific therapeutic goals might include reduction of pathological grief, improved marital or family function, decreased loneliness, or enhanced coping with social role transitions. For behavioral treatments, specific goals might include increased assertiveness, improved social problem solving, or increased involvement in pleasurable activities. Specific goals for cognitive behavior therapy (CBT) generally include reductions of cognitive symptoms. Such changes may be targeted at a superficial (automatic negative thoughts), intermediate (dysfunctional attitudes, attributional style), or deeper (basic assumptions, schemata) level of cognition. Both Aaron Beck's theory and available empirical evidence suggest that more specific and enduring changes in depressive vulnerability may necessitate modification of deeper cognitive structures.

A third goal of combined treatment is modification of maladaptive personality traits or patterns. The approach taken here varies as a function of the model of therapy used but, in essence, requires recognition of the behavioral, attitudinal, and interpersonal deficits and excesses that comprise the personality pathology. It seems unlikely that such enduring characteristics are readily modified during the first six to twelve sessions of therapy, and in practice, personality-disordered patients may warrant a longer course of psychotherapy and concurrent maintenance pharmacotherapy.

A final goal for combined treatment is improved medication compliance. Improved compliance maximizes the chances of achieving or maintaining a medication response. Strategies for meeting this goal include discussion in therapy about more general issues of stigma (for example, "Taking medication means I'm weak"), family pressure (for example, "My spouse wants me to get off this drug as soon as possible"), and annoyance with side effects (for example, "This weight gain is unbearable. I'll get depressed again just worrying about getting fat!").

Outcome Studies

The efficacy of combined psychotherapy-pharmacotherapy strategies has been the subject of both qualitative and quantitative reviews using meta-analysis. Generally speaking, there is little doubt about the effectiveness of combining pharmacotherapy and the newer forms of time-limited psychotherapy in major depression. However, the cost-efficiency of routinely using combined treatment remains in doubt, as discussed below.

Combined strategies have been compared against monotherapies in studies of behavior therapy, interpersonal psychotherapy, cognitive therapy, and standard care as provided by general practitioners. In one study of interpersonal psychotherapy and amitriptyline, combined treatment had a significantly greater effect than the components on symptom reduction during an acute-phase trial of depressed women. In two longer-term studies of the continuation and maintenance phases of treatment, however, the combined strategy offered no long-term antidepressant benefits when compared with pharmacotherapy alone. With respect to specific additive benefits, some evidence suggests that IPT-treated patients also showed a late-appearing improvement in social adjustment.

Studies of the combination of behavior therapy and pharmacotherapy have been limited to several trials of acute and continuation phases of treatment. To date, no evidence of additive antidepressant effects have been forthcoming, although several studies have reported a more rapid benefit for the combined strategy. Evidence of a specific additive effect also was found in one study combining social skills training and the tricyclic amitriptyline: patients receiving the behavioral intervention showed significant improvement in assertiveness skills when compared with those treated with amitriptyline alone.

The combination of CBT and pharmacotherapy has been studied in a number of clinical trials. On the basis of these studies, the additive effect of CBT and pharmacotherapy has been shown to be modest, at best (for example, a two- to three-point difference on the Beck Depression Inventory). There are, however, at least two exceptions to this general conclusion. First, the combination of CBT and standard care by a general practitioner has consistently been shown to be superior to standard care alone. Second, the combination of CBT and antidepressants has been shown in two trials to improve the outcome of depressed patients initially treated as inpatients. In one of these studies, the additive benefit was delimited to depressed patients with high pretreatment levels of dysfunctional attitudes.

Additive-specific effects as a result of combined acute-phase treatment have not been convincingly established across various combinations of psychotherapy and antidepressant pharmacotherapy. In two studies, patients who received CBT and pharmacotherapy had less risk of relapse following medication discontinuation than patients who received pharmacotherapy alone. Moreover, in one study, the combination of CBT and pharmacotherapy resulted in significantly greater improvements on measures of hopelessness and cognitive distortion than pharmacotherapy alone. In a fourth study, the combination of social skills training and amitriptyline produced significantly greater improvement on behavioral indices of assertiveness than amitriptyline alone.

Despite such glimpses of the potential value of combined treatment, it is hard to reconcile the research evidence with the American Psychiatric Association "Practice Guideline" recommendation that most patients should receive combined treatment. Rather, the best evidence for combined treatment comes from studies of severely impaired patient groups, such as inpatients. The research literature may present a somewhat biased view, however. Specifically, research studies often exclude patients with the most chronic, refractory, or complicated forms of depression. Because such patients are, on average, less responsive to monotherapy strategies (whether pharmacological or psychotherapeutic), they would represent ideal candidates for combined therapy.

Another approach to maximizing the cost-effectiveness of combined treatment is to stagger or stage the interventions in sequence. Thus, pharmacotherapy might initially precede psychotherapy in more severe depressive states. The research literature yields one example of such a strategy in which a brief course of CBT was fruitfully added after successful antidepressant treatment. In this study, Giovanni Fava and colleagues found that the goals of brief therapy (to treat residual symptoms and lessen the risk for relapse following medication withdrawal) were achieved when compared with a pharmacotherapy alone control group.

Conversely, antidepressant medication may be held back at least two months for treatment of patients with milder depressions in order to provide the opportunity for psychotherapy alone to work. This approach also obviates compliance problems for the many patients who are initially opposed to taking antidepressants.

Tapering or terminating the components after a successful course of combined therapy also has been studied. In a 1990 study of recurrent unipolar depression, Ellen Frank and her colleagues found that continued monthly interpersonal psychotherapy after discontinuation of antidepressant medication had a significant effect on reducing the risk of recurrence, particularly when the therapist-patient dyads were able to maintain a high level of therapeutic intensity. Overall, however, maintenance pharmacotherapy (following termination of psychotherapy) had a statistically and clinically more robust effect than maintenance psychotherapy (following termination of pharmacotherapy) for patients with highly recurrent depressions enrolled in this study.

Practical Guidelines for Combined Therapy

1.   *Diagnosis:* Be sure to make a *DSM-IV* diagnosis, a *family systems* diagnosis, and an individual case formulation (from a dynamic, interpersonal, or cognitive behavioral perspective). Without a diagnosis, the appropriate drug will not be prescribed. So, too, without a map of the family system dynamics, the clinician will be lost in the quagmire of historical and interpersonal pathology.

2.   *Goals:* Be sure to set target symptoms for all modalities. The issue here is to determine which symptoms are likely to be medication responsive and which may be responsive to individual or family interventions. Without this delineation of target symptoms, it is impossible to know which treatment (or combination) is effective.

3.   *Untoward Effects:* Be aware of the side effects of drug therapy and family/individual psychotherapy, as well as their interaction. For example, a syndromal response to medications may allow the identified patient to discuss issues that were previously too emotionally charged for careful family discussion. Needless to say, untoward effects must be monitored at each session. For example, medication side effects (for example, sedation or tremor) that are unpleasant also may decrease the patient's ability to socialize inside and outside the family.

4.   *Sequencing Effects:* Be aware of when and in what sequence to use each of the modalities. For instance, in psychotic depression, the primary clinician will want to medicate first and then evaluate for psychotherapy. A depressed psychotic patient who is paranoid might not be able to tolerate family therapy until he or she has benefited from pharmacotherapy; such a patient would be too suspicious to benefit from treatment beforehand. In some conditions (Axis II disorders or dysthymia), one may want to start with psychotherapy and then add medication. In some cases, one would want to wait until the identified patient has established a relationship with the therapist; this is especially true of depressed adolescents.

5. For whom is combined psychotherapy and pharma-cotherapy *not* indicated? Obviously, this combination is not for everyone. We believe in the principle of therapeutic parsimony. If one modality is effective, then do not add the second. To be explicit, for some clinical situations, we start with therapy; for others, medication; in still others, we start both simultaneously and may withdraw one (or both) modalities sequentially over time. At the very least, putting aside the power of a family inter-vention by itself, the family systems approach is a very efficacious way to increase compliance.

MANAGED CARE IMPLICATIONS

The impact of managed care on the treatment of depressed patients is still unfolding. From the managed care perspective, combined treatment models are on the horns of the dilemma. Said in another way, this most rapid and effective approach to treatment is also the most expensive, at least in the short run.

In ambulatory care settings, such as HMOs, models of treat-ment selection that provide the illusion of cost-efficiency are almost reflexively adopted. In this scenario, combined treatment strategies may be withheld from patients with mild to moder-ately severe depression in favor of serial trials of time-limited psychotherapy and pharmacotherapy. The least expensive model of pharmacotherapy is provided by a general practitioner, rather than by a psychiatrist. Patients with nonpsychotic depression thus may be triaged by a mental health worker or family doctor and referred, on the basis of patient preference, service availability, or agency policy, for either psychotherapy or pharmacotherapy. The combined strategy may thus be reserved for patients who do not respond to either monotherapy. Because many of the costs of depression are hidden (days lost from work or days of impairment in social role), the apparent cost-effectiveness of these less expen-sive initial forms of treatment warrants careful consideration. For example, a "cost-efficient" treatment plan that begins with a generalist's prescription of low-dose tricyclic antidepressants is likely to have manifold costs because of high rates of attrition and subsequent chronicity. For more severe depressions, particularly those warranting hospitalization or day treatment, combined therapy will remain the rule, rather than the exception. For these individuals, the more rapid effects of pharmacotherapy are capitalized on as the psychosocial treatment plan slowly segues from supportive to more active interventions.

In contrast to twenty years ago, the question (at least for most Axis I conditions) no longer is *whether* drugs should be combined with psychotherapy. The evidence from controlled trials over the past twenty-five years attests to the efficacy of drug therapy and, significantly but less convincingly, of psychotherapy. Now the question is *what* to combine for which patients and families. The next generation of controlled studies of combination therapy is now in progress.

The essence of the combined treatment approach includes (1) education about the disorder (the signs and symptoms, causes, and both biological and psychosocial treatments); (2) improvement of communication and interpersonal skills; (3) control of dysregulated neurochemical/neurobehavioral processes; and (4) resolution of cognitive, dynamic, and systems issues that create increased illness vulnerability. The essence of the pharmacological intervention, when combined with the family intervention, is to normalize the illness (as with lithium in bipolar disorder) and suppress symptoms in the individual. Thus, somewhat paradoxically, family therapy ultimately and indirectly can promote medication compliance, while medication can improve interpersonal function.

In summary, we believe that both drug therapy and psychotherapy are necessary, but each by themselves may not be sufficient to treat most of the chronic psychiatric illnesses that we face in contemporary clinical practice. Further research will only help sharpen our clinical guidelines.

REFERENCES

Barnett, P. A., & Gotlib, I. H. (1988). Psychosocial functioning and depression: Distinguishing among antecedents, concomitants, and consequences. *Psychology Bulletin, 104,* 97–126.

Chiles, J. A., Carlin, A. S., Benjamin, G. A. H., & Beitman, B. D. (1991). A physician, a nonmedical psychotherapist, and a patient: The pharmacotherapy-psychotherapy triangle. In B. D. Beitman & G. L. Klerman (Eds.), *Integrating pharmacotherapy and psychotherapy* (pp. 105–118). Washington, DC: American Psychiatric Press.

Clarkin, J. F., Glick, I. D., Haas, G. L., & Spencer, J. H., Jr. (1990). Inpatient family intervention for affective disorders. In G. I. Keitner (Ed.), *Depression and families: Impact and treatment* (pp. 121–136). Washington, DC: American Psychiatric Press.

Conte, H. R., Plutchik, R., Wild, K. V., & Karasu, T. B. (1986). Combined psychotherapy and pharmacotherapy for depression. *Archives of General Psychiatry, 43,* 417–479.

DiMascio, A., Weissman, M. M., Prusoff, B. A., Neu, C., Zwilling, M., & Klerman, G. L. (1979). Differential symptom reduction by drugs and psychotherapy in acute depression. *Archives of General Psychiatry, 36,* 1450–1456.

Fava, G. A., Grandi, S., Zielezny, M., et al. (1994). Cognitive behavioral treatment of residual symptoms in primary major depressive disorder. *American Journal of Psychiatry, 151,* 1295–1299.

Frank, E., Kupfer, D. J., Perel, J. M., Cornes, C., Jarrett, D. B., Mallinger, A. G., Thase, M. E., McEachran, A. B., & Grochocinski, V. J. (1990). Three year outcomes for maintenance therapies in recurrent depression. *Archives of General Psychiatry, 47,* 1093–1099.

Frank, E., Kupfer, D. J., Wagner, E. F., McEachran, A., & Cornes, C. (1991). Efficacy of interpersonal psychotherapy as a maintenance treatment for recurrent depression: Contributing factors. *Archives of General Psychiatry, 48,* 1053–1059.

Glick, I. D., Clarken, J. F., & Goldsmith, S. J. (1993). Combining medication with family psychotherapy. In B. Beitman (Ed.), *Combined treatments: The American Psychiatric Press review of psychiatry* (Vol. 12, pp. 585–610). Washington, DC: American Psychiatric Press.

Haas, G. L., Glick, I. D., Clarkin, J. F., Spencer, J. H., Lewis, A. B., Peyser, J., DeMane, N., Good-Ellis, M., Harris, E., & Lestelle, V. (1988). Inpatient family intervention: A randomized clinical trial: II. Results at hospital discharge. *Archives of General Psychiatry, 45,* 217–224.

Hersen, M., Bellack, A. S., Himmelhoch, J. M., & Thase, M. E. (1984). Effects of social skill training, amitriptyline, and psychotherapy in unipolar depressed women. *Behavior Therapy, 15*, 21–40.

Hollon, S. D., Shelton, R. C., & Loosen, P. T. (1991). Cognitive therapy and pharmacotherapy for depression. *Journal of Consulting Clinical Psychology, 59*, 88–89.

Keitner, G. I., Miller, I. W., Epstein, N. B., & Bishop, D. S. (1990). Family processes and the course of depressive illness. In G. I. Keitner (Ed.), *Depression and families: Impact and treatment* (pp. 1–29). Washington, DC: American Psychiatric Press.

Klerman, G. L. (1983). Psychotherapies and somatic therapies in affective disorders. *Psychiatric Clinics of North America, 3*, 85–103.

Klerman, G. L. (1991). Ideological conflicts in integrating pharmacotherapy and psychotherapy. In B. D. Beitman & G. L. Klerman (Eds.), *Integrating pharmacotherapy and psychotherapy* (pp. 3–20). Washington, DC: American Psychiatric Press.

Manning, D. W., & Frances, A. J. (1990). Combined therapy for depression: Critical review of the literature. In D. W. Manning & A. J. Frances (Eds.), *Combined pharmacotherapy and psychotherapy for depression* (pp. 3–33). Washington, DC: American Psychiatric Press.

Thase, M. E., Simons, A. D., McGeary, J., et al. (1992). Relapse after cognitive behavior therapy of depression: Potential implications for longer courses of treatment? *American Journal of Psychiatry, 149*, 1046–1052.

Weissman, M. M., Klerman, G. L., Paykel, E. S., et al. (1974). Treatment effects on the social adjustment of depressed patients. *Archives of General Psychiatry, 30*, 771–778.

Weissman, M. M., & Paykel, E. S. (1974). *The depressed woman: A study of social relationships*. Chicago: University of Chicago Press.

Weissman, M. M., Prusoff, B. A., DiMascio, A., et al. (1979). The efficacy of drugs and psychotherapy in the treatment of acute depressive episodes. *American Journal of Psychiatry, 136*, 555–558.

Wright, J. H., Thase, M. E., & Sensky, T. (1992). Cognitive and biological therapies: A combined approach. In J. H. Wright, M. E. Thase, A. T. Beck, & J. W. Ludgat (Eds.), *Cognitive therapy with inpatients: Developing a cognitive milieu* (pp. 193–218). New York: Guilford Press.

ABOUT THE AUTHORS

Carol M. Anderson, Ph.D., is professor of psychiatry at the University of Pittsburgh's School of Medicine, Department of Psychiatry. She is the author of more than fifty-one articles and chapters and the coauthor of five books, including *Schizophrenia and the Family, Mastering Resistance,* and *Flying Solo.* She has received awards for distinguished contributions from both the American Family Therapy Academy and the American Association for Marriage and Family Therapy. Her current research interests focus on women with depression or anxiety.

Jules Bemporad, M.D., is currently professor of clinical psychiatry at Cornell University College of Medicine and director of the Children's Day Hospital, Westchester Division. He is also Supervising and Training Psychoanalyst at the Psychoanalytic Institute of New York Medical College. In the past, he has been affiliated with Columbia and Harvard Universities. Bemporad is the author of more than one hundred books, articles, and chapters, including *Severe and Mild Depression: The Psychotherapeutic Approach* (with S. Arieti), which has appeared in five foreign editions. In addition, Bemporad is editor-in-chief of the *Journal of the American Academy of Psychoanalysis* and serves on the editorial boards of *Development and Psychopathology* and the *Harvard Mental Health Letter.*

Charles DeBattista, D.M.H., M.D., is associate director of the Mood Disorders Clinic at Stanford University. His main research interests include the utility of antidepressant drugs and electroconvulsive therapy in the treatment of major depression, and he is actively involved in teaching and writing in these areas.

Sona Dimidjian, M.S.W., is a family therapist at the Family Therapy Center, Western Psychiatric Institute and Clinic. Her publications and clinical interests lie in the areas of depression, women's development, and gender issues.

Ira D. Glick, M.D., is professor of psychiatry in the Department of Psychiatry and Behavioral Sciences at the Stanford University School of Medicine and chief of Inpatient and Partial Hospitalization Services at the Stanford University Hospital. He is the author or coauthor of more than one hundred articles and chapters and seven books, including *A Model Curriculum in Psychopharmacology* and *Affective Disorders and the Family.*

Joan Luby, M.D., is instructor of psychiatry at Washington University School of Medicine, Child Division. She completed her residency and fellowship training at Stanford University, where she received training in group psychotherapy from Irvin Yalom, M.D., and coauthored a chapter with him on the group psychotherapy of depression. Her primary interest is in infant and preschool psychiatry in which parent and infant interpersonal interactions are a primary theme. She is currently director of the Infant/Preschool Psychiatric Clinic at St. Louis Children's Hospital and director of residency training in child psychiatry at Washington University School of Medicine.

John C. Markowitz, M.D., is associate professor of clinical psychiatry at Cornell University Medical College and associate attending psychiatrist at New York Hospital. He is the author of "Interpersonal Psychotherapy: Current Status" (with M. M. Weissman) in *Archives of General Psychiatry;* "Psychotherapy of Dysthymia" in *American Journal of Psychiatry;* and "Interpersonal Therapy of Mood Disorders" (with M. M. Weissman) in *Clinical Neuroscience.*

Apryl Miller, L.S.W., is director of the Family Therapy Center, Western Psychiatric Institute and Clinic. Her clinical and research interests lie in the area of family life cycle development, depression, and gender issues. She has extensive experience training and supervising family therapists in both outpatient settings and in-home projects.

Alan F. Schatzberg, M.D., is Kenneth T. Norris, Jr., Professor and chair of the Department of Psychiatry and Behavioral Sciences at Stanford University and a world authority on the biology and treatment of depression. He is the author of six books on depression and pharmacotherapy, including *Manual of Clinical Pharmacology.*

Holly A. Swartz, M.D., is an instructor in psychiatry at Cornell University Medical Center and Clinical Affiliate of New York Hospital. She is a Reader's Digest/New York Community Trust research fellow, coeditor of *Time-Limited Psychotherapy*, and author of a chapter in *Psychiatry* (S. Tasman, J. Kay, and J. A. Lieberman, Eds.).

Michael E. Thase, M.D., is associate professor of psychiatry at the University of Pittsburgh School of Medicine and the Western Psychiatric Institute and Clinic (WPIC). His research interests pertain to the assessment and treatment of mood disorders, including the short-term and prophylactic efficacy of pharmacotherapy and cognitive therapy in relationship to the psychobiological correlates of depression. Thase has directed the Cognitive Therapy Clinic at the University of Pittsburgh since its inception in 1987. In 1988 he also become director of WPIC's Mood Disorders Module and associate director of their Mental Health Clinical Research Center. He has authored or coauthored more than 180 scientific articles and book chapters and is coeditor of the book series *Handbook of Outpatient Treatment* and of *Cognitive Therapy with Inpatients: Developing a Cognitive Milieu.*

INDEX

A

Activity scheduling, 49–50
Additive effects, 188–189, 201, 202
Adjustment disorder with depressed mood: in case examples, 99–100, 101, 116–119; described, 97–98; individual psychotherapy for, 116–119; intervention in, indications for, 116
Adolescents, depressed: autonomy of, 26, 28–29; combined treatment for, 204; family psychoeducation with, 20–22; family therapy with, 28–29
Agency for Health Care Planning and Research, 63
Agenda: in cognitive behavior therapy, 36, 43; in interpersonal group therapy, 138–139. *See also* Goals
Agenda group, 138
All-or-none thinking, 39
Alliance, therapist-patient: in cognitive behavior therapy, 34, 43–46, 49–50, 58–59; in combined treatment, 192–195; in family therapy, 10–11, 17; in individual psychotherapy, 97, 103, 104–105; in interpersonal psychotherapy, 76–77, 89, 91; and medication compliance, 104. *See also* Collaboration
Altruism, 126, 141–142
American Psychiatric Association, 183, 202
Amitriptyline. *See* Elavil
Amoxapine (Asendin), 165, 167, 175, 176
Anafranil (clomipramine), 165, 166
Anderson, C. M., 1–32
Anhedonia, behavioral techniques for, 49–50

Anticholinergic side effects, 166, 167
Antidepressants. *See* Medication
Anxiety disorders: dysfunctional attitudes in, 37; irrational thinking in, 39–40; medication for, 168, 171
Arieti, S., 127, 128
Arrythmia, 167
Asendin (amoxapine), 165, 167, 175, 176
Assessment/diagnosis: in combined treatment, 204; of depression types, 98–102; of family strengths and weaknesses, 14–15; in family therapy, 10–16; in individual psychotherapy, 98–102; in interpersonal psychotherapy, 79–81; of severe/psychotic depression, 102
Assortive mating, 26
Attitudes, dysfunctional: cognitive-behavioral approaches to, 36–38, 60–61, 141–142; psychodynamic approach to, 110–111, 113–115
Attitudes towards depression, 4–5; reframing technique and, 11–14
Attributional style, 38
Attributional Style Questionnaire, 38, 61
Atypical antidepressants, 170–171; dosing for, 172; indications for, 171; side effects of, 171–172
Atypical depression, 84; medication for, 166, 171, 177–178
Autobiography, 60
Automatic negative thoughts (ANTs), 36, 45; identification of, 54–58; monitoring of, 53; rational response technique for, 59–60; testing the accuracy of, 58–59
Autonomy, of adolescents, 26, 28–29
Avoidance, cognitive, 40

B

"Beating the Blues: Recovery from Depression," 48

Beck, A. T., 33, 35, 47, 58, 66, 128–129, 139, 185, 200

Beck Depression Inventory (BDI), 61, 134, 140–141

Behavioral models of depression, 41–42. *See also* Cognitive behavior therapy

Behavioral techniques, 48–53; combined with medication, 201–202. *See also* Cognitive behavior therapy

Bemporad, J. R., 95–120, 127

Bereavement: combined treatment for, 191; versus depression, 95–96; interpersonal treatment of, 82–83; uncomplicated versus complicated, 81–82. *See also* Grief; Loss

Betcher, R. W., 136

Biology of depression, 154–157; genetic structure and, 96; neuro-cognitive abnormalities and, 40–41; neurovegetative symptoms and, 102, 134–135. *See also* Somatic therapy

Biopsychosocial model of depression, 185–187

Blood pressure, and medication, 166–167, 169, 172

Bowlby, J., 73, 110

Brain structure, 155

Bupropion (Wellbutrin), 170, 171, 172, 177–178

C

Catastrophic thinking, 39, 62

Catatonia, 174

Catharsis, 82

Character pathology: in case example, 99–101; and chronic depression, 96–97, 99–101, 109–115; and combined-treatment goals, 200; and individual psychotherapy, 96–97, 99–101, 109–115; and interpersonal psychotherapy, 86–88, 91

Childhood, effects of, on adult depression, 107, 110–114, 119. *See also* Individual psychotherapy

Children: depressed, family therapy for, 20–22; impact of depressed parents on, 4. *See also* Family

Chronic depression: and character pathology, 109–110; cognitive dysfunctions in, 36; defined, 96–97; individual psychotherapy for, 97, 109–115. *See also* Character pathology; Dysthymia

Clomipramine (Anafranil), 165, 166

Cognitive behavior therapy (CBT): and behavioral models of depression, 41–42; behavioral techniques in, 48–53; and cognitive model of depression, 34–41; cognitive techniques in, 53–61; combined with medication, 202; duration of, 34; effectiveness of, 63–65; goals of, 200; homework assignments in, 47–48, 54, 58, 60, 140; and managed care, 65–66; outcomes assessment in, 61; principles of, 33–42; process of, 42–48; prophylaxis of, 65; response to, correlates of, 64–65; sessions of, first, 43–47; sessions of, structure of, 36, 43; sessions of, subsequent, 48; termination of, 62. *See also* Combined treatment

Cognitive-behavioral group (CBG) therapy: duration of, 140; effectiveness of, 134, 142; goal setting in, 140–142; format of, 140; outcomes measurement for, 142; phases of, 141; principles of, 139–140

Cognitive impairment, 91

Cognitive model of depression, 34–41, 44–46, 139–140

Cognitive techniques, 53–61, 140. *See also* Cognitive behavior therapy

Collaboration, between psychotherapists and pharmacotherapists, 159–160, 183–185, 192–195

Collaborative empiricism, 34, 43–44, 49–50, 58–59. *See also* Alliance; Cognitive behavior therapy

Combined treatment, 183, 206; collaboration in, 192–195; complementary effects in, 187–190; delivery methods for, 183–185; and family interaction, 195–199; and family therapy, 191, 197–199; goals of, 199–201; guidelines for, 204–205; indications for, 205; and managed care, 205–206; medication-group therapy, 143–144; medication-individual psychotherapy, 101, 102, 103, 115; medication-interpersonal psychotherapy, 89–90, 188, 201; medication-psychoeducation, 8, 206; negative interactions in, 189–190; sequencing in, 204; staggered, 203; theoretical justification of, 185–187, 191

Competence: and behavioral rating techniques, 50–51; and dysfunctional attitudes, 37; and family relationships, 15, 27, 29; and role transition, 985

Complementary effects, 187–190

Compliance, medication, 103–104, 188, 189–190, 200–201, 203

Conflict, interpersonal, 83–84

Congruence, in family communication, 14, 15

Connection, between family and therapist, 10–11, 17. *See also* Alliance

Constipation, 166

Consultants, for medication management, 159–160, 184–185; effective collaboration with, 192–195

Contract, treatment, 16

Coping strategies: and cognitive behavior therapy response, 64–65; of family, 2–3, 7, 14–15, 18, 19, 20

"Coping with Depression," 47

Cost-efficiency, of combined treatment, 201, 203, 205–206. *See also* Effectiveness

Covi, L., 134, 142

Criticism, sensitivity to, 15

Cyclic antidepressants, 164–165, 177; biology of, 156–157; combined with individual psychotherapy, 108; dosing for, 167–168; effectiveness of, compared with cognitive behavior therapy, 63–64; indications for, 165–166; side effects of, 166–167; studies of, 164. *See also* Somatic therapy

Cyproheptadine, 163

D

Daily Record of Dysfunctional Thoughts (DRDT), 54, 56–57

DeBattista, C., 153–181

Delusions, 174–175

Dependency, 105, 127–128, 129

Deprenyl (selegiline), 168, 169, 170

Depression: acute, 36; behavioral models of, 41–42; biology of, 154–157; biopsychosocial process of, 185–187; cognitive model of, 34–41; educating families about, 17–20; influence of, on family, 2–7, 15; interpersonal relationships and, 71, 72, 73–76, 127–129; neurocognitive abnormalities in, 40–41; pathophysiology of, 185–187; symptoms of, 18, 20–21, 30; types of, 95–98, 158–159, 174–179. *See also* Adjustment disorder with depressed mood; Atypical depression; Chronic depression; Dysthymia; Major depression; Melancholic depression; Seasonal depressions; Severe depression

Depressive personality, 109, 196. *See also* Character pathology; Dysthymia

Desipramine (Norpramine), 165, 166, 167–168

Desyrel (trazodone), 170–171, 172

Diagnosis. *See* Assessment/diagnosis

Dimidjian, S., 1–32

Diversion techniques: in cognitive behavior therapy, 51–52; and individual psychotherapy, 105

Dobson, K., 63

Dominant other, 127–128

Dopamine, 155, 156, 157, 170

Downward arrow technique, 54, 55

Downward spiral: in behavioral model of depression, 41–42; and family relationships, 5–7, 18

Doxepin (sinequan), 165, 167

DSM-IV, 80, 102, 177, 204

Dysfunctional Attitude Scale (DAS), 37, 61

Dysfunctional attitudes, 36–38, 60–61

Dysphoria: in adjustment disorder with depressed mood, 101; behavioral techniques for, 50; in dysthymic disorders, 97

Dysthymia: and character pathology, 109–110; effectiveness of cognitive behavior therapy for, 63; individual psychotherapy for, 109–115; medication for, 115; nature of, 96–97. *See also* Character pathology; Chronic depression

E

Edinburgh Primary Care Study, 64

Effectiveness: of cognitive behavior therapy, 63–65; of cognitive-behavioral group therapy, 134, 142; of combined treatment, 201–203; determination of, in combined treatment, 190; of family/psychoeducational therapy, 30–31; of group therapy, 134, 142; of interpersonal psychotherapy, 72, 88, 90, 92; of medication, 63–64, 65, 142, 161. *See also* Outcomes assessment

Effexor (venlafaxine), 170, 171–172, 177

Elavil (amitriptyline), 165, 166, 167; biology of, 156, 157; combined with interpersonal psychotherapy,

201; combined with social skills training, 190, 201–202; effectiveness of, compared with cognitive behavior therapy, 64. *See also* Cyclic antidepressants

Elderly, depressed: caretakers for, 22; depressive pseudodementia in, 40; family psychoeducation for, 22; and medication side effects, 166–167, 172

Electroconvulsive therapy (ECT), 173–174; for melancholic depression, 177; for psychotic depression, 175–176

Ellis, A., 33

Emotional reasoning, 39

Empathy, 104

Empiricism, collaborative, 34, 43–44, 49–50, 58–59. *See also* Alliance; Cognitive behavior therapy

Emptiness, 132

Enzymes, 156

Etiology of depression: biological factors in, 154–157; in childhood, 107, 110–111; by depression types, 96–98; explaining of, to families, 17, 18; and interpersonal relationships, 127–128; psychosocial variables in, 1; stress-vulnerability model of, 17, 18

Evans, M., 65

Exercise, 51

F

Family: coping strategies of, 2–3, 7, 14–15, 18, 19, 20; and depressed children, 20–22; depression-related problems in, 25–26; influence of, on depression, 1, 20, 195–199; influence of depression on, 2–7, 15; negative spiral/sequences in, 5–7, 18; and psychoeducation, 8–10; self-preservation skills for, 19, 20; strengths and weaknesses of, 14–15; task allocation in, 24–25

Family systems, 204, 205

Family therapy: applying principles/maintaining gains phase of, 24–29; for children/adolescents, 20–22, 28–29; combined with medication, 191, 196–199, 204; connecting/assessment phase of, 10–16; effectiveness of, 30–31; for the elderly, 22; and family problems, 25–26; goals of, 9–10; limit setting in, 24–25; and managed care, 7–8; and marital issues, 26–28; phases of, 10; rationale for, 7–9, 30–31; session formats for, 22–24; support/information phase of, 16–24; termination of, 29–30; treatment contract for, 16. *See also* Combined treatment; Marital issues; Spouses
Farberow, N. L., 145, 146
Ferster, C., 33
Fluoxetine. *See* Prozac
Fluvoxamine (Luvox), 157, 161
Focus: negative, 40; somatic, 40
Frank, E., 203
Frederick, C. J., 145, 146
Freud, S., 95

G
Gastrointestinal (GI) upset, from medication, 162
Generalization, over-, 39
Genetic factors, 96, 154. *See also* Biology of depression
Gioe, V. J., 142
Glick, I. D., 183–208
Global Assessment Scale, 61
Goals: of cognitive therapy sessions, 36, 43; of combined treatment, 199–201, 204; of family/psychosocial therapy, 9–10; setting of, in cognitive-behavioral group therapy, 140–142; setting of, in interpersonal group therapy, 138–139; in treatment contract, 16
Graded-task assignments, 52, 141
Greenberg, R., 47

Grief: versus depression, 95–96; interpersonal psychotherapy treatment of, 81–83; in role transition, 85–86; in termination, 88. *See also* Bereavement; Loss
Group therapy: cognitive-behavioral, 139–142; combined with medication, 143–144; combined with individual, 148; interpersonal, 123–134; interpersonal, inpatient, 134–139; and managed care, 142–143; with multiple families, 22–23; and suicidality, 144–148. *See also* Interpersonal group therapy
Guilt, in family members, 21

H
Haldol, 175
Hallucinations, 174–175
Hamilton Depression Scale, 78, 80
Heart problems, and medication, 167
Hersen, M., 190
HIV-positive patients, 78, 92
HMOs. *See* Managed care
Homework assignments, 47–48, 54, 58, 60, 140. *See also* Behavioral techniques; Cognitive techniques
Hope, installation of, 126, 135
Hopelessness Scale, 61
Hormonal factors, 154
Howell, J., 48
Hypercortisolism, 63
Hyperpyrexia, 169
Hypertensive crisis, 169

I
Idealization, 127–128
Imipramine (Tofranil), 164, 165, 165–167; effectiveness of, compared with cognitive behavior therapy, 63–64; effectiveness of, compared with interpersonal therapy, 90. *See also* Cyclic antidepressants
Imperative statements, 39

Individual psychotherapy: for adjustment disorder with depressed mood, 116–119; assessment and diagnosis in, 98–102; combined with group, 148; combined with medication, 101, 102, 103, 108, 115; and depression, types of, 95–98, 120, 177; versus disease-focused treatment, 98–102; for dysthymic disorder, 109–115; for severe/psychotic depression, 102–109. *See also* Combined treatment

Information: booklets for, 23–24; providing family with, 16–24

Information processing: abnormalities in, 38–41; and automatic negative thoughts, 36; and group participation, 138

Inpatient group therapy, 134–139

Insomnia, from medication, 162, 170, 171–172

Interactive effect, 189

Interpersonal formulation, 80–81

Interpersonal group therapy, 123–134; cohesion in, 136; debriefing from, 130; effectiveness of, versus cognitive-behavioral group therapy, 134; engaging depressed members in, 131–133, 137, 138–139; format of, 130; here-and-now focus in, 130–131; inpatient, 134–139; interpersonal learning in, 127–129; member selection for, 124–125; outcomes measurement of, 133–134; therapeutic factors of, 125–126; therapists for, 129–130; turnover in, 135–136

Interpersonal inventory, 79–80, 84

Interpersonal problem areas: defined, 80; grief, 81–83; interpersonal deficits, 86–88; interpersonal role dispute, 83–84; role transition, 84–86

Interpersonal psychotherapy (IPT): assessment and diagnosis in, 79–81;

beginning phase in, 79–81; combined with medication, 89–90, 108–109, 188, 201; described, 71–72, 129; and differential therapeutics, 90–91; effectiveness of, 72, 88, 90, 92; effectiveness of, versus cognitive behavior therapy, 63–64; goals of, 200; here-and-now focus in, 73–76, 130–131; and managed care, 91–92; middle phase in, 81–88; patients' suitability for, 77–79, 90–91; problem areas addressed in, 80, 81–88; for relapse prevention, 88–89; termination of, 88–89; theoretical background of, 73; therapists of, 76–77; training in, 76; transference in, 91. *See also* Combined treatment; Interpersonal group therapy

Interpersonal relationships: impact of, on depression, 3–4, 71, 72, 127–129; learning from, importance of, 127–129; negativity and, 1, 2; as stressors, 71, 72, 73–76. *See also* Family; Interpersonal psychotherapy; Intimacy

Interpersonal role dispute, 83–84

Intimacy: devaluation of, 128–129; and marital issues, 27; and women's depression, 73. *See also* Interpersonal relationships

IQ, 65

Isolation: of family, 5; interpersonal psychotherapy for overcoming, 86–87, 132–133, 134–135; and severe depression, 104

K

Kibel, H. D., 147

Klerman, G. L., 72, 185

Kramer, P., 153

L

Labeling, 40

Learned helplessness, 38

Learned resourcefulness, 65
Limit setting: in family therapy, 24–25; in individual psychotherapy, 105
Lipman, R. S., 134, 142
Listening to Prozac (Kramer), 153, 186
Litigation, 154
Loss, 98, 100–101, 105–106, 135–136. *See also* Bereavement; Grief
Luby, J. L., 123
Luvox (fluvoxamine), 157, 161

M

Major depression, 78; diagnosis of, in case example, 100–101; effectiveness of cognitive behavior therapy for, 63; subtypes of, and somatic therapies, 174–179. *See also* Severe depression
Managed care: and cognitive behavior therapy, 65–66; and combined treatment, 205–206; and cost effectiveness, 183; and family therapy, 7–8; and group therapy, 142–143; and interpersonal psychotherapy, 91–92; and medication, 153–154
Mania: and electroconvulsive therapy, 174; from medication, 171
Marital issues: and combined treatment, 191, 195–199; and family therapy, 26–28; and interpersonal psychotherapy, 83–84. *See also* Family
Markowitz, J. C., 71–94
Mastery ratings, 50–51
Maxmen, J. S., 136
Medical model, 72, 77, 79, 80, 90. *See also* Interpersonal psychotherapy
Medication, antidepressant: biological basis of, 154–157; combined with antipsychotic medication, 175, 191; combined with family therapy, 191, 197–199; combined with group therapy, 143–144; combined with

individual psychotherapy, 101, 102, 103, 108, 115; combined with interpersonal psychotherapy, 89–90, 108–109, 188, 201; combined with psychoeducation, 8; combined with psychotherapies, 183–206; compliance with, 103–104, 188, 189–190, 200–201, 203; consultants for, working with, 159–160, 183–185, 192–195; dosing of, 163–164, 167–168, 170, 172; effectiveness of, 161; effectiveness of, versus cognitive behavior therapy, 63–64, 65, 142; indications for, 157–159, 161–162, 165–166, 168–169, 171; lag time of, 103, 161; maintenance, 203; and managed care, 153–154; side effects of, 162–163, 166–167, 169–170, 171–172, 204; trade versus generic names for, 160–161; types of, 160–161; use of, 186–187; withdrawal symptoms of, 164. *See also* Atypical antidepressants; Combined treatment; Cyclic antidepressants; Monoamine oxidase inhibitors; Selective serotonin reuptake inhibitors
Melancholic depression, 176–177
Meyer, A., 73
Miller, A., 1–32
Mind reading, 39
Modeling, by therapist, 52–53
Monitoring, self-, 48, 50, 53, 54–58
Monoamine oxidase inhibitors (MAOIs), 156, 168, 169; dosing for, 170; indications for, 168–169, 177, 178; side effects of, 169–170
Monoamine transmitters, 155, 156–157
Mood congruent symptoms, 174–175
Mood incongruent symptoms, 175
Mood monitoring, 48, 54
Mourning. *See* Bereavement; Grief; Loss
Mouth, dry, 166

N

Nardil (phenelzine), 156, 168, 169, 170, 178
National Institute of Mental Health (NIMH), 63, 90
Nausea, from medication, 171–172
Negativity: and family, 3; and relationships, 1, 2; in thought content, 35; in thought process, 39–40. *See also* Automatic negative thoughts
Neurocognitive abnormalities, 40–41
Neurons, 155
Neuroticism, 41
Neurotransmitters, 155–157
Neurovegetative symptoms: and group therapy, 134–135; and medication, 102, 158
Norepinephrine, 155, 156, 157
Norpramine (desipramine), 165, 166, 167–168
Nortriptyline (Pamelor), 165, 166, 167, 168

O

Obsessive-compulsive disorder, medication for, 162, 166
Occupational impairment, 158
One Flew Over the Cuckoo's Nest, 173
Orthostasis, from medication, 166–167, 169, 172
Outcomes assessment: for cognitive behavior therapy, 61; for cognitive-behavioral group therapy, 142; for combined treatment, 201–203; for interpersonal group therapy, 133–134. *See also* Effectiveness

P

Pamelor (nortriptyline), 165, 166, 167, 168
Panic disorders, medication for, 166, 168–169
Parkinson's disease, 169
Parnate (tranylcypromine), 156, 168, 169, 170
Paroxetine (Paxil), 157, 161, 163, 164

Patients: for interpersonal group therapy, 124–125; for interpersonal psychotherapy, 77–79, 90–91; psychoeducation goals for, 9
Paxil (paroxetine), 157, 161, 163, 164
Paykel, E., 196
Personality, 109. *See also* Character pathology
Personalization, 40
Pharmacotherapists, 159–160, 183–185; effective collaboration with, 192–195
Phenelzine (Nardil), 156, 168, 169, 170, 178
Phototherapy, 178
Physicians, 185
Piaget, J.–P., 36
Pituitary abnormalities, 154
Pleasure ratings, 50–51
"Practice Guideline for Treatment of Major Depression," 183, 202
Predictions, negative, 39
Procrastination, 41, 42, 52
Prolixen, 175
Prophylaxis. *See* Relapse prevention
Protectiveness, of family, 15, 18, 19
Protriptyline (Vivactil), 165, 166
Prozac (fluoxetine), 156, 157, 161, 162, 163–164, 177–178
Psychiatrists, 159–160, 183–185; effective collaboration with, 192–195
Psychodynamic psychotherapy, 107–108, 110–111; group, 134. *See also* Individual psychotherapy
Psychoeducation: agenda for, 17–20; benefits of, 30–31; in cognitive-behavioral groups, 141; of depressed children, 20–22; of elders, 22; and families, 8–9; in family therapy, 16–24; formats for, 22–24; goals of, 9–10. *See also* Family therapy
Psychotherapy, combined with medication, 183–206. *See also* Cognitive behavior therapy; Combined treat-

ment; Family therapy; Group therapy; Individual psychotherapy; Interpersonal psychotherapy; Medication

Psychotic symptoms: combined treatment for, 204; medication for, 165, 174–176; psychotherapy for, 96, 102–109

R

Rage, 132

Reality testing, 58–59, 141, 142

Reasons for Living Inventory, 46

Reassurance, by family members, 2, 3, 15, 18

Receptors, 155

Recurrence: and cognitive behavior therapy, 65, 66, 141; and family therapy, 8, 30; history of, and medication, 158; and length of treatment, 66. *See also* Relapse prevention

Reframing technique, 11–14

Rehearsal strategies, 52–53

Relapse prevention: in cognitive behavior therapy, 48, 62; in interpersonal psychotherapy, 88–89. *See also* Recurrences

Relationships. *See* Family; Interpersonal relationships; Marital issues

Relaxation training, 53

Restlessness, from medication, 162–163, 172

Role dispute, interpersonal, 83–84

Role-playing technique, 52–53

Role transition, 78, 84–86

Rumination, 136

S

Schatzberg, A. F., 153–181

Schemata, 36, 38, 54; identification of, 60; modification of, 60–61

Seasonal depressions, 178–179

Sedation, 162, 166, 171, 172

Seizures, from medication, 172

Selective serotonin reuptake inhibitors (SSRIs), 157, 161, 177; dosing for, 163–164; indications for, 161–162, 177–178; side effects of, 162–163

Selegiline (Deprenyl), 168, 169, 170

Self-esteem: among depressed women, 26–27; and dependency, 127–128; and group therapy, 126, 142; loss of, 98, 100–101; loss of, in case example, 105–108; loss of, in childhood, 111–112

Self-harm prevention, 103. *See also* Suicidality

Self-monitoring tasks, 48

Serotonin, 155, 156, 157, 170, 171. *See also* Selective serotonin reuptake inhibitors

Sertraline (Zoloft), 157, 161, 162, 164

Severe depression, 82; and compliance, 103–104; in group therapy, 124–125; individual psychotherapy for, 102–109; with psychotic features, 96, 102–109, 174–176

Sexual dysfunction, from medication, 163, 170, 171–172

Side effects: of atypical antidepressants, 171–172; in combined treatments, 204; of cyclic antidepressants, 166–167; of monoamine oxidase inhibitors, 169–170; of selective serotonin reuptake inhibitors, 162–163

Sinequan (Doxepin), 165, 167

Slife, B. D., 138

Social impairment, 86–88, 158, 195–196. *See also* Interpersonal problem areas; Interpersonal relationships

Social supports, 102

Socializing, 77–78, 82

Somatic focus, 40

Somatic therapy, 179; and biology of depression, 154–157; by depression types, 174–179; electroconvulsive therapy, 173–174; medication,

157–172; phototherapy, 178. *See also* Combined treatment; Electroconvulsive therapy; Medication
Somnolence, from medication, 162, 166, 171–172
Specifiers, 178–179
Spouses: conflict among, 83–84, 195–199; coping of, 2–3; depression-related problems of, 26, 196; impact of, 3–4; marital issues of, 26–28. *See also* Family; Marital issues
Steuer, J. L., 134
Stigmatization, 4–5, 125–126, 201
Stress-vulnerability model, 17, 18, 62, 98, 101–102
Stressors. *See* Family; Interpersonal relationships
Suicidal ideation: cognitive behavior therapy for, 46–47; and group therapy, 144–148; interpersonal psychotherapy for, 85–86
Suicidality: caused by medication, 165; and group therapy, 144–148; prevention of, with medication, 158; and psychotic depression, 175
Sullivan, H. S., 73
Support, in family therapy, 16–24, 25
Surmontil (trimipramine), 165
Swartz, H. A., 71–94
Symptoms: of depressed children/adolescents, 20–21, 28; of depression, 18; for families to monitor, 30; of severe/psychotic depression 102
Synapse, 155
Synergistic effect, 189

T
Termination: of cognitive behavior therapy, 62; of combined treatments, 203; of family therapy, 29–30; of interpersonal psychotherapy, 88–89
Thase, M. E., 33–69, 183–208
Therapists: collaboration of, with

psychiatrists/pharmacotherapists, 159–160, 183–186, 190, 192–195; for interpersonal group therapy, 129–130, 137; for interpersonal psychotherapy, 76–77, 87; reactions of, to suicide, 147–148. *See also* Alliance; Transference
Thought content, abnormalities in, 35–38. *See also* Automatic negative thoughts
Thought counting, 54, 58
Thought processing, abnormalities in, 38–41; and group participation, 138. *See also* Cognitive behavior therapy
Thought stopping, 51
Thyroid abnormalities, 154
Time-limited therapies. *See* Cognitive behavior therapy; Combined treatment; Family therapy; Group therapy; Interpersonal therapy; Somatic therapy
Tofranil. *See* Imipramine
Transference: in group therapy, 146–147; in individual psychotherapy, 97, 107, 113–114, 115; in interpersonal psychotherapy, 91; in relationships, 110–113
Tranylcypromine (Parnate), 168, 169, 170
Trazodone (Desyrel), 170–171, 172
Treatments: for adjustment disorder with depressed mood, 116–119; for chronic depression, 109–115; compared, 74–75; and differential therapeutics, 90–91; effectiveness of, compared, 63–65; explaining of, to families, 17, 19, 20; responsibility for, divided, 159–160, 183–185, 192–195; for severe/psychotic depression, 102–109; and types of depression, 96–98, 101, 158–159, 174–179. *See also* Cognitive behavior therapy; Combined treatment; Family therapy; Group therapy; Individual psychotherapy; Interper-

sonal psychotherapy; Somatic therapy
Tricyclic antidepressants. *See* Cyclic antidepressants
Trimipramine (Surmontil), 165

U
Universality, 125, 135

V
Vegetative symptoms. *See* Neurovegetative symptoms
Venlafaxine (Effexor), 170, 171–172, 177
Videotape training, 76
Visual imagery, 51
Vivactil (protriptyline), 165, 166

W
Weissman, M. M., 72, 185, 188, 196
Wellbutrin (bupropion), 170, 171, 172, 177–178
Whisman, M., 64–65
Withdrawn behavior, 132
Wolpe, J., 33
Women: and interpersonal dysfunction, 196; and intimacy, 73; and spousal relationships, 26–27

Y
Yalom, I. D., 124, 125, 138

Z
Zoloft (sertraline), 157, 161, 162, 164